Mt 84

TRADITION IN EXILE

UNIVERSITY OF TORONTO DEPARTMENT OF ENGLISH

Studies and Texts, No. 10

TRADITION IN EXILE

A Comparative Study of Social Influences
on the Development of Australian and
Canadian Poetry
in the Nineteenth Century

by

John Pengwerne Matthews

UNIVERSITY OF TORONTO PRESS

in association with

F. W. CHESHIRE • MELBOURNE

Foreword

by CLAUDE BISSELL

WHEN IN 1953 John Matthews entered the Graduate School of the University of Toronto, he had, for a graduate student, an unusually clear idea of where his main interests lay. He was an Australian, just arrived in Canada, who had taken his degree in English at Melbourne University, where he had developed an interest in his native literature. He had read enough Canadian writing to realize that there were literary parallels between the two senior dominions of the Commonwealth. This book, *Tradition in Exile*, thus sprang out of an idea early formulated and then developed and refined by an increasingly detailed knowledge of the subject. After taking his Doctor's degree in 1957, Matthews joined the Department of English at St. John's College, University of Manitoba, and is now Professor of English and Dean of Arts and Science. He is thus in a position to write as a Canadian, but with an Australian bias that remains inoffensively strong. I mention these biographical details because comparative studies can turn into arid exercises, distinguished more by the neatness of their logical pattern than by any light they shed on the subject, products more of the mechanical fancy than of the organic imagination. This is a book that bears upon it the marks of the delight taken by the writer in his subject, and of the fascination with which he has pursued its development.

This book derives in part from personal experience, from familiarity with the political and cultural climate of the two countries. But this is not the sole or indeed the main reason for its success. No amount of enthusiasm or first-hand knowledge can subdue a recalcitrant subject. The subject of this book is simple enough to be precisely stated and complex enough to invite subtleties. The book is a study in com-

parisons between the varying fortunes of a common cultural tradition that works itself out on two frontiers separated by thousands of miles, widely different from each other in natural décor, rarely aware of each other's existence except as geographical facts, but nevertheless responding to the compulsion of an inner logic that transcended the environment. This, then, is an essay in cultural comparison, and it demonstrates the point that comparisons are most effective and helpful when they deal with divergences that spring out of a strong common base. The comparative method in literature is more useful in revealing the broad picture than in illuminating the small details. It is therefore best used in the service of cultural history; and this is what Matthews has done in this book. Frequently he crosses over into the areas of politics and history—excursions that can be more readily made in dealing with a minor derivative literature than with a major one. Many of his observations and conclusions will command the attention of a social scientist no less than a humanist. In particular, he tells us a good deal about the nature of Canadian conservatism—not the specialized political brand, but the great national religion, our genius for taming natural impulses and for gilding even the shyest lily.

Although the book is not important for the reassessment it gives of individual writers or works, it does contain a good many lively and perceptive comments. Some sections, particularly those that deal with the cultural implications of the Canada First movement and the thin strain of nineteenth-century Canadian popular verse, are valuable additions to our knowledge of nineteenth-century Canadian literature. For the Canadian reader, the book will serve as an introduction to Australian literature, which remains largely unknown in this country. Like our own literature, it is uniformly free of masterpieces, but it has a directness and vitality not often displayed by our own writers. Matthews does not venture directly into the twentieth century, although he supports his argument at various points by references to the contemporary literary scene. One feels that this is the first section of a composite comparative study of Canadian and Australian literature, which is both a satisfying whole in itself and a lively prologue to a second book that demands to be written.

Preface: A Basis for Comparison

ONE OF THE most seductive things about a preface is the opportunity it gives an author to apologize in advance for what he is going to say. No matter how much confidence he may have in his case, no matter how convinced he is of the value of his contribution to knowledge, a preface provides the means for him to cover his retreat. In it, he may provide a measure of insurance against critics and readers alike. Is he accused of ignoring whole provinces of his subject? Of making outrageous value judgments? Of making no value judgments? The preface has taken care of it. The author must try to guard against all the attacks he can anticipate, and must seem modest and self-deprecating at the same time. Of course it can't be done, and every season one may witness thousands of writers, intoning with fearful pride, "Go little book . . .," as the only alternative to protecting their manuscripts by storing them under the mattress.

The historian of comparative literature has an additional need for the questionable protection of a preface. He faces at once the challenge of defining the limits of his subject, and this is very difficult to do when both his areas of research belong to a larger generic group. Australian and Canadian literatures are both parts of literature in English, as are the literatures of Great Britain, the rest of the Commonwealth, and the United States. But unlike the historians of English and American literature, workers in the Commonwealth field have often felt it necessary to justify the existence of their subjects. For too long they have either wilted or grown aggressive under the jocular or sympathetic remarks of their colleagues who, confident of the existence at least of both Shakespeare and Bacon solidly behind them, enquire with interest, "*Is* there a Canadian poet?" or incredulously, "You mean there is an Australian novel worth reading?" If this goes on long enough one begins to feel a part of the world of *Sarah Binks* in the ultimate nightmare of spending one's life compiling a comparative study of the literatures of Saskatchewan and Easter Island.

To be true to the tradition, then, I should attempt a double justification: first that the two literatures I want to compare *do* exist, and secondly that some useful purpose will be served by comparing them. If I could do that in a preface there would be no need to write the book. Both justifications, therefore, will have to stand or fall with the argument that the book presents: that there *is* a recognizable profile of Dominions' literature at present in existence, in spite of apparent contradictions and variations, and that more may be discovered about both Canadian and Australian letters when they are compared than when they are studied in isolation. If this is demonstrated, then both the value of the comparative method and the separate identities of the literatures on which this method has been used, will be established.

This book also attempts to introduce some aspects of the history of ideas to the comparative study of Commonwealth literature. In both Australia and Canada ideas and attitudes about social and literary traditions come from the same British roots. Where are the differences and where the similarities? What are the changes which the two environments worked upon them? Obviously these questions cannot be answered by the usual chronological and critical survey of the literary works alone. There must be an examination of the varying ideas of the English tradition which were a part of every settler's effects, and which became, in both countries, a tradition in exile.

In brief, as Canadian and Australian creative writing springs from common roots, what has each done with its inheritance? How has each responded to identical influences which continued to enter from abroad? And how has each moulded these traditions and influences into new and recognizable national patterns? These are the questions which this book will attempt to answer.

J.P.M.

Contents

Acknowledgments

THE AUTHOR acknowledges his special debt to President C. T. Bissell of the University of Toronto and to Dr. R. L. McDougall of Carleton University, Ottawa, for their generous interest, criticism, and guidance in the course of this undertaking. Thanks are also due to the Mitchell Librarian, Sydney, for making available by microfilm much Australian material not available in Canada, and to the Humanities Research Council of Canada for their grant in aid of publication from funds provided by the Canada Council.

TRADITION IN EXILE

This book is dedicated
in gratitude for his time, encouragement, and
constructive criticism to Professor

F. E. L. PRIESTLEY

who, I suspect, still believes that
if Miltonic poetic diction was good enough
to describe the geography of Hell
it should have been suitable for
nineteenth-century Australia

1. The Seas Between

IN THE NINETEENTH century there was very little direct contact between Canada and Australia. Dr. C. T. Bissell, in his article "A Common Ancestry: Literature in Australia and Canada," mentions Gilbert Parker's travel book on Australia and A. G. Stephen's slighter comments on Canada, but his parallels serve only to emphasize the degree to which, in the nineteenth century, any contact between the two countries was centralized through the common link with Great Britain. Governor Arthur went from Van Diemen's Land to Upper Canada; Governor Phillip was made responsible for the dispatch of supplies to Vancouver in his exploration of American northwest coastal waters. Yet neither of these events had as much impact upon Australian society as the frequent use of Australian ports—principally Hobart and Sydney—by American whalers.

In politics, although Canadian confederation was achieved thirty-four years before the union of the Australian states, the Canadian example was seldom invoked by Australian federalists, who, however, closely examined the American Constitution. There are good historical reasons for this. From the beginning, the history of nationalism in Australia reveals two distinct groups. There were those who fought for an increasing degree of independence within the British Empire, and there were those who would settle for nothing less than outright independence as a republic.

In the first group belonged most of the politicians, drawn at first largely from the landed class. William Charles Wentworth, with his plans for the establishment of a separate Australian peerage with a House of Lords at Sydney, might have had his grandiose ideas laughed out of court, but he marked a growing movement among the graziers for greater control over their own affairs. Their motives may have been economic ones, but they are not without their importance in the nationalist movement. Sir Henry Parkes, the so-called "Father of Federation," also worked with the landed class for a continued British connection, though he repeatedly insisted on his continued membership in the working class from which he had risen. It was largely due to his efforts in New South Wales that a majority in that state finally agreed to the proposed constitution.

The second group of Australian nationalists sought complete independence. To this group belonged the majority of the articulate working classes, particularly the rural workers of the outback and their spokesmen, who identified the British connection with economic and social injustice. The concept of "mateship" and egalitarianism, which had developed from the earliest convict days, reinforced the position of this group, which adopted republicanism as a part of its philosophy. Later still, the *Bulletin*, as we shall see, gave cohesiveness to this group by setting itself up as "The Australian National Newspaper" with republicanism and aggressive Australianism as the keynotes of its policy.

By 1900, however, both these groups looked to the United States rather than to Canada. Richard Jebb, in his *Studies in Colonial Nationalism*, remarks (p. 61):

There appears to be nothing except the sense of imperial security to account for the unnatural prolongation of the colonial system, and the colonialist attitude, upon the Australian continent. In Canada the unmistakable hostility of a powerful neighbour gave urgency to the vital question of the national future—to be, or not to be. Meanwhile the Australians, secure in their antipodean isolation, long remained immune from the external pressure which history associates with the birth of nations in the new world as in the old.

This is an oversimplification. It is true that there was no sense of urgency such as the Fenian raids provided for the Canadian federal movement. There was, however, in Australia after 1850 and even before then a greater sense of national consciousness than was to be found in Canada at any time in the nineteenth century. This must surely discount Jebb's accusation of "unnatural prolongation" of a colonialist attitude. Patrick Maloney, a Sydney poet, said in 1869, two years after Canadian confederation: "In Canada they have a nation, but no national feeling. In Australia we have national feeling in abundance, but no nation."[1]

To those Australian nationalists who wanted independence, the British North America Act was regarded as a political expedient imposed upon the Canadian people from above, rather than inspired by a spontaneous upsurge of national unity. They looked upon it as a measure which, with its provision for a Senate whose members were to be appointed for life, threatened to perpetuate in another form Wentworth's colonial aristocracy and to strangle the cause of the popular franchise for which they were fighting. It is not surprising that they looked instead to a flourishing United States which had thrown away colonial ties.

For very different reasons the British North America Act also failed to appeal to those Australian nationalists who wished to preserve the British connection. The pastoral interests, in control of the legislatures during the eighteen-forties, made the first attempt towards union when the New South Wales Legislative Council passed, in 1842, an Act to admit imports duty-free from New Zealand and Van Diemen's Land. The Act was promptly vetoed by the Colonial Office. Separate economic systems in each of the colonies were not only encouraged by British policy of the day, but were made mandatory. By the time that policy was reversed, powerful interests existed in each of the colonies to maintain the barriers. By the eighteen-sixties the tariff disputes between a free-trade New South Wales and a protectionist Victoria had discouraged federal planning by creating a suspicion that under a united government one would seek to gain control over the other. The British North America Act, providing for residual power to be left in the hands of the federal government and for the appointment of provincial lieutenant-governors by the Governor General in Council, threatened the carefully constructed framework of States' Rights. This fear of the consequences of centralization was reinforced in the smaller states by consideration of the overwhelming proportion of population and wealth contained in New South Wales and Victoria.

While therefore there was a popular nationalism which continued to speak of an Australian people and an Australian nation, there was a clinging to local autonomy, which it was feared would be

[1]*Australian Union*, 2.

lost through domination by other partners in the union. The nature of this regionalism, however, should not be mistaken. There was no Victorian or Tasmanian patriotism. A study of the earliest broadsheets will disclose a universal adoption of the term "Australian"—a tendency which was, of course, helped by the fact that the continent formed a natural geographical unit. The inter-colonial disputes might, in some instances, arouse bitterness, but they were of the same nature as disputes between the conflicting interests of bordering municipalities. The wider unit was always presumed, even though it was not there in fact. J. B. Stephens reflected this constant awareness in 1877:

> Already here to hearts intense,
> A spirit-force, transcending sense,
> In heights unscaled, in deeps unstirred,
> Beneath the calm, above the storm,
> She waits the incorporating word
> To bid her tremble into form.
> Already, like divining-rods, men's souls
> Bend down to where the unseen river rolls:—[2]

This was sentiment that both groups of nationalists could find palatable. However, in what way was this union to be brought about? States' Rights automatically suggested the similar controversy in the American Union, and so the American Constitution seemed to be the most likely place to search for a solution to the problem. There were provisions for sovereign power to remain in the hands of the states, and there was also an answer to the question of inequality in the size of state populations by the institution of a "States' House"—later called the Senate—which was elected rather than appointed. The acceptance of elected governors would have been too close to republicanism to be satisfactory, but as a reinforcement of the sovereign character of the states the next best thing was to have them appointed directly by the Crown, and not, as in the Canadian system, by the federal government. For a while the idea of an elected judiciary was considered, but it was soon rejected.

It is not true to say that the Canadian precedent was ignored. The framers of the Australian Constitution examined closely the federal constitutions of each of Canada, Germany, and Switzerland, as well as that of the United States. It was felt, as a result, that Australia

[2]G. Mackaness (ed.), *An Anthology of Australian Verse*, 346.

had obtained the best of all possible worlds, and an unmistakable air of smugness emerges from the statements of the drafters of the Constitution:

Never before have a group of self-governing, practically independent communities, without external pressure or foreign complications of any kind, deliberately chosen of their own free-will to put aside their provincial jealousies and come together as one people, from a simple intellectual and sentimental conviction of the folly of disunion and the advantages of nationhood. The United States of America, of Switzerland, of Germany were drawn together under the shadow of war. Even the Canadian provinces were forced to unite by the neighbourhood of a great foreign power. But the Australian Commonwealth, the fifth great federation of the world, came into voluntary being through deep conviction of national unity. We may well be proud of the statesmen who constructed a Constitution which—whatever may be its faults and shortcomings—has proved acceptable to a large majority of the people of five great communities scattered over a continent; and proud of the people who, without compulsion of war or fear of conquest, have succeeded in agreeing upon the terms of an indissoluble social compact.[3]

There were very few other direct contacts between Australia and Canada. The Eureka Stockade movement, which broke out on the Ballarat goldfields in 1854 and which led to the proclamation of the short-lived Republic of Victoria, contains the record of two Canadian names among the casualties, but literature has made little of this beyond the first stanza of a ballad printed in 1855, entitled "Victoria's Southern Cross":

> When Ballarat unfurled the "Southern Cross",
> Of joy a shout ascended to the heavens;
> The bearer was Toronto's Captain Ross;
> All frightened into fits red-taped ravens.[4]

Dr. Bissell has suggested[5] that in direct literary relations Canada has had more success than Australia in reaching a world-wide audience. Canada has her trio of international best-selling authors who are as well known in Sydney as in Toronto. Leacock, Service, and Mazo de la Roche are known extensively in Australia through the medium

[3]J. Quick and R. R. Garran, *The Annotated Constitution of the Australian Commonwealth*, 225–6.
[4]C. C. Ingleton (ed.), *True Patriots All*, 256.
[5]"A Common Ancestry: Literature in Australia and Canada," *U.T.Q.* XXV (January 1956), 131.

of British editions; but again, the relations have been channelled through the United Kingdom. Dr. Bissell remarks that "no Australian writer comes anywhere near enjoying the same kind of reputation in Canada." Yet Henry Handel Richardson, Marcus Clarke, Henry Lawson, D'Arcy Niland, and Patrick White enjoy considerable English audiences, and English editions of their works continue to appear. It might be true to say that in this century the orientation of literary taste in Canada has pointed more towards the United States and less to Great Britain, whereas in Australia the British literary tradition outweighs the American. This is in direct contrast to the nineteenth-century position. One of the first surprises which emerges from the comparison is the degree to which, during the last century, Canadian letters were influenced by the English tradition and relatively uninfluenced by the American. During the same period in Australia, the English tradition found few adherents, but the American one was stronger than it is now and certainly much stronger than it was in Canada.

This, then, is the introductory picture. There is very little direct contact in any field of endeavour, and little is gained by the effort to bring documented parallels into unwilling union. To the extent that a cultural history is also a history of gropings towards self-identification, we must see what has been done in each country when the same raw materials have been used. In both Canada and Australia the main tradition has been the British one, with American influences modifying it.

2. The Social Context

By 1788, when Governor Arthur Phillip and his seven hundred half-starved convicts crept ashore at Sydney Cove, the eastern Maritime sections of Canada were already the homeland of a proud race with an established history and set of traditions behind it. In this fundamental comparison of sets of values at the very time that the first seeds of the Australian colonies were being planted, we may see a very important difference which was to underlie the entire course of development of the English tradition in both countries.

The inhabitants of Nova Scotia were for the most part intensely British, including the expelled Loyalists from the newly independent American colonies, who had proved in the most tangible way the fervency of their adherence to the homeland. The nucleus of the Australian contingent, on the other hand, was composed of a set of malcontents who had arrived in their exile with nothing but bitterness for the country which had used them so harshly. It has long been fashionable for Australian historians to play down the convict origins of the country as an unfortunate incident, the effects of which have long been obliterated. They point instead either to the influx of free settlers, or to the economic and social effects of the gold rushes as the more important determining factors in Australian history. This reluctance to look deep into origins which were considered by most nineteenth-century historians as shameful and sordid has only recently been modified. From a cross-section of late Victorian histories of Australia, and even from those of the third decade of this century, one may obtain a bewildering variety of interpretations of the nature of the land and its people, and of the relative importance of the events and influences which caused them to be as they are. Even the well-known *Short History of Australia* by the late Professor Ernest Scott, which, from the time of its appearance in 1916, has undergone twenty-one printings and seven editions, avoids anything but bare reference to the facts when dealing with the convict period, and turns, we sense, with some relief to analysis of the social and economic impact of free settlers, the wool market, and the gold rushes. This standard work has also adopted, and to some extent has perpetuated, the official nineteenth-century attitude of trying to forget a lawless past and to minimize or to ignore any assertions that facets of Australian national character owe their existence to such unfortunate origins.

When speaking of the Eureka Stockade, an event which has admittedly reached a position of primacy among the mythologies of Australian egalitarianism, Professor Scott is guilty of strengthening a counter-myth which has perhaps been equally conducive to the clouding of the issues of early Australian history. He says:

> Among the Australian miners the Eureka Stockade incident has always been regarded as in some sense a "fight for freedom", and the fact that a liberalizing of the governing institutions occurred afterwards was connected with the event itself. But the rebellious features were contrary to the saner judgement of the miners, especially those of British origin. How much of it was really due to foreigners who had no respect for British methods of securing reforms, it is difficult to determine. The influence of the foreign element has been questioned, and Hotham's assertion that the mass of the miners were urged on by non-British agitators has been attributed to his anxiety to find an excuse for the mishandling of the situation by the Government. But Vern was a German; so was Thonen, another ringleader who was killed; and Raffaelo, who was arrested and brought to trial, was a red-headed Italian who seemed to hate all authority because he had been brought up to hate the Austrians.[1]

Brian Fitzpatrick, by no means a traditionalist in historical interpretation, has tended in this respect to follow the well-established path. In *The Australian People* (p. 22), he adds, as an *obiter dictum* on the foreign influences in the country: "Thus it was Irish, English, Scottish, German, Italian and other radicals—Canadians lay among the Ballarat Reform League dead at Eureka—who gave the world what is still called 'the Australian ballot' in the United States of America."

[1]Ernest Scott, *A Short History of Australia*, 223. We may compare this document with the dominantly Tory renderings of the rebellion in Upper Canada.

Perhaps it is not surprising that Scott's inference of the virtuous nature of the majority of the miners, "especially those of British origin," suborned by foreign agitators, should for so long have received ready acceptance. Australians have always been prone to xenophobia, and the cry of "foreign agitators" is not one with which we are unfamiliar today. But such an explanation will not do. Professor Crawford and the novelist-historian Kylie Tennant are among those who are only now beginning to challenge the old interpretation, to look back further for more satisfying explanations of the facts underlying Australian attitudes.

The basic fact remains that for the first twenty years of its existence the colony of New South Wales was a gaol, and nothing more than that in the eyes of the Colonial Office. Among the convicts the attitude towards the mother country was one of bitterness and resentment, and towards their gaolers and the dribble of free settlers who had begun to arrive in search of profitable pickings, one of hatred. There is an English broadsheet of 1790 headed by a cartoon drawing of George III asking "Where's everybody?" and being answered "Sent to Botany Bay Sire!" One verse of the accompanying song reads:

> Let us drink a good health to our schemers above,
> Who at length have contrived from this land to remove
> Thieves, robbers and villains, they'll send 'em away,
> To become a new people at Botany Bay.[2]

But what was intended as satire by the London balladist became largely true by virtue of the attitude of the convicts themselves. Even during the desperate first years, before the constant threat of famine was removed, there was a vision on the part of the Governor of what this part of the world might become, and an equal determination on the part of many of the convicts to reject Britain as she had rejected them. Governors who showed signs of desiring to make more of Sydney Cove than a replica of an English prison found willing co-operation from many of their charges. That Phillip and Macquarie proved to be the most successful of the early administrators lay largely in this attitude to the nature of their tasks, and to the measure of co-operation they were given by the convicts and their descendants. They received little encouragement either from the Colonial Office

2Ingleton (ed.), *True Patriots All*, 8.

or from the free settlers, and indeed Macquarie was recalled for treat-
ing his charges too well.

Under Macquarie, society, outside the close-quarter prisons, was
divided into three sections: (a) the free settlers or "exclusionists,"
(b) the convicts who had served their sentences in prison and who
were free within the colony, but were not permitted to leave it (these
were known as "emancipists"), and (c) "ticket-of-leave men," who
had not yet served their full prison sentences but who had been
granted remissions and who were allowed the run of the colony on
parole.

Macquarie erected large and impressive public buildings, built
roads and pleasure gardens, emancipated convicts, made public office
open to them, and enabled them to obtain land-grants. He employed
convict architects, lawyers, secretaries, and surgeons. The small
minority of free settlers who had expected to find themselves in a position of unassailable ascendency in a convict settlement protested bitterly, and through their influence in England succeeded in instituting
a commission of enquiry. Commissioner Bigge came out in 1819,
saw the plans for a large and impressive city which Macquarie was
putting into effect, and noted the type of meals served to convicts in
the new Hyde Park Barracks: "a most excellent dinner, Plum Pudding
and an allowance of Punch being given to them."[3] Macquarie was
recalled, and to mark the occasion the convict laureate, Michael
Massey Robinson, composed an ode:

> Our gallant Governor has gone,
> Across the rolling sea,
> To tell the King on England's throne,
> What merry men are we.
>
> Macquarie was the prince of men!
> Australia's pride and joy!
> We ne'er shall see his like again;
> Here's to the Old Viceroy![4]

It was true that they did not see his like again, but henceforth an
attitude of mind and a tradition of conduct established itself which
was never to be completely eradicated. The recall of Macquarie
marked the end of despotic rule, benevolent or otherwise, by the

[3]Kylie Tennant, *Australia, Her Story*, 41.
[4]Ingleton (ed.), *True Patriots All*, 95.

governor; henceforth governors were to be advised by a Council of settlers. For many years this event has been marked in Australian history as the beginning of constitutional government in the country, and, as such, a great landmark in the march towards self-determination; and in many respects it was. But the event was also in many ways parallel to the revolution of 1640 in England. Despotism had ended, but, as modern historians have pointed out, it was far from being an unmixed triumph of freedom for the whole nation. As the lower classes in England found little or no improvement in their lot under Cromwell, so the great majority of the population of New South Wales deplored the removal of the despot who had protected them against the wealthy free settlers, who now proceeded to dominate the new "constitutional" administration. As late as 1836 the emancipists were sending petitions to the British House of Commons for redress against what they called the "factious oligarchy" of the exclusionists:

That your Petitioners feel so strongly on this point that they would infinitely prefer a recurrence to the old despotic form of Government, under which the Governor for the time being combined the Legislative as well as the Executive authority in his own person, either to the present Legislative Council or to the still more numerous and irresponsible Non-elective [i.e., severely limited franchise] Council which is thus sought to be introduced in its stead.[5]

As a mark of their new freedom, the serving convicts found their working hours were extended from eight hours a day, for five days a week, as they had been under Macquarie, to twelve hours a day for six days a week under the new Governor, Sir Thomas Brisbane. Emancipist privileges were curtailed and land was available only to men of wealth who had no convict record. The reaction was immediate. The convicts, emancipists, and their descendants, who formed 85 per cent of the population and who regarded themselves as the only true Australians, closed their ranks against those whom they identified with the class in England responsible for their exile.

It is true that one of the "Pure Merinos,"[6] William Charles Wentworth, advocated a bi-cameral legislature to which ex-convicts

[5]C. H. M. Clark, *Select Documents in Australian History*, 333.

[6]"Pure Merinos" was a name coined by the emancipists and applied to the wealthy graziers, as a sneering reference to the pedigreed merino sheep which had been imported illegally from Spain via the Cape of Good Hope.

should be eligible for admission; but he also appealed for more free settlers to counter the emancipist majority. He warned of the probability of rebellion in New South Wales and pointed to the example of the American colonies. The people of New South Wales might turn from Britain and appeal for protection to the United States, and he questioned, quite gravely, whether such a rebellion could be put down by British troops. He looked at the Blue Mountains, close to the west of Sydney, and saw a bigger and more terrible Bunker's Hill. "Of what avail would whole armies prove in these terrible defiles, which only five or six men could approach abreast."[7] Judge Barron Field in 1820 warned: "I see the shadow of the spirit of American revolt at taxation arising in the shape of the petition for trial by jury by the Emancipists; they will next demand legislative assembly; and in the end declare themselves a nation of free-booters and pirates."[8] But there was no rebellion and by the eighteen-thirties the exclusionists were firmly in the saddle. The justices were all of their party and had summary powers to punish all non-capital offences by the members of the working class (which, by definition, included all those who had any convict record). This was the position and there was apparently no means of altering it. The colonial majority had no way of influencing the British Government in its decisions on land policy, and had no medium for expression of its grievances and opinions in the local legislature. One Alexander Harris, a mechanic, complained that the new land policy "suited pretty well the highest class, but nobody else; it prevented persons of small property from becoming farmers, and made a proletariat of them."[9]

This discontent and resistance found expression in other ways, and it is in these ways that the continuing influence of the attitudes that began with the convicts has become embedded in Australian social behaviour. First, there was a rejection by the emancipists of the contract-of-hire system, which had been normal practice for "ticket-of-leave" men in the early days of the colony. Under this system, convicts would be paroled to a free settler on the understanding that they would work for him under a contract for a definite sum for a set period. Upon their emancipation, however,

[7]Quoted by Tennant, *Australia, Her Story*, 58.
[8]*Ibid.*
[9]Fitzpatrick, *The Australian People*, 128.

they found that the free settlers still offered the same rates that had prevailed under the penal system. As, technically, the emancipist was as free a citizen within the colonial area as was the free settler, he resented perpetuation of a mode of employment which he had come to associate with the period of his imprisonment, and he took extravagant attitudes to underline his independence and his status of nominal equality.

The farming of small tracts of land on the fringes of the great estates attracted few volunteers. The laws were slanted in favour of the wealthy grazier rather than of the small agriculturalist, who would find himself too often dependent on the bounty of his wealthy neighbour, operating always on the margin of bare subsistence, and a prey to the capricious interpretation of numerous local by-laws.[10] There seemed to be only one escape left to them. They dissociated themselves from what they considered to be a semi-feudal state of affairs, took a perverse pride in owning virtually no property, and drifted to the outer areas of bush settlement where the entanglements of local by-laws and the whims of magistrates could not touch them without very great difficulty. Some of these men became bushrangers, the Australian version of highwaymen, and the legendary position which outlaws such as Ned Kelly and Captain Starlight have assumed in the popular mythology attests to the sympathy with which they were regarded by their "currency" compatriots.[11] The majority, however, resorted to contract work in the outback. They would roam from one sheep station to the next, refusing any type of binding term contract, undertaking piece-work for prearranged amounts. As often as the graziers would try to bring in from the coast labourers who would be more pliable to their wishes, they would find that the new workers had been persuaded not to report, or they would fade away before their contracts had expired. Gangs of bushworkers, who had acquired special skills which the station owner needed, would follow a nomadic existence around the countryside, largely free from the over-extended arms of the law, and protected by a rigid code of mateship which sternly forbade anything that might hint of betrayal of a mate to the squatters or to the police.

10Clark, *Select Documents*, 257.
11"Currency" was the term used to describe convicts, emancipists, and their native-born descendants.

This state of mind, which grew directly from convict solidarity and continued in the emancipists' descendants, was firmly entrenched long before Eureka. The graziers and squatters[12] assumed in the minds of these nomadic workers the same position held in the minds of their convict forbears by the gaolers and supervisors. Anything was justified which might frustrate the common enemy, but woe betide the convict who attempted to prey on his fellows. For survival there had to be complete trust between mates. The official account of the trial and execution in 1826 of Matthew Brady, the most notorious of the Tasmanian bushrangers, provides an interesting commentary on this code.

Brady had assumed a type of Robin Hood role in Tasmania. When Governor Arthur posted notices of reward for his capture, Brady would offer larger ones for the capture of the Governor. Finally the reward offered by the Government rose to one hundred guineas, three hundred acres of land free from any restrictions, or a free pardon and a passage to England. One of Brady's mates, Jefferies, betrayed him, unaware that the Governor's offer specifically excluded him and certain other leading members of the gang. After the capture of the outlaws, Jefferies was the subject of a most hostile demonstration as he was taken through the streets of Hobart, and Brady was given a hero's welcome. The official account, deploring this, goes on:

We regret to state that the Court during the trials was crowded with sympathizing ladies, who wept at the recital of Brady's sufferings, and palliate the enormity of his crimes. Brady's chivalrous behaviour to females had won their esteem; gentleness to the weak, and the brilliant feats of his career, had excited their imagination with pleasure. Following the pronouncement of death we must remark that petition followed petition for Brady's deliverance from the halter. His cell was besieged with visitors, and his table loaded with presents—baskets of fruit, bouquets of flowers, and dishes of confectionery were prepared by these fair admirers, and were tended in abundance to the gaoler for his distinguished captive. Brady's

---

[12]In the early stages of Australian land development large sheep holdings were granted to free settlers of means by the Government. When the vast Western Plains were opened many would-be graziers, irked by the red tape attending land grants, took off with their livestock into the interior and staked out their own claims to property. They were thus "squatters" in much the same sense as in Canada. When the Government caught up with them, however, their titles were usually confirmed, and the term "squatter" came to be applied by the bushworkers (as Furphy says on p. 151) to any large landowner regardless of his method of acquiring title, and, by association, to his manager if he was not resident. It thus came to be a term synonymous with "boss."

greatest vexation, he repeatedly stated, was being brought to Hobart Town in company with the monster Jefferies, and he bitterly grieved his fate that he should be hanged on the same platform with such a despicable creature.[13]

The doctrine of mateship, then, which has been the subject of such enquiry on the part of historians and sociologists, must be allowed to spring from a source very easily explained. It is an extension of the traditional "honour among thieves" which prevailed when the entire colony was no more than a prison. A state of mind was instilled then that was perpetuated long after the convict system had ended. First the convicts, then the emancipists, and after them the independent bushworkers, felt that they were the only true Australians, for they had moistened the land with their blood. As early as 1819 Judge J. H. Bent testified to the British Parliamentary Select Committee on the State of Gaols: ". . . the native youths, as they call themselves, those born in the colony, I have heard, claim the rights of the aboriginal inhabitants. They say they are solely entitled to have grants of land given to them in preference to persons from Europe; when I say native youths, I mean those who are born in the Colony, the descendants of persons sent there. . . ." To the question: "Is the opinion at all prevalent in the colony, that the colony is for the convicts and their descendants, and not for free settlers from the mother country?" Mr. Bent replied, "I have heard such opinions expressed."[14] He was to hear them again, more and more loudly as the years went by.

"Frank the Poet," a convict spokesman, remarked in 1829:

> The hardships we'd to undergo, are matters of record,
> But who believes the convict, or who regards his word?
> For starv'd and flogged and punish'd, depriv'd of all redress,
> The Bush our only refuge, with death to end distress.[15]

But more and more the Bush was to become a very real refuge, hallowed ground where sanctuary was available and where a stubborn rearguard action could be fought against the encroachments of the so-called governing class. Writing fifty years later, Joseph Furphy recorded the continuation of this attitude inherited by the free-lance bullock drivers of the outback. Willoughby, an Englishman, cannot

[13]Ingleton (ed.), *True Patriots All*, 109.
[14]Clark, *Select Documents*, 411.
[15]Ingleton (ed.), *True Patriots All*, 129.

understand why the drivers are so bitter about occasional fines for trespass, when the over-all profit of their operations makes them well able to afford such penalties.

Yet the solution is simple. The up-country man is decidedly open-handed; he will submit to crushing losses with cheerfulness, tempered, of course, by humility, in those cases where he recognizes the operation of an overhanging curse; he will subscribe to any good or bad cause with a liberality only exceeded by the digger; he will pay gambling debts with the easy, careless grace which makes every P. of W. so popular in English sporting circles—in a word, the smallest of his many sins is parsimony. But the penal suggestiveness of trespass-penalty touches the sullen dignity of his nature; and the vague, but well-founded fear of a law made and administered solely by his natural enemies makes him feel about as apprehensive as John Bunyan, though certainly more dangerous. Of course, Willoughby, born and bred a member of the governing class, couldn't easily conceive the dismay with which these outlaws regarded legal seizure for trespass—or possibly prosecution in courts dominated by the squatters.[16]

Eureka was no more than a logical continuation of an attitude already firmly established, and it would seem to be begging the question to speculate on the influence of foreign agitators at that event. The majority of historians focus their attention on Eureka as the starting point for Australian egalitarianism, and they do so as inheritors of a lingering nineteenth-century reluctance to face the harsher realities of an earlier period, when the basic division of society into two camps dictated the structure of the Australian class system. Although the squatters, as we have seen, were later to develop a nationalism of their own, they were never regarded as true Australians by the classes beneath them.

There is also evidence of some class feeling in the same period in Canada. Alexander McLachlan might proclaim that Jack was as good as his master, and the first neighbours of Mrs. Moodie might try to prove this by their boorishness. In so far as this tendency was a revolt from the restrictions of the English class system, there are similarities in its appearance in both Canada and Australia. Mrs. Moodie makes this comment:

The serving class, comparatively speaking, is small, and admits of little competition. Servants that understand the work of the country are not easily procured, and such always can command the highest wages. The

---

[16]Joseph Furphy, *Such is Life*, 37.

possession of a good servant is such an addition to comfort, that they are persons of no small consequence, for the dread of starving no longer frightens them into servile obedience. They can live without you, and they know well that you cannot do without them. If you attempt to practise upon them that common vice of English mistresses, to scold them for any slight omission or offence, you rouse into active opposition all their new-found spirit of freedom and opposition. They turn upon you with a torrent of abuse; they demand their wages, and declare their intention of quitting you instantly. The more inconvenient the time for you, the more bitter become their insulting remarks. They tell you, with a high hand, that "they are as good as you; that they can get twenty better places by the morrow, and that they don't care a snap for your anger." And away they bounce, leaving you to finish a large wash, or a heavy job of ironing, in the best way you can.[17]

In Canada the individual family marked the unit of settlement. The clearings, each of a hundred acres or so, scattered themselves across the forests and bushlands. In bad times, as Mrs. Moodie gratefully records, the help of neighbours was promptly forthcoming to those who had been accepted within the community. Yet self-help continued to be the predominant note in early Canadian pioneer life. The ideal was the establishment of a tiny family microcosm completely self-sufficient and independent. Haliburton's Old Judge makes the same point, and though his comments are intended to apply to Nova Scotia only, he substantiates Mrs. Moodie's evidence of life in Upper Canada:

There are no hamlets, no little rural villages, no collections of houses but for the purpose of trade; and, of course, there is no mutual dependence for assistance of defence; no system of landlord and tenant, of farmer and cotter, and, consequently, no motive or duty to protect and encourage on the one hand or to conciliate and sustain on the other; no material differ-ence in rank or in fortune, except in the capital, and hence no means to direct or even influence opinion; and, above all, no unity in religious belief, and, therefore, no one temple in which they can all worship together and offer up their united prayers as members of one great family to their common Father in Heaven. Interest, therefore, predominates over affection, and the ties of friendship are weak. Everyone lives by himself and for himself. People dwell on their own properties at a distance from each other, and every household constitutes its own little world; but even here the habit of early migration from the parental roof and a total want

---

[17]Susanna Moodie, *Roughing It in the Bush*, 223.

of local attachment added to a strong and confident feeling of self-reliance weaken the force of domestic love, and the heart suffers. Woman, we are told, was made for man; but alas! man in America was made for himself. He is independent of the world and can do without it. He is full of expedients and able to support himself. He can, and often does, remove far into the depths of the forest, where, alone and unaided, he erects his own house and ministers to his own wants.[18]

When one turns to Australia, one is confronted by the very striking similarity of initial outlook. Here, one cannot but say, is the same type of people with the same instincts, and a desire to follow the same course. The earliest convicts felt that the class boundaries of England had no application in the wild new country, and their favourite sport was to jeer, heckle, and parody the distinctions of society which some had attempted to transplant to new soil. Mrs. Moodie's first neighbours, recognizing her membership in a class to which they had formerly been forced to show extravagant respect, showed their own class-consciousness, though they would deny it, in the delight which they took in humiliating her. As Mrs. Moodie herself recognized, frontier life was not for those who wished to maintain the sensibilities of gentility founded on English conditions. In Canada it was economically possible for such people to realize their ambitions of independence; indeed their very lack of such sensibilities often proved an advantage to them in meeting the demands of their environment.

But in Australia, though the attitude might be identical, the environment dictated other means for its expression. The first ticket-of-leave men, encouraged by Phillip and Macquarie, took small land grants, and went into the bush to clear away the scrub, form small farms, and fulfil their ideals of independence; hundreds of small farmers from England arrived as free settlers to do the same thing. But the country defeated them. The climate of Canada, though far colder than the English, was still a northern one. The settlers were able to adapt themselves comparatively easily to the more intense, but familiar, round of the seasons. Water was never a problem, and the soil, though sometimes rocky, was rich, and responded in proportion to the labour expended in its preparation.

[18]T. C. Haliburton, *Sam Slick*, 346. Haliburton is, of course, writing in support of a special case, but the evidence he presents is valid enough to justify its use here in a wider context.

In Australia everything was different. Winter and summer the sun still beat down on the parched earth. Water was always a problem; rain, when it came, often arrived in such a deluge that all the top-soil, painfully scratched in preparation for the seed, would be washed away, and the task had to be begun again. In the height of summer, the gum-trees denied the gentle familiar shade of Canadian elms and oaks, and there was no lake nearby from which water could be drawn. The comparatively fertile lands around Sydney had early been allocated in large tracts to the wealthier settlers, who found that the profit from grazing was far greater than that from farming. One by one, the smaller farmers gave up. Their land was either appropriated by the grazing estates, or consolidated by the military government into large collective units operated by the convicts. As late as 1830, over 50 per cent of the grain food grown in the colony came from government-operated farms where there were no labour costs to contend with. In spite of this, the cost of bread in New South Wales was always proportionately much higher than the cost of meat, and it was not until the huge wheat farms of the western plains came into operation that agriculture could operate successfully without government subsidy.

Obviously, the first attempt to achieve self-sufficiency and independence on the part of the free settler without means failed in Australia, where it largely succeeded in Canada. The next step was dictated to him, and usually meant the end of his dreams. Many free settlers and their families became the dependents of the larger estates; for in Australia, while large land grants accompanied by large initial capital meant correspondingly large profits, the marginal level of production remained far above the heads of those with small grants and virtually no capital. Here is the origin of another facet of that class bitterness still to be found in the country. Already present in the convicts and their descendants, it was reinforced in the smaller free settlers who found themselves, after the failure of their first enterprise, in a state of equal or greater dependency than that which they had endured in England. Those of them who rebelled joined the nomadic bush-workers, dependent for their special position in bush life upon their membership in a class or group. The ideal of personal self-sufficiency had to be exchanged for that of the doctrine of mateship and for the self-sufficiency of their class. An attack upon it or on one of its members threatened all the others. Paradoxically, the principles of unionism in Australia had their origins in the frustrated dreams of man living by and for himself, of which Haliburton speaks.

The free nomadic bushworkers had a horror of becoming permanently attached to a station, of becoming what Furphy was later to call "a wage-slave"; with the contract work of shearing and bullocking, there was at least the vestige of self-respect that came from calling oneself a "contractor," and they looked with pity and some scorn upon those who had surrendered their independent status to work as the servants of one employer. How different from Mrs. Moodie's description of the weakening of class barriers in the Canadian bush is this account of Australian station organization:

In the accurately graded society of a proper station, you have a reproduction of the Temple economy under the old Jewish ritual. The manager's house is a Sanctum Sanctorum, wherein no one but the high priest enters; the barracks is an Inner Court, accessible to the priests only; the men's hut is an Outer Court, for the accommodation of lay worshippers; and the nearest pine-ridge, or perhaps one of the empty huts at the wool-shed, is the Court of the Gentiles. And the restrictions of the Temple were never more rigid than those of a self-respecting station. This usage, of course, bears fruit after its kind.[19]

The fruit of which Furphy speaks is to be seen in the rising tension between the squatters and those who served them. He goes on to outline the development of the master-servant relationship in Australia, and again one may see the same ambitions of independence. But here these ambitions were frustrated, whereas they were given free rein in Canada.

The squatter of half-a-century ago [1820] dominated his immigrant servants by moral force—no difficult matter, with a "gentleman" on one side and a squad of hereditary grovellers on the other. He dominated his convict servants by physical force—an equally easy task. But now the old squatter has gone to the mansions above; the immigrant and old hand convict to the kitchen below; and between the self-evaluation of the latter-day squatter and that of his contemporary wage-slave there is very little to choose. Hence the toe of the blucher treads on the heel of the tan boot, and galls its stitches. The average share of that knowledge which is power is undoubtedly in favour of the tan boot; but the preponderant moiety is just as surely held by the blucher. In our democracy, the sum of cultivated

---

[19]Furphy, *Such Is Life*, 225.

intelligence, and corresponding sensitiveness to affront, is dangerously high and becoming higher. On the other hand, the squatter, even if pliant by disposition, cannot spring to the strain; social usage being territorial rather than personal; so here, you see, we have the two factors which should blend together in harmony—namely the stubborn tradition of the soil, and the elastic genius of the "masses"—divorced by an ever-widening breach. There are two remedies, and only two; failing one of these, something must, sooner or later, give way with a crash. Either the anachronistic tradition must make suicidal concessions, or the better-class people must drown all plebeian Australian males in infancy, and fill the vacancy with Asiatics.[20]

In Canada, Jack may be as good as his master and have the power to show it without fear of reprisal. Because of this, the inferiority feeling which is the initial cause of any violent expression of equality has no continuing motive, and aggressiveness dies away. The result can be, as Canada has shown, a community with very little class-consciousness or bitterness, for it is futile to keep insisting on the obvious. But in Australia there is an equal conviction that Jack is every bit as good as, if not a great deal better than, his master. There was, however, no equivalent to the Canadian method of realizing this, except for the highly precarious expedient of following the path of the nomadic bushworkers. The sense of injustice which has sprung from this frustration has led to a highly aggressive insistence on egalitarianism, an insistence which is felt to be necessary only because the economic conditions for its attainment have not been realized. As both town life and regular employment on a grazing property appeared to endanger the bushman's independence, the only alternative was to join the roving bushworkers; married men made caravans and trailed their families over the countryside from job to job, while the unmarried ones went singly or in pairs on foot. These "sundowners" formed the nucleus of what was to become the Great Bush Myth in Australia. They, far more than their settled brothers who were eventually to outnumber them, were to exemplify the aggressive egalitarianism of the Australian character; and even now, when their numbers have greatly diminished and when members of the Australian Workers Union (consisting chiefly of shearers and other seasonal workers) are among the most highly paid members of the community, their traditions have become the basis for a national mythology.

[20]Ibid., 255–6.

To a lesser extent Canada has an equivalent mythology. The Rising of 1837 has been paired with the Eureka movement in Australia, and in spite of apparent contradictions, the pairing is a valid one. The self-reliance of what Professor Underhill has termed "the intelligent yeomanry" of Upper Canada was threatened by insurgents who were fighting fundamentally against abuses that were not unknown to their Australian counterparts. Eureka was fought against a group of professional soldiers, while the 1837 Rising in Upper Canada was put down by a militia largely drawn from the ranks of the backwoodsmen themselves. It was as though economic conditions had made a Salisbury Oath effective in Canada and not in Australia. The settler who had achieved self-sufficiency was by nature a conservative, for he owed his independence to a government that left him alone to work out his own salvation. The Canadian settler's sense of responsibility and his fear of the implications of Jacksonian democracy was reinforced by intelligent self-interest coupled with a sentimental attachment to Great Britain.

This Canadian attitude was largely reflected in Australia by the larger landowners, who found themselves in very similar circumstances. The protection and encouragement of their sheep-runs was the principal benevolence of the government, and the class division fostered a close connection with Britain, both emotional and economic. They felt little kinship with the descendants of felons or the transient and ragged members of the nomadic bushworking class. Early in the century, the Bigge Report deplored the lack of a middle class, of a sturdy yeomanry, in Australia. The programme for the encouragement of emigration of free settlers, for long was not, as we have seen, successful in fostering such a class. Greater government intervention became an established tradition, but there was nothing new in this. For the first thirty years of its life the colony was without any large number of free settlers, and the government regulated every facet of life. After the failure of first parties of the potential middle class, they too were dependent upon the government for relief, but by this time the Colonial Office had made the mistake of imagining that New South Wales was ready for gradual transition to the type of government emerging in the Canadian colonies.

Assistance was given to the large landholders in the early stages of their enterprise. The wool industry was becoming an increasingly valuable one, and it was recognized that facilities had to be offered in the way of land grants to attract the capital and energy necessary to further it. After this initial aid, however, the graziers were on their own and were happy to be so. But again, as we have seen, this did not work on small Australian farms. Sir Thomas Brisbane, who succeeded Macquarie, reacted violently from the latter's system of governmental paternalism and attempted to apply a system, which had worked admirably in Canada, to a people whose environment was wildly different. From these seeds have sprung much of the Australian attitude that it is the task of the government to undertake a wide variety of responsibilities which in Canada are accepted as the province of the individual.

Accordingly, the ties of loyalty between settler and home-government passed through a sea change in Australia. The embittered smaller settlers believed that the government had betrayed them by providing the means to begin but not to maintain their enterprises. The police troopers, agents of that government at the local level, who were frequently called in by the large landowners to protect their property rights, became identified with the forces of repression. There was never a hint of anything resembling the public respect and affection shown by the Canadians for their red-coated Mounties. In Canada the articulate citizen regarded the policemen as his natural ally. The small settler was a small capitalist with property rights of his own to be protected. But the Australian trooper is always the villain of the piece, and resistance to him and to the squatter who lurks behind him is not only morally defensible but glorious. "Waltzing Matilda," where the swagman, discovered by the squatter and the three troopers in possession of a stolen sheep, commits suicide in the billabong rather than submit to capture, is an interesting commentary on this attitude.

Price Warung, in *Tales of the Old Regime*, quotes two verses of a convict oath that throw some light on the values of the prisoners:

> Hand to hand,
> On earth, in Hell,
> Sick or Well,
> On Sea, on Land,
> On the Square, ever.

Stiff or in Breath,
Lag or Free,
You and me
In Life, in Death,
On the Cross, never.[21]

The bushworkers were the natural legatees to this necessity for what later jargon has come to call "class solidarity." As "On the Square" and "On the Cross" were interpreted from the standpoint of convict morality as distinct from that of their wardens, so the bushworkers had their own standards which were not the same as those of the squatters and the police. It was "right" for bullockies to steal water and grass for their teams, but unspeakably heinous to steal from a comrade.

These conditions provide the basis for literary comparisons, as distinct from social ones. By 1830 the distinctions in the Canadian and Australian societies that were to diversify their common inheritance had already become apparent. Two widely different environments were shaping men and their attitudes. But it must not be forgotten that in the case of the free settlers to each country, those attitudes were at first identical. That they were to become, in such a short space of time, direct opposites of one another is one of the most interesting features of the comparison.

The great waves of migration which reached both countries in the early decades of the last century, though built on different foundations, provide the common factor of population. In Australia the economic environment and the attitudes of the convicts and emancipists were waiting to work upon the newcomers. In Canada, specifically in Upper Canada and the Maritimes, the newcomers found societies based also upon the values of those who had been there before them—including the influence of the United Empire Loyalists, who were responsible for the direct continuation into Canadian society of seventeenth-century English Puritanism, modified and perhaps narrowed by way of New England.

It has been said that a large proportion of Scots came to Canada, while most of the Irish went to Australia. The statistics do not support this contention. While it is true that in any one decade the figure for

21Quoted in Vance Palmer, *The Legend of the Nineties*, 58. "On the Square" was an expression in use among the convicts meaning loyalty and dependability. "On the Cross," conversely, meant treachery and double-dealing.

emigrants from the three main divisions of the British Isles might vary considerably between Canada and Australia, there is no significant difference to be drawn between their distribution in the two countries by 1850.

If the environment, then, could produce such striking differences in a common racial stock with similar attitudes, what was the result when a common literary tradition imported with them was subjected to the full vigour of these influences? We are now perhaps in a position to examine this question in detail.

3. The Eighteenth-Century Inheritance

Where Sydney Cove her lucid bosom swells,
Courts her young navies, and the storm repels;
High on a rock amid the troubled air
Hope stood sublime, and wav'd her golden hair;
Calm'd with her rosy smile the tossing deep,
And with sweet accents charm'd the winds to sleep;
To each high plain she stretched her snowy hand,
High-waving wood, and sea-encircled strand.
"Hear me," she cried, "ye rising Realms! record
"Time's opening scenes, and Truth's unerring word.—
"*There* shall broad streets their stately walls extend,
"The circus widen and the crescent bend;
"*There*, ray'd from cities o'er the cultured land,
"Shall bright canals, and solid roads expand. —
"*There* the proud arch, Colossus-like, bestride
"Yon glittering streams, and bound the chafing tide;
"Embellished villas crown the landscape-scene,
"Farms wave with gold, and orchards blush between. —
"*There* shall tall spires, dome-capt towers ascend,
"And piers and quays their massy structures blend;
"While with each breeze approaching vessels glide,
"And northern treasures dance on every tide!" —
Then ceased the nymph—tumultuous echoes roar,
And joy's loud voice was heard from shore to shore —
Her graceful steps descending press'd the plain,
And peace, and art, and labour, join'd her train.[1]

> Erasmus Darwin, "Visit of Hope to
> Sydney-Cove, Near Botany-Bay," 1789.

[1]Ingleton (ed.), *True Patriots All*, 5.

DARWIN'S POEM, published in England not twelve months after the establishment of the first settlement, is an excellent example of the official verse tradition which the colony was to inherit. Darwin had, of course, never seen Sydney Cove, and though the bursting optimism of the poem might, thirty years later, have been mistaken for a report of Governor Macquarie's planning committee, it must have appeared strange to any of the thousand men who were balancing on the edge of starvation at the time of its appearance. Nevertheless, the theme was a dominant one in some circles. Although they wrote in cautious and sober prose, both Phillip and Macquarie were to propound their visions of "another Britain in the southern seas"—and they were to be reprimanded for it. A sink for surplus felons was all that was required. However, in poetry this type of sentiment was satisfactory, for the ideal, even the sublime, was the prerogative of poetry, and no one expected the Colonial Office to carry it into effect.

Michael Massey Robinson, an Oxford graduate transported for forgery, was the convict "poet laureate" of the early colony, and he composed official odes for royal birthdays which reflected the same type of spirit, although there is good reason to imagine him with tongue in cheek for many of these works. One may compare the lines from his Prologue to a Sydney theatrical performance:[2]

> From distant climes o'er widespread seas we come,
> Though not with much eclat or beat of drum,
> True patriots all; for be it understood,
> We left our country for our country's good;
> No private views disgraced our generous zeal,
> What urg'd our travels was our country's weal;
> And none will doubt but that our emigration
> Has prov'd most useful to the British nation.[3]

with this from his Ode for the Queen's Birthday, 1816:

> True to the great Example of their Sires,
> Where Duty calls, and native Ardour fires; —
> Advent'rous Britons still that Impulse feel,
> Which prompts to Glory, and their Country's Weal!
> But not, alone, on Ocean's vast Domain

[2]J. K. Ewers (in Creative Writing in Australia, 31) follows the common error of attributing this passage to the actor Barrington.
[3]Ingleton (ed.), True Patriots All, viii.

> They glean the Spoils his deep dark caves contain,
> Or where the Harpoon's lengthen'd Line is hurl'd,
> Grapple the Giants of the watery World —
> Tracts of untravers'd EARTH their Toils explore,
> And add new Triumphs to AUSTRALIA's Shore![4]

As Robinson received a reward of two cows from the government herd for his verse-making, presumably his odes proved acceptable in official circles. However, in addition to these more ceremonial productions, Robinson also composed a large number of other works, openly satirical in nature. It is only in the last fifteen years, following the collection and publication of his odes, that research has established his claim to other verse of a more openly pungent nature. The odes have been largely dismissed as "stilted and lifeless echoes of the eighteenth century"[5] and as verse "of historical interest but small merit."[6] If the reader takes them at face value, he will have little difficulty in agreeing with Green's verdict; but it is impossible to avoid seeing the similarity, even to the use of identical phrases, between Robinson's official and his satirical verse. It is more probable that this convict, who in his other poetry is so obviously infected with the prevailing custom of poking fun at authority, incorporated in the odes a rich vein of irony, which was completely overlooked by a bored officialdom.

On the face of it, Michael Massey Robinson in his official odes would seem to celebrate the settlement of New South Wales as an idyllic process which had begun to sweep steadily towards its goal, attended by a solid phalanx of personified Virtues whose chief occupation was to inspire a group of devoted and idealistic settlers to fulfil a plan pre-ordained by the Almighty. One may find a ready equivalent in Canada in Oliver Goldsmith's *The Rising Village*. The general tone is astonishingly similar to that of the convict poet. Compare Robinson's selfless heroes to Goldsmith's. Here is the Australian version:

> Far brighter Trophies ALBION's Heroes bore,
> When Glory call'd them to a distant Shore:

[4]Mackaness (ed.), *Anthology*, 320.
[5]H. M. Green, *An Outline of Australian Literature*, 19.
[6]Rex Ingamells, *Handbook of Australian Literature*, 10.

When, on the raging Bosom of the Deep,
They watch'd the giddy Mast's impending Steep;

....

Taught the reluctant stubborn Glebe to yield,
And in the Desert sprung the cultur'd Field.[7]

And here is Goldsmith's account:

What noble courage must their hearts have fired,
How great the ardour which their souls inspired,
Who, leaving far behind their native plain,
Have sought a home beyond the western main;
And braved the terrors of the stormy seas
In search of wealth, of freedom, and of ease!
Oh! none can tell but they who sadly share
The bosom's anguish and its wild despair,
What dire distress awaits the hardy bands
That venture first on bleak and desert lands. . . .[8]

In style the two works are much the same; yet, from these passages, but for Goldsmith's references to the search for wealth, freedom, and ease, one might well take his to be the convict's lament, and Robinson's the account of the prosperous settlement of a rising village. That Goldsmith's work was itself in imitation of his great-uncle's famous poem would support the conclusion that in both countries the eightenth-century tradition has been imported directly, and has been used in the same way by second-rate poets to describe the settlement of Englishmen in new lands; which, fundamentally, was experience common to newcomers in Canada and Australia. But the fact remains that before 1820 not only were the physical conditions of the settlements themselves widely different in nature, but the two systems under which the transplantation of migrants was effected had virtually no points in common.

In Nova Scotia, Goldsmith, setting out to "describe the hardships the early settlers experienced, the difficulties which they surmounted, the rise and progress of a young country, and the prospects which promise happiness to its future possessors,"[9] had ostensibly the same

[7]Mackaness (ed.), Anthology, 320–1.
[8]A. J. M. Smith (ed.), Book of Canadian Poetry, 68.
[9]Desmond Pacey, Creative Writing in Canada, 10.

aim as Robinson in his series of odes. As exercises in the application of a poetic convention to a new physical environment, Goldsmith's works are perhaps the more successful. If Robinson's poems are interpreted in the light of satires, however, a new evaluation is necessary. The very commonplaces form an ironical indictment of the official interpretation of the facts of convict life. In such circumstances the complete avoidance of any mention of hardship (however noble) has an added significance. Goldsmith, whether or not he was successful, does attempt to trace the very real miseries which beset the early settlers. Robinson, though the wretchedness which he had himself seen and experienced must have far outweighed anything in Goldsmith's knowledge, makes no mention of it at all. The two sides of his poetry do not represent an elaborate hypocrisy; rather do they emphasize the difference between the official and the actual, a difference glaringly apparent. He was protected by the assumption itself. The administration, even had its suspicions been aroused, could not have censured such exaggerated praise of itself, and the very exaggeration, so wildly at variance with the facts, displayed an obvious criticism as effective as the more direct "pipes" and broadsheets.

The poems, taken as a whole, show the effects of an incipient nationalism upon an established convention. If the odes are read as a series of official verses, they are attempts to deal in optimistic terms with the future of the new country. Taken as satires, they are significant as adaptations of the conventional eulogy used for the purpose of satire—a process made quite familiar by Pope. In either case the poetry is of interest as the first evidence of a celebration of the native scene in terms of the imported tradition. The same is true in Goldsmith's case, yet the native scene which he had to describe imposed some obvious distinctions.

The Nova Scotia he was describing was a community which was representative of the highly developed cultural centres of Halifax, Windsor, and Annapolis, surrounded by a hinterland which represented very different standards of values. In these centres the stratification of society on English lines was advanced; the level of journalism, as evidenced by such men as Howe and Haliburton, was high, and the upper classes extremely literate, if not literary. In the hinterland, the social pattern described by Mrs. Moodie in the backwoods of Upper Canada applied with few local variations. Class-consciousness was strong at first, with a considerable degree of suspicion in the attitude of the settlers towards strangers; however, this diminished as the concept of equality was taken for granted. There is no more a picture of the development of this type of society in *The Rising Village* than there is of the convict in Robinson's odes. The scene presented by Goldsmith to his audience among the Halifax upper classes is that of the struggle of the diligent rustic, couched largely in English terms, with local variants where applicable, though the variants, again, are explained in English terms. The hinterland of Nova Scotia was thus *explained* to its own capital city in English terms. This had to be so, for the literary standards of Halifax were purely English ones, and the medium of description and interpretation had remained English during the century of the colony's existence. The rustics so described would neither understand nor be expected to understand the manner in which they had been represented.

In Canada, as in Australia, the particularity of the local scene was at first interpreted through the generality of the English tradition. Great thoughts, should they happen to be present, could remain general. They would emerge without the need to distinguish a particular local variety of nature manifesting herself. This was not difficult in the case of Canada. The scenery, vast and wild as it was, was not unlike parts of the European scene. The seasons, though intensified, were essentially the same, and came in regular succession during the accustomed months of the year. The need for accurate differentiation did not present itself as an acute problem.

In Australia it did from the beginning. The English-trained eye had few starting points from which to work. The trees shed their bark instead of their leaves; the seasons were back-to-front, and the distinction between them not clearly marked; the native animals were like mutations from a biologist's nightmare, and the soothing generalities of a diction based upon European nature were glaringly wrong. Vance Palmer has suggested that Barron Field, in his *First Fruits*, resorted to amused detachment as the only solution to a problem too big for him. As we shall see, Tompson, Harpur, and Kendall, the only three poets of note in the first seven decades of the century, were also troubled about this search for a starting point, and the lack of the need for this concern in Canada may be a contributing factor to the more impressive output and achievement of Canadian poets in the same period. They too were imitative, but they did not have as far to go as the Australians in achieving a measure of self-identification within the English tradition. They could coast along comfortably for a while on a tradition imported and only slightly adapted. It was not so obviously an importation, so completely un-suitable, as it was for the Australians. This is the first important point to note in considering the all-important question (discussed more fully later[10]) of the process by which a poet in a new environment learns to look at nature.

For corresponding reasons, the nineteenth century in Australia was to produce a quantity of prose, particularly prose-fiction, better than that produced in Canada over the same period. Prose, lacking the restrictions of poetic form and diction, is less susceptible to tradition, less rigid in its modes of expression. The early non-fictional prose written in both countries is of excellent quality; the majority of the letters, journals, diaries, and descriptive accounts of life in the country are readable and accurate. They need only to be made accessible to the general reader by collection and publication to assume the posi-tion of importance in our literatures that they already hold in the minds of those specialists who have had access to the manuscripts. One legacy of the eighteenth century which prevailed was the careful observation and recording of experience, and early Canadian and Australian literature was at its best when the feelings and imagination were not self-consciously involved in finding formal means for their expression. As Vance Palmer has said of the settlement period in Australia: "If the bulk of its essays, verse and pseudo-novels were swept away, no loss would be felt; there is little in them that has even historical value. But it is different with the journals of thoughtful men of action like Sturt and Leichardt, and the careful observations of that Scots tradesman, Alexander Harris."[11]

This is an extreme view, but much the same could be said of the numerous Canadian journals of exploration, and such special records as the Jesuit Relations. In Nova Scotia, at the same period, this was also true. Thomas Haliburton's *General Description of Nova Scotia* provided a prose equivalent to Goldsmith's *The Rising Village*, with

[10]See chap. IV.
[11]Vance Palmer, *Legend of the Nineties*, 57.

Haliburton more successful in achieving his aim than Goldsmith had been.

Expository prose is confined by less rigid restrictions than is poetry, and prose of this type offers itself as a medium especially suitable in the interpretation of a new environment. For as great poetry may mark the zenith of creative writing, so bad poetry may sink to a corresponding nadir. Prose may not fly so high in its successes, but neither does it fall so low in its failures. The plain style provides as admirable a means of communication as it is possible to achieve between men of common language. It is relatively free from the straitjacket of poetic diction which, from one source, may develop as a convention attached to a specific physical environment. For its success poetry must be dependent upon a diction which is held in common among the majority of readers, and this is particularly true of descriptive poetry, which relies for its success upon the evocation of mood and emotions. These in turn are usually dependent upon a common frame of reference. While the greatest poetry may rise above such considerations, creating its own field of reference, it is still based firmly upon them. It is possibly only when such factors are so well established that they may be taken for granted that great poetry can emerge. Second-rate poetry does not rise to such heights and so is almost entirely dependent upon the appropriateness and skill with which technique and subject-matter are joined, in a particular frame of reference. Competent prose, on the other hand, may be more successful in working cautiously from the known to the unknown. For, while it too must be bound to some extent by the traditions of comprehension based on the reader's own experience, it does not contain as many restrictions inherent in the form itself as does poetry. The need for an objective correlative does not arise to the same degree.

All this, of course, refers to prose outside the novel, which, as an art form, has imposed its own set of conventions and restrictions. Fenimore Cooper's early novels, Richardson's *Wacousta*, and Mrs. Moodie's works of fiction reveal the influence of a supposed necessity to conform to traditions based upon an environment very different from their own. In Canada, as we shall see in chapter vii, the restrictions of these traditions were also imposed later upon expository and descriptive prose published in such periodicals as the *Literary Garland*.

Thomas Chandler Haliburton was able to adapt the best of both worlds to suit his purpose, for while his *General Description* does not make such vivid reading as Alexander Harris's *Settlers and Convicts* or Cunningham's *Life in the Colony of New South Wales*, he prepares the way for successes greater than either of these. Unlike Harris and Cunningham, Haliburton is concerned with speculation on the principles and anomalies that arise when a civilized race transplants itself to an uncivilized country. Reason would seem to dictate a pattern of development which could be assumed to follow; but, in fact, it does not. The tracing of the causes of this apparent contradiction, and allotting the blame for it, provide a unity to the work which is lacking in the more disjointed Australian productions.

The appearance of *The Clockmaker* series has no parallel in Australian literature. Haliburton, possessed by a fierce local patriotism, strongly imbued with the traditions of Tory aristocracy, made no secret of his double purpose: of arousing his countrymen to new energy and ambition in fulfilling the potentialities of the colony, and at the same time of convincing the Colonial Office that the settlement was not, and did not deserve to be treated as, the Cinderella of the Empire. To accomplish this aim he succeeded in blending two traditions with such originality that his work marks the first genuine contribution of Canadian letters to literature in English.

Haliburton set out to portray, by a series of sketches, his views on the social, political, and economic problems of Nova Scotia. In carrying out his intention of attacking what he considered the dangerous concern for reform prevailing in the colony, Haliburton drew upon the English traditions of Swift and Burke. Nova Scotians would do well to attend more to their own immediate practical problems, and not waste their time and energies pursuing political will-o'-the-wisps. To point the moral, Haliburton created the figure of the irrepressible Yankee, Sam Slick. It was a far cry from the polished admonishments of Swift and Burke to the rough sophistry of a New England pedlar, and in making the adaptation, Haliburton drew upon a second, this time American, tradition.

There was already a rapidly developing American mythology of folk-heroes. Davy Crockett had become the centre of one such collection of legends, involving tall tales and feats of heroic proportions. Buffalo Bill, Paul Bunyan, and Kit Carson were to succeed him in later decades as representatives of American civilization advancing westward into the unknown. Jacksonian democracy had emphasized the virtues of the "natural" man, and the self-conscious aspects of frontier life had been elevated to a type of authenticity by the employment of certain genuine pioneers as symbols of the new "natural" Everyman, or, more accurately, the new Superman.

Accompanying the element of exaggeration in American humour was the element of fraud. Life was highly competitive and it was necessary to outwit others or be outwitted oneself. This in turn led to a high regard for "smartness" or "slickness" as a factor determining one's place in frontier society. Charles Dickens complained in the eighteen-forties that in America smartness was extolled at the expense of honesty, and Trollope later found the same thing. He was told: "On the frontier a man is bound to be smart. If he ain't smart he's better go back East; perhaps as far as Europe. He'll do there."[12] Frauds and swindles were the basis for delighted appreciation.

One finds the same attitude in Australian humour. The Australian bushman, feeling himself to be the only real Australian, took delight in outwitting, by means of his native cunning, the squatters and police, who had only the artificial benefits of their money and their authority to uphold them. The Australian nomadic worker was the equivalent to the "natural man" of the American frontier. However, in the United States, because of the absence of the need for class feeling that arose in Australia, fraud could be perpetrated legitimately against any individual, regardless of his class. In Australia it was a case of the triumph of one group—usually the bushmen—over its natural enemies.

In *The Clockmaker* can be found the Canadian compromise, the epitome of this "slickness" used for a moral purpose, developing a subtlety that contrasts strongly with the more blatant dishonesty openly praised in the frontier tales of the United States. The Yankee pedlar with his wooden nutmegs was a well-known figure in American humour by the beginning of the nineteenth century, and in such a character Haliburton found the goad he could apply to the inert elements of Nova Scotia life.

We do not know if Haliburton was familiar with the work of Hugh Brackenridge, but there is an interesting parallel to be drawn

12Anthony Trollope, *North America*, 1, 188.

between *The Clockmaker* series and Brackenridge's *Modern Chivalry: or the Adventures of Captain Farrago and Teagus O'Regan*, published in Boston in 1815.[13] Farrago is a frontiersman, from western Pennsylvania, who has acquired an Irish servant, Teague. These two go visiting the East, and their adventures occasion the satirical description of a number of prominent New England institutions. Teague is suspected of being a philosopher and professor of Greek, and narrowly avoids election to the Pennsylvania State Legislature. This work, in turn, is an adaptation of the Don Quixote model, and Teague marks a half-way point between Sancho Panza and Sam Slick. He is neither as naive as Cervantes' character, nor as shrewd as Haliburton's. Like Sam, Teague has the gift of swift repartee and comic exaggeration, together with the Irish ability to reveal obvious but hitherto disguised absurdity by seemingly innocent description. As Sam Slick feels he is more more than a match for the Nova Scotians, so Teague is convinced of Yankee simplicity. Like Haliburton, Brackenridge was a patrician who was fully aware of the excesses of democracy, yet also opposed to the smug stolidity of many New England institutions. He regarded the frontier with great enthusiasm, and felt that the greatest hope for real democracy lay not in institutions but in the hard-working and independent pioneers of the West. It was to these that he addressed himself: "It is Tom, Dick and Harry in the woods that I want to read my book."[14] Haliburton would have little sympathy with this aspect of Brackenridge's beliefs, for the author of *Modern Chivalry*, despite his strictures on his fellow countrymen, remained a fervent admirer of the type of society evolving in the United States. Sam Slick, on the other hand, represented all those traits of bumptiousness which Haliburton so detested, and while his self-confidence and ingenuity are characteristics that Nova Scotians would do well to copy, he is the caricature of a national prototype that Haliburton did not admire. But as Will Honeycomb provided the Spectator with many opportunities for criticizing the traditions of morality and breeding surviving from Restoration days, remaining himself a not unsympathetic character, so Sam Slick provided Haliburton with a means of combining his social message with entertainment.

[13]Hugh Brackenridge, *Modern Chivalry* (ed. C. M. Newlin), New York, 1937. See also Quinn (ed.), *The Literature of the American People*, 191.
[14]Quinn (ed.), *The Literature of the American People*, 191.

Haliburton's combination of the particular and the universal brought him great success not only within the bounds of Nova Scotia, for Haliburton gave his English readers a picture of the type of American they had already visualized. He confirmed and brought to life their own prejudiced conception of the typical Yankee. At the same time, the sketches were expressed with such easy and apparently appropriate wit that English readers began to believe that a new and original form of creative writing was emerging from their colony in North America. Ironically, from this impression that at last there was a book authentically North American in spirit, rather pseudo-European, sprang the association of Sam Slick's humour with the United States and its literature, rather than with a Canadian commentary upon it. The nature of the humour of Sam Slick has been discussed so often that recapitulation would serve no useful function here; it is more to the point to insist upon the synthesis between the tradition of entertaining sketches joined to a didactic purpose, and the already established New England tradition of "wisecracks" and "smart alecks."

Haliburton concerned himself with the middle classes in Nova Scotia: the educated, the merchants, and the yeomanry. Unlike Brackenridge, he did not call upon every "Tom, Dick, and Harry" as the hope of the colony. His was not an emotional appeal to the masses, but a reasoned plea for each member of society to play his part in the station of life in which he found himself. Inevitably, he found his greatest audience among the middle classes.

To summarize—Nova Scotian, or rather Halifax, society at the turn of the eighteenth century had already assumed the elements of stratification to be found in English provincial circles, and had developed a degree of sophistication, security, and leisure sufficient for the development of an appreciation of cultural values. This was ground prepared for easy adaptation of the English tradition. This tradition joined the native pungency of the North American tradition which contrasted strongly with the more rigid social climate of Halifax, and produced the originality of Haliburton. *The Clockmaker* series mark more than a starting point in Canadian letters, for in some ways they mark an end as well. Haliburton's Sam Slick marks the beginning of a true integration of the British and the North American traditions. Unfortunately, for some considerable time, he also marks the end. His is the Canadian equivalent of the native characterization to be found at the end of the century in Henry Lawson's Australian short stories, which were to have no parallel development in Canada at that time. The way had been prepared for a distinctively Canadian literary tradition, but no one followed the lead. It was for Mark Twain to follow on, and to annex for American literature the type of character that Haliburton had created. Canadian critics could not see the difference between the synthesis that Haliburton had created and the unadulterated American slick humour south of the border. As a result, Canadian writers and critics drew back in well-bred horror from the distasteful crudities of the frontier, and looked, more resolutely than ever, eastward across the Atlantic to the source of all good things.

In the Australia of 1835 there was no audience, the equivalent of Haliburton's, ready to be addressed. The middle class was virtually non-existent; the upper class of large landowners and wealthy merchants had little interest in literary subjects, and the lower classes, except for their ballads, were as yet inarticulate. The inhabitants of New South Wales seemed to have neither time nor inclination to consider a discussion of the manner in which life should be conducted; for them it was enough that life should be conducted at all in such circumstances. Literature, the upper classes felt, was all very well when there was time for it, but it was softening, and this was a time for hardness. The wealthiest of all the "Pure Merinos," John Macarthur, in a letter to England reflects the attitude of the landowners:

With respect to numbers I fear that my flocks must remain stationary, unless an unexpected change should be made in the system of managing the prisoners. It is now the most difficult thing to keep a small number in any kind of order and I am of the opinion that he who should employ many, would injure instead of improve his fortune. I am endeavouring to break James and William in by degrees to oversee and manage my affairs. They appear to be contented with their lot, but I by no means think them well calculated for it. They have not sufficient harshness of character to manage the people placed under their control, and they set too little value upon money, for the profession of agriculture, which as you know requires that not a penny should be expended without good reason.[15]

The spirit of the Australian colonies was not one to encourage

[15] J. Macarthur to W. Davidson, September 3, 1818. Clark, *Select Documents*, 270.

romantic dreams of new horizons and the touch of the eighteenth century was slow to depart. As Vance Palmer says: "They held to the eighteenth century and took care that its attitudes should prevail long after they had broken down overseas; that is to say after the defeat of Napoleon had made it unnecessary to close ranks against the ideas of the French Revolution and of such English supporters of it as Shelley, Hazlitt and Byron."[16]

The Australian landowner had definite and practical ideas on how an outpost of civilization was to be maintained, and he was not concerned with any literary discussion on the niceties of civilized living. The ideas of the French Revolution were far from being academic questions half-a-world away. The defeat of Napoleon made no difference to the inhabitants of a prison settlement. For the government and the graziers there had always to be constant vigilance, as there must be in any gaol. As late as 1828, 46.4 per cent of the population of New South Wales were convicts in full custody, not counting ticket-of-leave men, emancipists, and their families. The free settlers and graziers, those who had no convict associations, together with military forces, guards, and government officials, made up only 15.7 per cent of the total number.[17]

In such an atmosphere bitterness was inevitable, but there was no Shelley on hand to ennoble the bitterness to transcendent idealism for the convicts, nor a Hazlitt to propose to the graziers concepts which would overturn their economy and closed society. What there was can perhaps be suggested by a comparison of two authors, William Wentworth and Barron Field.

William Charles Wentworth, the parodied "Earl of Vaucluse," was born in 1791 at Norfolk Island off the New South Wales coast. In England to complete his education, he wrote his long poem *Australasia* in 1822 as an academic exercise for the Chancellor's medal at Cambridge. Enthusiastically, he invokes an Australian Muse:

> No child of song has yet invoked thy aid
> 'Neath their primeval solitary shade,—
> Still, gracious Pow'r, some kindling soul inspire,
> To wake to life my country's unknown lyre,
> That from creation's date has slumbering lain,

16Palmer, *Legend of the Nineties*, 56.
17Clark, *Select Documents*, 406.

Or only breathed some savage uncouth strain;
And grant that yet an Austral Milton's song
Pactolus-like flow deep and rich along,—
An Austral Shakespeare rise, whose living page
To nature true may charm in ev'ry age;—
And that an Austral Pindar daring soar,
Where not the Theban eagle reach'd before.[18]

If his ambitions for the future of Australian literature were great, his
hopes for her future place in world affairs were even greater:

And, Oh Britannia! should'st thou cease to ride
Despotic Empress of old Ocean's tide;—
Should thy tam'd Lion—spent his former might—
No longer roar, the terror of the fight:—
Should e'er arrive that dark, disastrous hour,
When, bow'd by luxury, thou yield'st to pow'r;
When thou, no longer freest of the free,
To some proud victor bend'st the vanquish'd knee;—
May all thy glories in another sphere
Relume, and shine more brightly still than here;
May this—thy last-born INFANT—then arise,
To glad thy heart, and greet thy PARENT eyes;
And AUSTRALASIA float, with flag unfurl'd
A new BRITANNIA in another world![19]

Many of the late Nevil Shute's ideas were thus anticipated by over
130 years. It must not be forgotten that these sentiments were
expressed only thirty-four years after the first landing, and they
mark the measure of difference between the native-born Australian
on the one hand, and the English administrator, temporarily exiled,
on the other.

Barron Field, the first Justice appointed to the colony, was very
much the exile waiting to return home. An intimate in the English
literary circles that included Leigh Hunt, Charles Lamb, Wordsworth, and Coleridge, Field was amused with speculations about the
manner in which a poet could approach the task of describing such a
country. There was no real starting point, and so this itself became the
basis for his own attempts. It was a huge joke that after the botanists
of Europe had picked, squashed, dried, and classified tens of thousands of plants, and assigned to them impressive Latin names, here,

[18]Bertram Stevens (ed.), *Anthology*, 3–4.
[19]G. B. Barton (ed.), *Poets and Prose Writers of New South Wales*, 29.

at Botany Bay, were thousands more waiting for them, mocking their hopes of ever reaching an end. Then too:

> Still fewer (perhaps none) of all these Flowers
> Have been by Poet sung. Poets are few
> And Botanists are many, and good cheap.[20]

Perhaps these were Titania's flowers, for if Puck could throw a girdle round the earth it must have passed over Botany Bay. When he came to the fauna there was nothing else to do but sit back and laugh. How could one apply the familiar terms of English pastoral poetry to the kangaroo?

> She had made the squirrel fragile;
> She had made the bounding hart;
> But a third so strong and agile
> Was beyond ev'n Nature's art;
> So she join'd the former two
>   In thee, Kangaroo!

Could a stirring hunting song be written about it?

> Better-proportion'd animal
> More graceful or etherial,
> Was never followed by the hound,
> With fifty steps to thy one bound.

Whimsy is the only defence of the cultivated sensibility when confronted by the "divine mistakes" of the Australian continent:

> When sooty swans are once more rare,
> And duck-moles the Museum's care,
> Be still the glory of this land,
> Happiest Work of finest Hand![21]

Charles Lamb assured him that "both Wordsworth and Coleridge were hugely taken with your Kangaroo"[22] but parody cannot sustain poetic flights for long.

When Field looked about him for inspiration in more serious mood, there was nowhere to begin. Not only were the physical aspects of the landscape unfamiliar, but, to him more important, there were no associations which could be brought to mind in it. The only historical place was the point where Captain Cook had landed, so he wrote

[20]Richard Edwards and Roderick Shaw (eds.), *Barron Field's First Fruits of Australian Poetry*, 3.
[21]*Ibid.*, 10, 11.
[22]*Ibid.*, 24.

two sonnets on that, and then turned to one on ships of the type that would take him away from this land

> where nature is prosaic,
> Unpicturesque, unmusical, and where
> Nature-reflecting Art is not yet born;—
> A land without antiquities, with one,
> And only one, poor spot of classic ground,
> (That on which Cook first landed)—where, instead
> Of heart-communings with ancestral relicks,
> Which purge the pride while they exalt the mind,
> We've nothing left us but anticipation,
> Better (I grant) than utter selfishness,
> Yet too o'erweening—too American;
> Where's no past tense, the ign'rant present's all;
> Or only great by the *All hail, hereafter!*
> One foot of Future's glass should rest on Past;
> Where Hist'ry is not, Prophecy is guess—[23]

To Wentworth, the native-born, anticipation was certainly strong, and perhaps "o'erweening" too. He did not attempt landscape poetry, and so we do not have an equivalent to set against Field's helplessness in the face of natural description. His Australian muse failed him at Cambridge, however, for he ran second in the Chancellor's medal competition to W. M. Praed. It is interesting to note an Australian critic's comments on this event, written in 1866:

A comparison of the two productions will suggest doubts to some readers as to the justice of the award. In local colouring, at least, Wentworth's is altogether superior, as might be expected. Nothing can be more absurd than some passages in Praed's in which he attempts to describe the character and customs of the aboriginals. He seems hardly to have been aware of the distinction between New Zealand and New Holland; for he first takes the reader to the one, and then hurries him off to the other,— mixing up convicts and Maories as if they were members of the same community.[24]

There will be occasion to refer to this emphasis on "local colouring" again, but it is significant that at so early a stage there should be such an emphasis on the distinctness of the Australian scene and on the difficulties of interpreting it.

---

[23]*Ibid.*, 15.
[24]Barton, *Poets and Prose Writers of New South Wales*, 19.

Wentworth was sincere in his local patriotism. Though one of the young lions of Sydney society, he was already full of plans for exalting his homeland, and he saw his best method of preparation of this task in a voyage to England. He wrote to his father's patron, Lord Fitzwilliam, before leaving: "I am sensible to the claims it [Australia] has upon me—claims which, in its present despised and indigent situation, I should blush even to be supposed to be capable of neglecting. In withdrawing myself, therefore, for a time from that country, I am actuated by a desire of better qualifying myself for the performance of those duties that birth has imposed."[25]

Already he saw himself as one of the new (and, he hoped, official) nobility of Australia, filled with a sense of responsibility towards the peasants, but confident of his assured position among the governors. His patriotism, therefore, was directed towards a vision—in Field's terms, an "anticipation." The extravagance and rhetoric of his ideas of Austral Miltons and Shakespeares, and his apology for the existing "savage, uncouth strain" was typical of his nature. Full of confidence he went to London, and, as Vance Palmer says, examined the House of Commons with interest, and the House of Lords with enthusiasm.[26] He went to Paris conscientiously to "enlarge his knowledge of the world," but found on returning to London that not only had his father, in his youth, been forced to leave England on a charge of robbery under arms, but that his mother had been a Norfolk Island convict, and that he himself was probably illegitimate. The "Pure Merino" was not quite so pure after all, as the Sydney emancipist newspapers exclaimed with delight.

This discovery brought about the most profound change in the erstwhile rhetorical patriot of the graziers. He read Shelley and Byron, and talked about the world being "on the eve of some great general revolution";[27] and he changed his ideas on future political institutions for Australia—particularly changed were his views on the role that emancipists should play in society. Whereas before his discovery he would not admit their right to participate in political power, expecting them to accept gratefully the benevolence of those who knew better than they, now he was willing to advocate the right of

[25]Vance Palmer, *National Portraits*, 39.
[26]*Ibid.*, 41.
[27]*Ibid.*

emancipists to full voting privileges. After a year at Cambridge he returned to Sydney prepared to fight the "family compact" theories of the exclusivist government of which he had formerly been such a strong supporter. He determined, instead, to head the emancipist group in the colony, and to do this he established the *Australasian*, which, with the support of the majority of the emancipists, quickly became the most influential journal in the colony, attracting support from all those who opposed either autocracy or oligarchy. Governor Darling tried to suppress him by making him a member of the exclusivist Executive Council, but Wentworth became a popular agitator, and the great ghost of popular revolution haunted the government and the exclusivists. Darling tried to ban the *Australasian*, but the Chief Justice disallowed the edict; Darling was recalled, and Wentworth stood as the great champion of the emancipists and convicts.

But as the cries for universal rights, revolution on the American pattern, and even expulsion of the exclusivists rose among his followers, he felt he had gone too far. He was still a large landowner, and he began to have second thoughts. As a result, his modified programme supported responsible government and free institutions, but free institutions founded on a basis of property rather than on the rights of man. When Wentworth petitioned for trial by jury and elected legislatures, a deputation of exclusivists, headed by Macarthur's son, went to London to assure the Colonial Office that these things were not desired and that only "a small irresponsible group in the colony" wished for them.

By the thirties more and more of the emancipists were pressing for the abolition of the transportation of convicts, for the large supply of free labour which the system supplied to the large properties was confirming the monopoly of the graziers over the use of land, and widening the economic gap between them and the rest of society. As time passed the breach between Wentworth and the exclusivists closed. Wentworth was now a wealthy man, and he retired from public life. The emancipists treated him as a "Lost Leader" and bitterly commented on his betrayal of their interests.[28] By 1840 Wentworth

[28]It is interesting to compare Wentworth with Canada's Howe who was also regarded as a "Lost Leader" when he opposed Confederation.

was in favour of keeping the convict system, the land system, and even of importing coolies from India to supplement the labour supply. The wheel had come full circle, and the emancipists turned instead to the new radical movement headed by a young mechanic named Henry Parkes.

At the height of his influence, Wentworth's function in his community was not unlike that of Haliburton in Nova Scotia, but Wentworth's community was very different from Haliburton's. It was not until the eighteen-fifties that anything resembling a middle class in the English sense appeared on the Australian scene, and even then it was a poor thing compared to its flourishing counterpart in Canada. Therry's *Reminiscences*, an account of life in Sydney during the fifties, reflects the desperate attempts of the wealthier merchants and their wives to join the closed circle of the "First Families" of "squatto-cracy." Institutions are described in terms of their English models, and pathetic efforts are made to assert the advanced status of colonial civilization: "At races and public balls in the circuit towns, at the time of the assizes, agreeable reunions and other festive entertainments take place as in England. They lack of course the advantages and influence incident to the society at the seat of Government—Sydney; but the general features of "town and country" society are identical."[29]

Therry goes on, however: "The various observances of precedence in New South Wales, as in most colonial societies, are attended with great, sometime with ludicrous precision."[30] But although one is reminded of the parallel illustration in Haliburton's *Old Judge*, describing the dinner given for the Governor, Australian "Society" before 1860 consisted of a very small group trying desperately to uphold traditional etiquette among a populace who mocked them for their pains.

From all this it is possible to put forward some propositions about the pattern of development emerging in the two countries. Unable to shake itself free from the inhibitions already besetting some eastern United States writers, the authors in the Canadian Maritimes did not follow the lead which Haliburton had given. Not only were they looking fearfully over their shoulders at Europe, they were also

[29]Clark, *Select Documents*, 431.
[30]*Ibid.*, 432.

watching developments to the south with alarm and misgivings. A closer identification with England was even more necessary than it had been before, and as it became so politically and economically, so too culturally. They were not quick enough in seizing the advantages Haliburton had given to Canadian writers (if, indeed, they were even recognized as advantages), and they would not bemean themselves by seeming to follow an American pattern. It was far better to look across the Atlantic, to follow a more exalted model.

From this point there begins the custom which was to contrast strongly with the Australian practice. In Canada, cultural patterns were to be imported from England, filtered through the cities, and discussed (usually very well) by provincial critics, then fed out to the frontiers. The frontier itself for long was not recognized as a valid subject for serious creative writing. With the deliberate repudiation of native inspiration and with the study of the central tradition came, for the educated frontier settlers, a sense of belonging—of security within an established culture—which made their exile more endurable.

In Australia there was a continual struggle against the importation of the central tradition—a struggle that, as we shall see, was not in its early stages a successful one. Here the inspiration was reversed. The frontiers became almost the only valid subjects for creative writing, and this writing in turn was fed back into the cities for evaluation and comment.

The career of William Wentworth might in some ways be a symbol of the attempt to imitate the Canadian process. That it ended in failure was a measure of the difference between the two environments.

4. The Poetry of Adaptation

IT IS DIFFICULT to separate nationalism from the search for a native tradition. As we shall see in a later chapter, such Australian writers as Lawson, Furphy, Dyson, Paterson, and O'Dowd had more in common with Whitman and Poe than they had with their Canadian contemporaries. Tompson, Harpur, and Kendall, on the other hand, though less successful than Lampman, pursued goals similar to his. The period of transition—that portion of a nation's literary history when the parent tradition is beginning to evolve into a new and recognizable shape—cannot be rigidly defined. To many critics Canada and Australia have not, even yet, produced work of quality and magnitude sufficient to justify a claim to a separate body of national literature. The classification must, then, be an arbitrary one; and as it is used here will be taken to represent that period when the eighteenth-century English tradition imported into both Canada and Australia begins to react to literary changes taking place in Great Britain, and to modifications imposed by the colonial environment.

A study of the poetry of Joseph Howe could have been made during the discussion of the eighteenth-century inheritance; it could also be argued that his work belongs to an analysis of Canadian nationalism in poetry. It is included here because, although he owes as much to the Goldsmith tradition as did Goldsmith's grand-nephew, part of his poetry shows signs of adaptation to environment greater than those found in The Rising Village.

Most discussions of Howe's poetry begin with the qualifying statement that his prose is much better. Professor Pacey says: "Where . . . [the prose] is fresh, idiomatic, and flexible, . . . [the poetry] tends to be

conventional and stiff. He did not take himself seriously as a poet. . . ."[1]
This tends to confirm the point previously made about the relative
adaptability of poetry and prose, and for that reason the poetry
is worth examining. The most notable single poem is the unfinished
"Acadia," which, while similar in theme to Goldsmith's *The Rising
Village*, is the more successful work. Both Goldsmith and Howe
reflected the influence of the later eighteenth-century English tradition in which the more rigorous classicism of an earlier time was modified by an inner change. As the invasion of sentimentalism had
transformed the moral life, so the literature, and particularly the
poetry, was transformed by the gradual appearance of themes based
on sentiment, which came to take their place beside the classical
motifs.

After sentiment had become associated with everyday surroundings,
with landscape, and with the darker aspects of human fate, it spread
to those objects that affected, not the senses directly, but the imagination through the senses.[2] The artefacts of past eras and civilizations
provided admirable starting points for re-creating absent reality
according to preconceived pattern. Monuments, ruins, inscriptions,
all served to stimulate the imagination away from the restrictions of a
prosaic present to an imaginative and delightfully misted past. It was
the absence of such crutches to the imagination that Barron Field
lamented so bitterly in Sydney, and which made him despair of the
lot of the Australian poet. Wentworth, who dwelt on "anticipation"
instead, could not be considered in terms of this tradition truly
"poetic." It was true that Australian poets could, by use of their
imaginative powers, annex the history and mythologies of the Old
World from which they had come, but the vital link was missing.
The physical presence, the "heart-communings with ancestral relicks"
and the meditation upon classic ground, which "purged the pride
while they exalt the mind" was impossible here. And without it
"prophecy"—that highest voice of the poetic spirit—was impossible, and
mere anticipation took its place.

The Canadian Goldsmith was faced with the same problems, but
his great-uncle's poem, *The Deserted Village*, had given him what
he hoped would be a link between the use of poetic tradition in the

[1]Pacey, *Creative Writing in Canada*, 18.
[2]Legouis and Cazamian, *A History of English Literature*, 831.

Old World and the New. *The Deserted Village* portrays an idealization of the immediate past, of an idyllic rustic existence torn asunder
by the greed of the powerful, and of the emigration of the villagers
to the horrid and exotic shores of North America, where they could
look forward to nothing but bats, snakes, Indians, scorpions, and
tigers. The sentimental possibilities of the parting scene are fully
exploited, but it is with such people as these that the Muse of Poetry
belongs, for she too is emigrating. She requires honesty, simplicity,
piety, loyalty, and love for her nourishment, and as there is all too
little to be found in England, Goldsmith bids her farewell as she
leaves for the strange lands "Whether equinoxial fervours glow, Or
Winter wraps the polar world in snow."[3] Goldsmith is reinforcing
Steele's plea for simplicity, echoing Rousseau in affirming that what
give value to life are the common emotions, perhaps instincts, in
respect to which men differ hardly at all and which he imagines to
exist in a purer and less perverted form in the simple, uneducated
man than in the enlightened and sophisticated. Again, like Rousseau's,
Goldsmith's moral valuations turn upon the worth of these common
feelings: the affections of family life, the joy and beauty of mother-
hood, the satisfactions of such homely arts as tilling the soil, the
universal feeling of religious reverence, above all, the sense of a
common lot and the sharing of a common life—all that men call the
"realities" of everyday living. By contrast, science is the fruit of idle
curiosity; philosophy is mere intellectual frippery; the amenities of
polite life are tinsel. The hero of Rousseau's primitivism was not
the noble savage; it was the bewildered and irritated bourgeois, at
odds with a society that despised and looked down on him, conscious
of his own purity of heart and the greatness of his own deserts, and
profoundly shocked at the philosophers to whom nothing was sacred.
By some strange logic of the emotions Rousseau joined in an
equal condemnation both the social order that oppressed him and
the philosophy which had attacked the foundations of that society.
Against both he set up the pieties and the virtues of the simple heart.[4]
Goldsmith, on the other hand, looked for the nearest equivalent to
the noble savage to be found in England; and there he was, in the
simple pattern of country village life.

[3]*The Deserted Village*, lines 419–20.
[4]Legouis and Cazamian, *A History of English Literature.*

When the Canadian Goldsmith and Joseph Howe came to write their poems about their own transatlantic community one can distinguish the manner in which each employed this same material. The Canadian Goldsmith took the peasants of his great-uncle's poem and traced a virtual reconstruction of their former village in the new surroundings. Some of the externals have changed, but even in the descriptions of the physical surroundings one could imagine that the fondly remembered scenes of the elder Goldsmith had been revived with few variations. The Indian is "the fearless beast of prey"[5] as he had been in the English poem.[6] All that had really been done was to work out the theme in reverse, as the title itself would indicate. Instead of looking back on a rustic idyll and contrasting it with the wickedness of the present, *The Rising Village* looks back on a period of struggle and strife in which virtue and industry have triumphed, and which has led to paradise regained. Perhaps paradise regained can never be as convincing and moving an experience as paradise lost, and perhaps this is only another way of stating Field's distinction between poetry based upon a noble conception of the past, and upon an anticipation of the future. Goldsmith aggravates the offence by assuming that the Golden Age could be found in the present—an assertion very few are bold enough to make about their own age. Added to this, an absence of verbal felicity in the Canadian poem makes the verse appear, as A. J. M. Smith has put it, "familiar without being memorable."[7]

Howe's *Acadia* begins with essentially the same things to say. The poem records the growth of Nova Scotia, but from the point of view of one who has never known any other homeland. Howe had the advantage over Wentworth in that Nova Scotia was not, as completely as New South Wales, a land without history. Howe could look back on the settlement of Nova Scotia not as the record of a successful transplanting of a desirable type of community which once flourished three thousand miles away (complete with its own resident Muse of Poetry), but as the merging of a number of elements which have all contributed their savour to form a new type of society which exacts a loyalty all its own. Howe is not echoing Wentworth's

[5]Smith (ed.), *Book of Canadian Poetry*, 69.
[6]*The Deserted Village*, lines 355–6.
[7]Smith (ed.), *Book of Canadian Poetry*, 68.

plea for an indigenous Milton or a native Shakespeare; his aims are
more limited but more significant of his purpose. His theme is that
there is no place like home, but there is the difficulty in a colonial
environment of determining just where home really is. His invocation
is to Foscari, to the exiled sons of Israel, and to Burns and Moore,
rather than to the Muse of Poetry. Though the theme is far older
than Rousseau's doctrines, one is reminded of his statement: " Il est
certain que les plus grands prodiges de vertu ont été produits par
l'amour de la patrie: ce sentiment doux et vif, qui joint la force de
l'amour-propre à toute la beauté de la vertu, lui donne une énergie qui,
sans la défigurer, en fait la plus héroique de toutes les passions."[8]
Howe's own apologia is similar:

> And bless the feeling, for it ever leads
> To sacred thoughts and high and daring deeds;
> 'Twas that illumed his eye when Nelson fell,
> 'Twas that which urged the unerring shaft of Tell,
> Inspired the plaintive and the patriot strains
> That Burns pour'd freely o'er his native plains,
> And breathes the influence of its sacred fire
> O'er many a chord of Moore's seraphic lyre.
> With daring hand that feeling bids me now
> Twine a rude wreath around my Country's brow,
> And tho' the flowers wild and simple be,
> Take, my Acadia, those I twine for thee.[9]

Daring or not, with the invocation over, Howe goes on to describe
briefly the countryside in each of the seasons, and though his description of nature carries with it no distinctive Canadian imagery, it rein-
forces the assertion previously made that the Canadian seasons, though
more intense than their English counterparts, were not very different
from them. The winter is hard, but it is invigorating and healthy, a
robust climate that clears the head:

> Still there is health and vigor in the breeze
> Which bears upon its wings no fell disease
> To taint the balmy freshness of the air
> And steal the bloom thy hardy children wear.
> No withering plague spreads o'er thy smiling plains
> In fearful horrors and soul-sickening pains,

[8]Oeuvres de J. J. Rousseau, "De l'Economie politique," IV, 410.
[9]Joseph Howe, Poems and Essays, 6.

No wild tornado, with its voice of wrath,
Spreads desolation in its fearful path;
No parching Simoon's warm and sickly breath
Casts o'er thy hills the pallid hues of death;
But Health thy rosy youth to labour cheers
And teaches age to brave the blight of years.

It is not, like Australia's climate, a bewildering array of the extremes of nature, bewildering, not to a native Australian, but to one accustomed to the European succession of seasons.

Here is the raw material; now it must be peopled; and Howe portrays an ideal picture of Micmac life, the noble savage as he lives (p. 14). The joys of simple life are held up for admiration here as they were in *The Deserted Village*:

> . . . Complete their frugal feast, for rich content,
> Which thrones have not, makes rich the Indian's tent.

The coming of the British interrupted this idyllic existence, but the newcomers were not the villains of the piece, as one sometimes feels they are in Mair's portrayals of Indian life. They were hardy and adventurous too, but through ignorance they desecrated the most holy beliefs of the Indians. Neither party is the real villain; each acted according to its lights. Howe's poem, divided into three parts, attempts to alternate these sympathies. The first section presents the Indian case. The second describes the simple pioneering life of the early settlers, and includes the often-quoted passage of the Indian massacre of a pioneer family, a description which approaches nearer to realism than anything achieved in the Canadian Goldsmith's works, but which still exacts the last drop of pathos from the situation. The struggle with the French, and their expulsion from Acadia, are themes touched on with sympathy. In particular, the fate of the dispossessed French settlers closely resembles the lot of the inhabitants of *The Deserted Village*. The third section of the poem describes the contemporary view of society, and is, perhaps, the weakest of the three. The strain of love-in-a-cottage is repeated; the perils of a fisherman's life and the anxieties of the waiting family are rehearsed, and the motif re-established that no matter how far they may wander, the sons of Nova Scotia always feel the ties of their birth-place pulling them home. To the native son every prospect pleases, and even the

works of man, in his new pious simplicity, are not vile. The races, it
is asserted, have merged into one, and all is peace. Industry comple-
ments rather than despoils the natural landscape (p. 35):

> But has not time—that drowned the din of arms
> Defaced Acadia's wild and simple charms,
> Broke the deep spells of woodland solitude
> And banished nature with a hand too rude?
> Oh! no, together Art and Nature reign,
> Smile on the mountain top and deck the plain.

The diction, as is to be expected, is conventional, and at times absurd.
Though most of the landscape may be described, without incongruity,
in terms of English nature, it is more difficult to fit native animals
into the scene. The adaptation to a new environment of traditional
descriptions of animals in an English spring may have some curious
results. We have already seen that Field could only use the kangaroo
in parody. Unfortunately Thomas Campbell, in his "Lines on Emigration" (to New South Wales), produced in 1828 the touching picture
of the youth who

> . . . petted birds still brighter than their bowers,
> Or twined his tame young kangaroo with flowers.[10]

Howe's description of the fearless cariboo is close enough to the
familiar Stag at Bay to be believable if not informative, but one has
difficulty in accepting the picture of the ponderous square-dance
brought to mind when (p. 100)

> . . . the gay moose in jocund gambol springs,
> Cropping the foliage Nature round him flings.

His shorter poems are remarkable only for their renewed emphasis
on the local patriotism felt by colonists making their pilgrimages to
England. "Making Land," which was written in 1838 on the occasion
of Howe's first sight of England, reflects the reverence and awe with
which the native-born colonist approached what had always been
referred to as the Homeland. Field's antiquity had suddenly blossomed
into a physical presence, and this process is celebrated in much the
same terms by both Canadian and Australian writers. But Howe
found, as Henry Handel Richardson's Richard Mahoney was to find,

[10]Thomas Campbell, Poetical Works, 284.

that, though obeisances be made, the architecture admired, and the
sense of history inhaled, the place was not really home after all. On
the same trip Howe found himself amid the glories of the Rhine and,
in spite of himself, began to make comparisons (p. 79):

> But yet, three thousand miles away,
>   Some gentle streams there are,
> That here, midst all this proud array,
>   To me are dearer far.

"The Streams," "My Native Pines," "Home," "Coming Home," all
reflect this local nationalism which is quite distinct from the more sen-
tentious patriotism of "The Flag of Old England." The public poetry
of rhetorical patriotism stands or falls with the poet's ability to catch
the reader's imagination with a line or a phrase. It is seldom as
successful as the private poetry of personal loyalty reflecting only the
poet's own beliefs, and expressed, not as an exhortation, but as an
act of faith. This dualism, seen in Howe, between local and imperial
patriotism is a recurring problem in the history of Canadian poetry.

Charles Heavysege was to escape the pitfalls of patriotic verse
by avoiding it altogether. By concentrating on universal themes which
were virtually independent of time and place, he could stand within
the central tradition unaffected by the problems of adaptation to
native environment. *Saul*, much admired by eminent contemporaries,
stood within the tradition of the nineteenth-century closet-drama, and
dealt not with Canadian but with Biblical themes. But, as Bailey's
Festus, which had seemed to Tennyson one of the supreme achievements of English poetry, sank to obscurity within ten years of its
appearance, Heavysege's *Saul* did not outlast its author.

Charles Sangster adopted a position of compromise between central
tradition and native background. His emphasis is upon universal
themes, but he shows the influence of the local scene. Mrs. Moodie
called him "the Wordsworth of Canada," but the analogy is not a
happy one, for it would assume a depth of poetic vision far beyond
Sangster's limited perception. The value of his work lies in his
attempts to describe the Canadian scene. Tentative though it was,
Sangster's sensibility in his nature verse furthered the adaptation of
the central tradition to the native scene. To English readers his
descriptions were strange and exotic, but they could sense the variations on a familiar theme. As Haliburton had presented an American

who had conformed to pre-set ideas on American national character, Sangster provided a picture of the Canadian forests sufficiently vague and undefined in detail to allow preconceptions full play. The terms for description are still English terms: trees are always "stately," eagles "proud," the isles of the St. Lawrence are "clad with soft verdure," and the stag goes on his way "with lordly stride." But occasionally, against the muted background of terms common to both Canadian and English nature, come flashes of the scarlet of Canadian autumn, with the homestead "like a white tent" seen through the openings of the trees.[11] Yet the poet is still the objective observer, seeking, with varying degrees of success, to focus his sights upon the new country— new, not in Sangster's case to the eye, for he was Canadian-born, but to the expression of what he saw. The first results inevitably were, for us, blurred general impressions.

The title poem of Sangster's first volume, *The St. Lawrence and the Saguenay*, is an interesting example of the type of adaptation that had to be made. Sangster uses the Spenserian stanza to describe what A. J. M. Smith calls "a kind of sentimental journey, or Childe Harold's pilgrimage, in which the poet and some fair but imaginary companion sail down the great river and respond with appropriate emotions to the beauty and variety of the scenery or the sacredness of historical associations."[12] The work met with lavish praise from the local press, and at the back of Sangster's second volume, *Hesperus*, which appeared in 1860, are some four pages of extracts from newspaper and periodical reviews of *The St. Lawrence and the Saguenay*. At first sight the reviews would seem to be unanimous in praising Sangster for his ability to depict the Canadian scene: "The work is essentially Canadian . . . ," "This is a book that, as a Canadian, we are proud of . . . ," "our Native Bard," "a credit to Canadian literature. . . ." Such phrases might represent the delighted discovery of one who had at last given to an inarticulate country a national poetic voice, accurately representing its aspirations and interpreting its distinctive features. Yet the poetry itself is clearly imitative. It is not enough to explain the apparent paradox by saying that the critics were too parochial, too anxious to overpraise a native son. This was true in some cases, but the judgment bestowed on the writing of local poets was, for the most part, exacting. The answer may be found,

[11]Charles Sangster, *The St. Lawrence and the Saguenay*, 128.
[12]Smith (ed.), *Book of Canadian Poetry*, 100.

quite logically, in the climate of opinion which has already been discussed. Sangster was praised not for his faithful reproduction of the local scene in terms readily comprehensible to its inhabitants, but because he appeared to have attained skill in writing poetry within the parent English tradition, skill sufficient to enable him to rank with minor contemporary English poets. It was not the Canadianism of his poetry that was praised, but the fact that he had written presentable poetry within the English tradition, and was, at the same time, a Canadian. Within this context, the statement that "he may be regarded as the Canadian Wordsworth"[13] indicates the pride that was felt in the Canadianism of the poet rather than in that of his poetry.[14] If we accept this contention—that Sangster was proudly hailed because he was *not* different from English poets—the contrast between Canadian and Australian attitudes to poetry becomes striking.

It is useful to take A. J. M. Smith's definition of a "colonial" attitude towards literature as the starting point for discussion. Briefly, he defines the spirit of colonialism in literature as one that gratefully accepts a place of subordination, and which looks elsewhere for its standards of excellence, being content to imitate, timidly and conservatively, the parent tradition. Unlike the literature of true nationalism which, he affirms, rises out of the local realism of the pioneer, colonialism manifests itself in abstract and conventional patriotic poetry, and where the work is set ostensibly within a local framework, the description is inevitably abstract in order to avoid accusations of parochialism. As a result, a sense of inferiority and doubt is engendered. Even more dangerous, in turning away from the despised local present, writers may turn, not towards the mother country, but towards an exotic idealized crystallization of impossible hopes and "noble" dreams. As Smith puts it, "the romantic spirit, indeed, is encouraged by a colonial sense of inferiority."[15]

To the educated English visitor in 1860 it is possible that Australia

[13]Review by *London National Magazine*, end papers of *Hesperus* volume.
[14]This question, which is expounded by A. J. M. Smith in "Colonialism and Nationalism in Canadian Poetry Before Confederation," Canadian Historical Association, *Report*, 1944, 74–85, will arise again in later chapters. The points made by Dr. Smith when he discusses the differences between colonial and national attitudes have striking parallels in Australia, and support the contentions put forward in the third chapter of this book.
[15]*Ibid.*, 75.

would appear far more provincial than Canada. Canadian periodicals fostered a wider and more intelligent interest in all aspects of contemporary literature than did their Australian counterparts. The *Australasian Chronicle*, the *Gazette*, and the *Sydney Observer* were preoccupied with local affairs almost to the exclusion of anything else. The complaint of George Hart that he must "rely upon the English publications, for the Sydney productions do not deign to keep us informed of any literary progress beyond the confines of this colony,"[16] could not have been uttered in Canada with any justification. Excessive preoccupation with local events might seem to be one of the hallmarks of colonialism, and George Hart has so interpreted it. Yet within the terms of Smith's definition, Australian literature was less colonial than the Canadian. This apparent paradox is resolved by the definition which Smith offers. Within its terms, Hart is the one who shows a colonial spirit by despising the local scene and looking beyond for the source of all good things. The Australian attitude would be infinitely depressing to one of Hart's wide and cosmopolitan tastes, but it would be parochial rather than colonial in nature. The reception which the poems of Charles Harpur received illustrates this attitude.

The earlier poems of Harpur, which began to appear in Sydney publications in 1842, were subjected to a type of criticism very different from that afforded to Sangster in Canada. Where he appeared to imitate English poets, he was censured, and where he appeared to be trying to avoid such imitation he was praised. His successes were held to be those portions of his poetry in which he was *not* the Australian Wordsworth. A contemporary reviewer noted his uncertain technical skill, but felt this was a matter for congratulation as it at least proved that he was not slavishly imitating anybody! "Harpur is self-taught, self-relying, self-contained. Content with Nature herself, he puts aside many of her professed exponents—as David rejected Saul's rich and well-tempered cuirass, 'These things are excellent, but I have not proved them. Leave me to my sling.'"[17] Such efforts must be encouraged:

No mean advantage this, that already the Genius of Australia begins to walk unaided—already her poets begin to look at Nature through the

---

[16]G. Hart to W. Saunders, September 2, 1851; *Letters From Australia*, 28.

[17]"Australian Literature (No. III), Charles Harpur," *Colonial Monthly* (February, 1869), 448.

naked eye, tracing the poetry of life in the spontaneous remorse of the
brutal murderer, and the power of Nature's worship to develop [sic]
the soul of man. Thus may they create for Australia a literature and a
muse all her own. While, then, we revere and cherish old-world models,
let our criticisms of the rising, untaught, young giants of the soil, be
neither formal, minute, or pedantic.[18]

Harpur is a good example of a poet trapped between an unsuitable
poetic idiom and an environment which he desperately wishes to
interpret. Charles Tompson, who had published his *Wild Notes
from the Lyre of a Native Minstrel* in 1826, the first book of poetry
by a native-born Australian to be published in that country, had
contented himself with highly conventional verses. Most of his poems
were patriotic ones, based on the familiar appearance of Australia's
guardian gods and goddesses who prophesied the future greatness
of the country. Harpur was not content to imitate such empty rhetoric.
He experimented with words and images in the attempt to describe
Australian nature more accurately. His greatest contribution as a poet
is historical in nature. He is important for the influence he was to
have on his successors, and as a reflection of the criticism of his day;
but there are isolated instances where he did come close to finding
what he was looking for. An early attempt, "Midsummer Noon in the
Australian Forest," captured more effectively than any preceding
poem the stifling breathlessness of the Australian bush on a still
summer day. The poem ends:

> Every other thing is still,
> Save the ever-watchful rill,
> Whose cool murmur only throws
> Cooler comfort round repose;
> Or some ripple in the sea
> Of leafy boughs, where, lazily,
> Tired summer, in her bower
> Turning with the noontide hour,
> Heaving a slumbrous breath ere she
> Once more slumbers peacefully.
>
> O 'tis easeful here to lie
> Hidden from noon's scorching eye,
> In this grassy cool recess
> Musing thus of quietness.[19]

18[Ibid., 452.
19Mackaness (ed.), *Anthology*, 130.

There was still the use of "bower," "rill," "slumbrous breath," clichés that Harpur was to avoid in his later poetry. From this orthodox beginning, Harpur went on to "The Creek of the Four Graves," his most ambitious poem, where he again attacked the problem of description of the Australian scene, and again he achieves an elusive type of success. It was his fate always to be on the edge of sustained achievement. In this extract from "The Creek of the Four Graves," Harpur is trying to describe the sudden Australian sunset, and the equally sudden moonrise, together with the curious optical illusions, leaping shadows, and apparent sharp magnification which are features of the abrupt transition between day and night in the Australian bush, and which today still startle those who are not used to the absence of the gentle glow they have come to associate with twilight in other lands. In this passage Harpur begins with a description of dusk couched in conventional terms, but passes from this with increasing success to an isolation of the distinctive features of the scene before him, and to a real attempt to express these features in vivid imagery (p. 131):

Eastward at last
The glow was wasted into formless gloom,
Night's front; then westward the high massing woods
Steeped in a swart but mellow Indian hue,
A deep dusk loveliness lay ridged and heaped,
Only the more distinctly for their shade,
Against the twilight heaven—a cloudless depth
Yet luminous with sunset's fading glow;
And thus a while in the lit dusk they seemed
To hang like mighty pictures of themselves
In the still chambers of some vaster world.

Meanwhile the cloudless eastern heaven had grown
More luminous, and now the moon arose
Above the hill, when lo! that giant cone
Erewhile so dark, seemed inwardly aglow
With her instilled irradiance, while the trees
That fringed its outline, their huge statures dwarfed
By distance into brambles and yet all
Clearly defined against her ample orb,
Out of its very disc appeared to swell
In shadowy relief, as they had been
All sculptured from its surface as she rose.

> Then her full light in silvery sequence still
> Cascading forth from ridgy slope to slope,
> Chased mass by mass the broken darkness down
> Into the dense-brushed valleys, where it crouched,
> And shrank and struggled.

These near successes were few. Harpur's limited achievement is indicative of the task that the academic poet had to face in Australia. The ballad was already assuming a position of pre-eminence with both the critics and the reading public, and there was an impatience with the painstaking efforts of more serious poets, who could not help including echoes of a parent tradition that was generally held to be unsuitable to Australian conditions.

G. B. Barton, in the sixties, commenting on Harpur's contributions to Australian poetry, quoted with approval one of Harpur's bush-ballads, and added: "The following ballad of bush life, entitled "Ned Connor", is so well executed as to make us wish that Mr. Harpur had written more in the same style, instead of soaring into cloudier heights. Both this and the preceding poem are perfect examples of local colouring."[20]

Such critics as Barton did not disapprove of serious poetry *per se*, but they were fumbling their way towards an idea of the best manner in which Australian poetry could develop. If the more simple poetic forms such as the ballad could be successfully naturalized, then perhaps it would be better to work up from there slowly, rather than plunge into a rhetorical nature poetry that brought to mind every time it appeared a sweating Wordsworth cowering behind the eucalyptus. Barton further chided Harpur: "Apparently disdaining the more common sources of inspiration he has striven to emulate the lofty flights of Wordsworth: and while he has grasped at objects placed beyond his reach by nature, he has left behind him those which might have been attained with ease."[21]

Limited and parochial though such views may seem in isolation, perhaps many of the Australian critics had a greater instinctive awareness of the growing pains of a national literature, and of the crudities and limitations it must suffer before it can stand on its own feet. The most difficult question which arises during this discussion is: what

[20]Barton, *Poets and Prose Writers of New South Wales*, 45.
[21]*Ibid.*, 48.

constitutes the national element in poetry? Is it merely subject-matter, biological and geological peculiarity? It is a refusal to use "alien" metrical forms and stylistic devices? Can one assume that a poet in Canada or Australia who imitates an English model could have been a better poet, or a more national one, by refusing to imitate?

We can state confidently that Wordsworth, writing of the English Lakes District, uses an idiom that is no longer employed in twentieth-century poetry, but to anyone who has seen the country he was describing there can be no question of the appropriateness of his language. This is to fall victim to the "inevitability" of great poetry, which rises above place even though it is rooted in it. It has been suggested that Milton was able to describe Hell very successfully using the English poetic diction of the seventeenth century, and that therefore it might very well have been an adequate medium to interpret the Australian landscape. But at once the answer suggests itself that Satan was unable to publish a critique of the reliability of the description from the point of view of a local inhabitant, and the majority of Milton's present readers are as yet unable to speak on the subject with authority. The local inhabitants of Australia, on the other hand, were quite capable of reporting back when they felt what they called the "local colouring" was wrong. It was initially a negative criticism, but it had to be. They could say that they felt the application of English poetic diction to Australian nature was completely inappropriate, but if they had been able to say positively why this was so, or what could be done about it, there would have been no problem to worry about.

Canadians did not feel they had such a problem because they could look at nature and apply the familiar phrases to it without any jarring of the sensibilities; there was no urgency to find a new set to take the place of the old. Canadian critics, usually with university backgrounds, judged against the central tradition which, they felt, applied anywhere English was spoken. Australian critics and writers, usually without university training, looked for a way out in fostering an idea of Australianism which was, as might be expected, treated in non-academic terms. Subject-matter was the first test, particularly in nature poetry. It was absurd, they maintained, for poets to write of glens and moors and cedars if they had never seen any; and, they maintained, it did not matter if a poet or novelist was hailed in

England for representations of the Australian scene. If it did not pass the test for authenticity from the Australians themselves, the work was false.

Nationalism in literature must, in its early stages, be self-conscious and awkward. It judges by standards rightly held to be very dubious ones by supporters of absolute, that is, non-national, principles. One might say that both Chaucer and Shakespeare, though both obviously influenced by foreign predecessors, produced their greatest works in an atmosphere of rebellion against servile imitation, and built upon the efforts of dozens of less talented and fumbling writers, now forgotten, who cleared the way. If a national literature is to come into existence, the earlier these fumblings, painful though they are, are begun, the earlier the unself-conscious vision of the poet, who does not have to keep looking at his feet, may have free play.

While it is not necessarily true that a nationalist poet is better than a non-nationalist one, a great poet has never arisen from a climate where imitation is accepted as the natural course for a writer to follow, nor from one where there have not been, at some time, agonized efforts to adapt foreign influences to a new environment, in other words, some form of literary nationalism. There is no reason to say that a Canadian or Australian poet, imitating an English model, could have been a better poet by refusing to imitate; but he is, by imitating, lessening the chances that his successors will learn from his mistakes, and so emerge more quickly from the crudities of nationalism to a position where the production of great poetry is possible.

It becomes easier to see why Canadian poetry in the nineteenth century is more impressive than its Australian counterpart. Poets and critics in Canada adopted more rigid standards, and assessed the *poetry* rather than the Canadianism or appropriateness of the poetry. A national Canadian poet did not have to be distinctively Canadian at all, but he did have to be recognizably a poet. This may seem to be a very happy state of affairs. To judge by absolute standards without reference to purely local considerations may indicate a high-minded and laudable standard of literary criticism. There are still many critics today who insist that a Canadian author must stand apart from his community, and bear comparison with the best that is produced in the language. If he chooses to write in English, he must be judged beside his English and American colleagues. It is difficult to quarrel with this view; there is no more depressing tendency than the one to praise local products because they are local rather than because they are good. But there is a middle ground, and it is the only one for the critic of Dominions' literature to adopt. In Canada, the absolute, the "non-national" view, imposed a set of values upon its writers which we must, if we are to be honest, now recognize as false. No single institution imported from England and transplanted to Canadian soil survived the journey unchanged. In spite of all the attempts to reproduce English traditions, and no matter how doggedly these attempts were repeated, there was never complete success. To a greater or lesser degree the country worked its own change upon them. The whole social histories of Canada and Australia are records of the introduction of outside influences and institutions, and of the adaptations that were wrought upon them to make them suitable to the new environment. Sometimes the change was small, sometimes altered out of all recognition; but, great or small, there was always a change.

English critics, judging an English minor poet, would consider first his sensibility, his poetic insight, his ability to interpret his surroundings and his experience into fresh and significant terms. If they raised the question of his relation to his physical environment, most of them would be ready to admit a great variety of relations; for instance, formal and idealized pastoral is recognized as fully as realistic description. So that the question of the manner or degree of relation to the physical environment is, in a sense, independent of the ability of the poet. But in nineteenth-century Canada and Australia this was not so.

In Canada the separation of the two was not recognized, while in Australia poetic ability was judged in terms of "local colouring." It is obvious that there are no Canadian or Australian poets great as Milton and Pope and Wordsworth and Keats are great. There is only a succession of figures who, small by the standards of the world stage, are comparatively large in their own small spheres. But admitting that these are all minor poets, it is surely more enriching to the tradition of the language for them to be minor figures within their own frame of reference, working as a part of their own environment, which no one else knows as well as they do, than it would be for them to be minor English poets—minor poets of the English scene, of which they have no real knowledge, and on which they can have nothing of real significance to say.

No one who has seen the St. Lawrence can affirm confidently that Sangster's interpretation has added to their insight, or that his poetry has succeeded in striking, not merely a "distinctively Canadian note"—for that may consist in no more than scattered references to maple leaf and cariboo—but a note that a Canadian may recognize as a part of the experience of life in his own country. Heavysege with his *Saul* was probably more successful as a *poet* than Sangster, for *Saul* had nothing to do with a Canadian setting, and the failure to interpret it is not as obvious as it is with Sangster's work. Yet Sangster is the more important, historically, because of his failure. He, at least, was working in an area which had to be developed if there was to be any Canadian literature at all. But his importance within the framework of Canadian poetry is very different in kind from that given to him by his contemporary critics.

Thus, despite the different reception each received, Sangster and Harpur were each performing the same function for the literature of his country. Harpur was more conscious of his role because of the greater gulf he had to span. He fell between the two stools; Australian critics were judging Australianism rather than poetic merit, and in seeking both he succeeded in neither. Sangster also failed both in real poetic achievement and in Canadianism; not because he had so far to go, but because he was unaware that any gulf existed.

5. The Poetry of Colonial Romanticism and the Problem of the Literary Nationalist

O Poesy! for thee I hold my pen,
That am not yet a glorious denizen
Of thy wide heaven—should I rather kneel
Upon some mountain-top until I feel
A glowing splendour round about me hung,
And echo back the voice of thine own tongue?

KEATS

WHEN GOLDSMITH tried to reconstruct the rising village from the material of the deserted one, the new site imposed its own restrictions, in addition to those ingrained in the poetic medium itself. Poets in the United States were finding the same difficulty; political independence inspired a nationalism that demanded a national culture for its expression. Canada was to have her "Canada First" group, and the *Bulletin* school served the same function in Australia. The United States, the first to sever the political ties of dependency, demonstrates very clearly the difficulties and dangers of establishing a conscious nationalism in literature; and as Canada and Australia were to share many of the problems which worried the Americans, it would be as well to examine them.

Washington Irving wrote in his diary in 1817: "There is an endeavour among some of the writers of the day (who fortunately have not any great weight) to introduce into poetry all the common colloquial phrases and vulgar idioms—In their rage for simplicity they would be coarse and commonplace. Now the language of poetry cannot be too pure and choice."[1]

This is a sentiment that we are to hear again in Canada, where it is listened to with such respect that it predominates, and in Australia, where the articulate bushmen, with their contempt for the academic, completely ignored it. The United States was the scene of a conflict between the two worlds of almost total acceptance and total rejection of this proposition. The extremes to which some advocates of rejection of the British tradition in the United States would go is revealed in the story, revived by Cunliffe,[2] of the delegates to the Continental Congress who moved that the United States should cease to employ the English language; and this is a sequel to an amendment from another delegate, Roger Sherman, that the United States should keep English as its official tongue, and should force the English themselves to learn Greek. But these facetious attempts to deal with the problem of language were only part of the wider American dilemma. Both factions were equally proud of their country, but the arguments of either side, when pressed to their conclusion, were equally galling to American pride. If the English tradition were copied, the results would be inevitably provincial; yet if the attempt were made to start afresh, how much could be accepted and how much rejected? Where was the starting point to be set? American pride smarted under such comments as those of Sydney Smith in the *Edinburgh Review* of December 1818:

Literature the Americans have none—no native literature, we mean. It is all imported. They had a Franklin, indeed; and may afford to live for half a century on his fame. There is, or was, a Mr. Dwight, who wrote some poems; and his baptismal name was Timothy. There is is also a small account of Virginia by Jefferson, and an epic by Joel Barlow—and some pieces of pleasantry by Mr. Irving. But why should the Americans write books, when a six weeks' passage brings them in our own tongue, our sense, science and genius, in bales and hogsheads?

The same scornful and condescending question was asked of both Canada and Australia, though in Canada it was often echoed by the Canadians themselves. In all three countries, however (with Canada weakest in her representation here), for most of the nine-

[1]Van Wyck Brooks, *The World of Washington Irving*, 78.
[2]Marcus Cunliffe, *The Literature of the United States*, 42.

teenth century, writers continued to give their answers to this question. As early as 1786 Freneau wrote an indignant poem called "Literary Importation," in which he bewailed the tardiness of American intellectual independence, as though such a thing could be brought about as easily as the political changes made during the preceding decade:

> It seems we had spirit to humble a throne,
> Have genius for science inferior to none,
> But hardly encourage a plant of our own:
> > If a college be planned,
> > 'Tis all at a stand
> Till to Europe we send at a shameful expense,
> To send us a book-worm to teach us some sense.
>
> Can we never be thought to have learning or grace
> Unless it be brought from that horrible place
> Where tyranny reigns with her impudent face;
> > And popes and pretenders
> > And sly faith-defenders
> Have ever been hostile to reason and wit,
> Enslaving a world that shall conquer them yet.[3]

The negative approach was carried through in defiance of Sydney Smith by William Channing, who said "it were better to have no literature, than form ourselves unresistingly on a foreign one."[4] While Noah Webster, who was to enshrine North American variations from the standard language in meaning, usage, and spelling as the next best thing to a separate American tongue, announced in 1789 that there was virtually nothing worth copying anyway: "Great Britain . . . should no longer be our standard, for the taste of her writers is already corrupted and her language on the decline."[5]

Such extremes are, of course, absurd, but they are an inevitable companion to newly acquired political independence. Charles Mair and his group were to wave the flag almost as vigorously, though the strength of their position was not as clear-cut as Webster's. The flag was still a British one; and while they were aware of the value of their inheritance and of the uselessness of repudiating it altogether,

[3]Prescott and Sanders (eds.), *An Introduction to American Poetry*, 90.
[4]Cunliffe, *Literature of the United States*, 44-5.
[5]*Ibid.*, 45.

their task was made more difficult by lack of agreement about where they were going, as well as about how to get there. Webster and his compatriots had no doubts on that score. The political break had simplified their position to a consistent patriotism, and made it comparatively easy quite soon for such a man as Emerson, in "The American Scholar," to rescue literary nationalism from jingoism and to provide it with an intellectually respectable basis upon which to build.

Cries for intellectual independence in Canada and Australia, on the other hand, became associated with similar political moves, whether or not this was in the minds of the writers themselves. "Canada First" became embroiled in the Annexation, Independence, and Imperial Federation controversies; and in Australia the *Bulletin* school flirted with republicanism for most of the nineties. If a situation arises where the search for a national cultural identity leads to association with politics, the issues become seriously clouded. A poet can hardly do his best when all his efforts to be original are regarded as evidence of treason.

The position of the intellectual radicals in the United States was, therefore, much easier than that of their counterparts in the two colonial groups. Where political dependence remains it is difficult to avoid literary imitation. In Australia, where, as has been shown, a tradition of governmental interference in many aspects of private life was the rule of the original settlement—a rule which called forth active resentment from those who had gone as far as they dared in declaring their independence from it—a more original spirit was to emerge. A distrust of British imperialism, and an active dislike of those to whom the mantle of local power had descended, caused a greater cultural independence than in Canada. For the first six decades of the century there is the spectacle of two forces in Australian letters, the one traditionalist (though without the university associations common to the equivalent group in Canada) and the other popular. It is not until the end of the century that the two groups show signs of merging.

In the United States the traditionalist, or academic, side of the controversy was vigorously represented by literary conservatives of no small ability. Theirs was the position largely adopted by Canadian writers, who, compared to their American colleagues, were conservative in politics as well as in literature. Irving's attitude, that it is the act of a small child to break a valuable possession because one does not like the donor, was reflected by many American writers. The editor of the Philadelphia *Port Folio* was not being unpatriotic (though he was accused of being so then) when he accused Benjamin Franklin of being "the founder of that Grubstreet sect, who have professedly attempted to degrade literature to the level of vulgar capacities, and debase the polished and current language of books, by the vile alloy of provincial idioms, and colloquial barbarism, the shame of grammar, and akin to any language rather than English."[6]

The fact remains that American literature of the period was obviously derivative and second rate, and while the literary nationalists claimed that any creative work that was so derived could not be anything but inferior, the more conservative writers asserted that this was not necessarily so. It is a familiar argument; in Canadian and Australian literary circles echoes of it still ring. The United States has long since emerged from these growing pains to reach that enviable position of maturity where creative writing has developed its own traditions and can proceed unself-consciously to build upon them. Undoubtedly political independence speeded the process, but the example of the literary history of the United States can provide some instructive lessons. Australia stands closer to the United States than does Canada in this process of development. Where Whitman asserted that America would create a new *kind* of literature,[7] Furphy, with his "bias: offensively Australian"[8] unconsciously echoed him, and Bernard O'Dowd flailed his arms for a Poetry Militant as late as 1909: ". . . at no time in the history of the world was the need for the Permeator Poet, the projector of ideals, the Poet Militant, greater than in the present reconstruction of all things beneath the wand of Evolution theories, and in no place greater than in this virgin and unhandicapped land of social experiments, embryonic democracy, and the Coming Race, Australia!"[9] Had Australia possessed an eagle as a national symbol, Whitman's disciple O'Dowd would undoubtedly have invoked it to soar. Yet such was the hiatus in literary development that O'Dowd's arguments appeared fifty-four years after the publication of

[6]*Ibid.*, 43.
[7]*Ibid.*, 45.
[8]Joseph Furphy, *Such Is Life*, 385.
[9]Bernard O'Dowd, *Poems*, 8.

Leaves of Grass.[10] The arguments, now newly consolidated, were not unknown to the Australian scene, however.

By 1860 an indigenous "folk" literature, crude, uncouth, idiomatic, was already the most virile and the most widely accepted expression of Australian creative writing. Australian poets who experimented, as Harpur did, in the more academic and traditional forms met with a mixed but largely indifferent reception. There were small "literary" cliques in the cities (none in the country) to encourage what they called "Polite Letters in Australia,"[11] but unlike their counterparts in Canada, they received little support even from the educated classes of the colony. They wrote their verses, but found it difficult to obtain publication for them. They called for an Australian Keats and a local Wordsworth, but since the early days of William Charles Wentworth few had echoed them. It is all the more surprising, therefore, to find that Kendall, the best nineteenth-century Australian poet to write in the English tradition, came from a circle far removed from these self-appointed guardians of the cultural flame.

Henry Kendall (1839–82) was born in Ulladulla on the New South Wales coast. In a small and primitive country town he received only the most elementary education, but he became the protégé of James Michael, a solicitor, the man who was to have the greatest influence on his life. As Furphy's *Such Is Life* reveals so eloquently, it was possible in mid–nineteenth-century Australia to find men of high intellectual capacity and broad learning in the most unlikely places. James Michael was one of these. As Harpur had done, Michael was constantly experimenting with diction and metre to adapt the English poetic tradition to the Australian environment, though he was objective enough to assess the merit of his work more dispassionately than most. He sensed a gift for words in his young companion, lent him books, and interested him in what Harpur was trying to do. Kendall was an enthusiastic pupil, but his developing obsession for poetry left him ill-equipped to handle the business of making a living in a small Australian town. After Michael's death, Kendall entered the civil service, resigned, went to Melbourne, and earned a most precarious

[10]Whitman's influence was delayed nearly everywhere. It is not exceptional that half a century intervened between the appearance of *Leaves of Grass* and O'Dowd's excited discovery of it in Australia at the turn of the century.

[11]See the dedication to Nicol Stenhouse, in J. S. Moore's *Life and Genius of James Lionel Michael*.

living at free-lance journalism, odd jobs, and clerkships. This was the employment pattern that he was to follow for most of his life. Whenever he could, he left the city and camped in the bush, writing poetry until his money ran out and he was forced to return to earn some more. Like Harpur's, his critical reception was a mixed one, and he lamented, in effect, that he was piping to a generation that would not dance. This was not quite true; it was dancing, but to a tune different to and less sophisticated than his. As Harpur's had been, Kendall's poetry was imitative, but his poetic ability was greater and more intense than that of his predecessor. Combined with this was a curiously fervent nationalism; he wanted to be the first successful interpreter of Australia to his countrymen. A contemporary, Henry Halloran, wrote a poem called "The Bards' Colloquy" made up of a dialogue (on the Poet's Mission) between himself, Harpur, and Kendall. Kendall is made to give an impassioned speech on Fame as the object of his poetry:

> . . . the single aim,
> Stirring this weak heart, is that mine should be
> Among my countrymen a household name.[12]

Kendall studied the English poets intensively, more for their technical secrets than for their content. His seventh sonnet on "The Stanza of Childe Harold" reveals a much deeper interest in the form of the stanza itself than in Byron—in the way "wild words were wedded to wild melody." How to do this for his own country was his persistent question. The twelfth sonnet, "Alfred Tennyson," reveals the manner in which Kendall played with the evocation of mood:

> The silvery dimness of a happy dream
> I've known of late. Methought where Byron moans,
> Like some wild gulf in melancholy zones,
> I passed tear-blinded. Once a lurid gleam
> Of stormy sunset loitered on the sea
> While travelling, troubled like a straitened stream,
> The voice of Shelley died away from me.
> Still sore at heart I reached a lake-lit lea,
> And then the green-mossed glades with many a grove,
> Where lies the calm which Wordsworth used to love;
> And lastly, Locksley Hall, from whence did rise

[12]Barton, *Poets and Prose Writers of New South Wales*, 214.

A haunting song that blew, and breathed and blew
With rare delights. 'Twas *there* I woke and knew
The sumptuous comfort left in drowsy eyes.[13]

These are sweets to be sampled, and, if possible, adapted. In this respect Kendall was perhaps more literary than the earlier Canadian poets, more devoted to the analysis of poetic techniques. As he says in the prefatory sonnet to his volume of 1869:

> So take these kindly, even though there be
> Some notes that unto other lyres belong,
> Stray echoes from the elder notes of song;
> And think how from its neighbouring native sea
> The pensive shell doth borrow melody.
> I would not do the lordly masters wrong
> By filching fair words from the shining throng
> Whose music haunts me as the wind a tree!
> Lo, when a stranger in soft Syrian glooms
> Shot through with sunset treads the cedar dells,
> And hears the breezy ring of elfin bells
> Far down by where the white-haired cataract booms,
> He, faint with sweetness caught from forest smells,
> Bears thence, unwitting, plunder of perfumes.[14]

Kendall's poetry is a strange mixture of good and bad, the bad being nearly always those poems in which he has remembered the strains of the "other lyres" too vividly. He is at his best when he writes simply of those things he knows intimately. He spent most of his time among the moist forests and the mountain slopes of eastern Australia, and, as a result, his poetry presents a more idyllic picture than the ones portrayed in the harsh realities of Lawson and Paterson, who lived mainly among the alternating droughts and floods of the western plains of New South Wales. Kendall's interpretation was a valid one, intensely felt, and there is today an increasing affection for his work. Such poems as "Bell-Birds" seemed to employ for the first time an imagery still traditional but recognizably Australian.

The bell-bird is found only in the south-eastern forests of Australia, where it lives by the sides of streams and waterfalls. Its song consists of a long single note, very mellow and yet very penetrating. Many travellers in the early days, lost in the bush and in search of water,

[13]Henry Kendall, *Poems*, 74.
[14]*Ibid.*, 4.

were saved by following the sound of the bell-birds; and even today
thirsty hikers are grateful to the cool liquid note that guides them
unerringly to water.

> By channels of coolness the echoes are calling
> And down the dim gorges I hear the creek falling;
> It lives in the mountain, where moss and the sedges
> Touch with their beauty the banks and the ledges;
> Through breaks of the cedar and sycamore bowers
> Struggles the light that is love to the flowers.
> And softer than slumber, and sweeter than singing,
> The notes of the bell-birds are running and ringing.
>
> Welcome as water unkissed by the summers,
> Are the voices of bell-birds to thirsty far-comers,
> When fiery December sets foot in the forest,
> And the need of the way-farer presses the sorest,
> Pent in the ridges for ever and ever,
> The bell-birds direct him to spring and to river,
> With ring and with ripple, like runnels whose torrents
> Are toned by the pebbles and leaves in the currents.[15]

More and more, his poems came to deal with Australian scenes. In
"The Austral Months," a poem in twelve parts, Kendall made the
first attempt to describe one of the great departures from the English
tradition that beset any Australian poet of nature. February, the
"blue-eyed last of Summer" whose "memory beams through all the
year," July, the bleak, wild-faced, carrying echoes from the Pole, are
replaced finally by the songs of September, the harbinger of
Australian spring.

> Grey winter has gone, like a wearisome guest,
> And behold for repayment,
> September comes in with the wind of the West,
> And the spring in her raiment.[16]

The year is ended on a triumphant note for December, the month of
Christmas and midsummer, when, for Australians, the sun stands
in the sky directly overhead, a symbol of the world of light that comes
with the birth of Christ. In this bright season the streams sing their
hosannas and the winds are full of gentle anthems; in this poem the

[15]Ibid., 9.
[16]Ibid., 77.

series rises to such an effective climax that one feels midsummer must be the only appropriate time for Christmas to be celebrated.

Anticipating one of Judith Wright's themes by some eighty years, Kendall wrote a long narrative poem on the theme of the remittance man, a familiar figure on the Australian scene of a century ago. "The Glen of Arrawatta" describes the hero's attempt at the life of the pioneer, an attempt which followed the traditional steady decline into failure and despair, until at last he dies, surrounded by mocking aborigines, the most backward savages in the world, but people who have at least managed to survive in such a land. His remains are eventually found and hurriedly buried in the bush. Back home in England his fate becomes the subject for legends. This is how the poem ends:

> But while the English Autumn filled her lap
> With faded gold, and while the reapers cooled
> Their flame-red faces in the clover grass,
> They looked for him at home: and when the frost
> Had made a silence in the morning lanes
> And cooped the farmers by December fires,
> They looked for him at home: and through the days
> Which brought about the million-coloured Spring,
> With moon-like splendours, in the garden plots,
> They looked for him at home: while Summer danced,
> A shining singer, through the tasselled corn,
> They looked for him at home.
>   And he
> Whose fate was hidden under forest leaves
> And in the darkness of untrodden dells
> Became a marvel. Often by the hearths
> In winter nights, and when the wind was wild
> Outside the casements, children heard the tale
> Of how he left their native vales behind
> (Where he had been a child himself) to shape
> New fortunes for his father's fallen house;
> Of how he struggled—how his name became,
> By fine devotion and unselfish zeal,
> A name of beauty in a selfish land;
> And then, of how the aching hours went by,
> With patient listeners praying for the step
> Which never crossed the floor again. So passed
> The tale to children.[17]

[17]Ibid., 47–8.

It is interesting to see how the note of irony comes into the work of this least ironical of Australian poets. As his work develops it is possible to see the influence of the prevailing literary climate growing stronger and stronger. The academic and experimental poems are accompanied by more long narrative poems dealing with incidents from Australian history, and told with less rhetoric and fewer heroics. Kendall also began to produce poems in the tradition of the bushman's anecdotes, the form that was to be perfected by Paterson, Lawson, and Dyson in the nineties. His portraits of some of the characters he came across during his wanderings in the bush would have been scorned by a Heavysege or a Sangster, but they are told deftly and with humour, and are directly in the tradition of bush realism which plays such an important part in the development of Australian literature. Perhaps the best of Kendall's bushman sketches are the pictures he gives of a bullock-driver, and a "splitter" or lumberman, the two bush occupations traditionally associated with fluent and colourful linguistic ability.

> The bard who is singing of Wollombi Jim
> Is hardly just now in the requisite trim
>   To sit on his Pegasus fairly;
> Besides, he is bluntly informed by the Muse
> That Jim is a subject no singer should choose;
>   For Jim is poetical rarely.[18]

Kendall attempted to make the best of both worlds. His major work was in the traditional form, and despite indifference from the public he devoted his life to the development of Australian poetry. It is unfair to say, with the American Professor Hartley Grattan, that he was "a barely respectable minor poet, leaning heavily on Wordsworth and Keats."[19] He avoided many of the pitfalls which wait for colonial poets; the rhetoric which cheapens so much of Sangster and Harpur was not used, and though in such poems as "Euterpe" and "Hy-Brasil" Kendall turned towards that exotic idealized crystallization of impossible hopes and "noble" dreams of which A. J. M. Smith speaks, he redeemed himself by the breadth of his experimentation and the success of many of his nature poems, in which he consciously set out to interpret Australian scenes for Australians themselves.

[18]Ibid., 192.
[19]Ewers, Creative Writing in Australia, 30.

An examination of the critical comments which Kendall received from his reviewers adds light to what mid–nineteenth-century Australian critics meant by "Australianism." It was, as we have said, first of all a matter of the subject on which a poet chose to write, and secondly the appropriateness of the images which he used to describe it. They felt that no matter how "poetic" an image was, only an Australian could judge whether the image was appropriate to Australia. There was, of course, a wide difference of opinion about this. A critic who wrote under the pseudonym "Evelyn" reviewed Kendall's *Leaves from an Australian Forest* in the *Colonial Monthly* in 1869. He defined, first, his frame of reference: "Among the things to be considered in looking at the new volume are: the range, purpose and quality of the present volume; and the nature of its claims as a distinctively Australian work of art."[20]

Apparently the latter was considered the most important, for the reviewer spends most of his time considering this. He discusses subject-matter and appropriateness, but obviously finds it difficult, as did all his fellow critics, to say *why* he thought certain images were appropriate to Australian landscape. He takes hold of Kendall's use of alliteration and tries to use it as an explanation:

. . . With Mr. Kendall alliteration is not so much a peculiar craft, wielded to cover deficiencies, but a necessity. His prose rings with it as freely as his verse, and in it the remarkable power of his descriptions of Australian scenery chiefly lies.

And it is a singular fact how aptly some of the physical characteristics of Australian nature can be thus reproduced. No one, for instance, can fail to apprehend the appropriateness of such expressions as "the breathless brazen sky", "runnels babbling of a plenteous fall", "the crimson days, and dull dead nights of thirst", "a sultry summer rimmed with thunder-cloud, and red with forest fires," or, "where the languid heavens quiver, o'er red depths of stirless air."[21]

If true, it is a "singular fact" indeed, and the critic's confidence that "no one can fail to apprehend the appropriateness" of the images he quotes is hardly explained by the quotations. More important, perhaps, than this, the review ends on the clinching note (p. 148): ". . . Mr. Kendall is far more than this. To him . . . Australia is home; England, its language and associations, foreign."

[20]*Colonial Monthly* (October, 1869), 142.
[21]*Ibid.*, 147.

Time after time this instinctive type of rationalization about appropriateness of imagery and the nature of that all-inclusive term "local colouring" raises its head in a similar way. It is very much easier to say what is not appropriate. An anonymous writer in the *Sydney Quarterly Magazine*, having expressed the usual approval of Kendall's "charm of local colouring," has no hesitation in lashing out at some of the non-Australian poems: "Well may we wonder how the author of *Araluen* could write such ludicrous rubbish as this [*To Damascus*], or a poem like *Saul at Gilboa*, where would-be grandiloquence is simple bathos, and the whole is like some ill-painted picture with discordant colouring and an utter lack of perspective."[22]

G. B. Barton, the dean of Australian critics in the sixties, solemnly added his comments on the same subject, praising Kendall for his lack of imitation. Note the renewed use of terms which, by now, should be familiar:

One striking merit of Mr. Kendall's poetry is, that its colouring is strictly local, and that he has endeavoured to give voice to the majestic scenery of his native land. *Whatever opinion may be formed of his poetry, it cannot be denied that it is distinctly Australian poetry* [my italics]. This is a hopeful sign; inasmuch as it speaks of a mind naturally original, and averse to imitation. He has not commenced the practice of his art by studying Tennyson, but by studying the wild and splendid scenery that surrounded him at his birth. His capacity in descriptive poetry is very great. . . . He has an artist's eye for a landscape, and if his shading is rather too dark, his outlines are none the less true. No local writer has reproduced the scenes familiar to us with so much effect. And again, he has sought inspiration in the characters and events of this country—endeavouring to paint the wild society of the interior as well as its peculiar scenery. He has chanted the savage melodies of the aboriginals—painted the sufferings of the explorers—and given a poetic interest to the life of stockmen. *These are facts which mark him out as an Australian poet* [my italics], and an original poet: for there is no writer in this field whom he could imitate.[23]

Two points emerge from this contemporary critical opinion. The Australianism of a poet is his most important attribute, and this is judged by subject-matter and appropriateness of language, the latter being very much a subjective matter. There is one more extract to notice before leaving the topic of the way in which Australian

[22]*Sydney Quarterly Magazine*, 6 (June, 1889), 106.
[23]Barton, *Poets and Prose Writers of New South Wales*, 193–4.

critics judged Australianism. It is very much to the point. W. H. O. Smeaton, looking back on "A Quartette of Australian Singers" (including Kendall) from the vantage point of 1889, had this to say in support of nationalist criticism:

Somewhat over a year ago an article of considerable power and literary merit appeared in one of the leading English monthlies, professedly reviewing Australian literature, both in its essential principles and body of examples. Once more we were regaled wth the *rechauffe* of an oft-reiterated mistake. Much that was otherwise of rare excellence in thought and expression was marred by the same error that has perverted the entire mass of English criticism on the subject in the past, viz. assuming that Australian song can be meted and judged by the same inspiring spiritual forces as that of the Motherland herself, and that Australian Singers, because they chance to form a part of that Empire on which the sun never sets, have therefore no distinctive characteristics and differentiating traits, imparting national individuality to their work.[24]

The writer goes on to point to the American example where cultural independence has been recognized, and claims the same right for Australia, quoting Marcus Clarke's "splendid demand for original canons by which to appraise the value of our distinctively National School of Australian Song."[25] Thus is commemorated a new poetry demanding a new criticism, with no one very sure of the characteristics of either, but agreed on the virtue and necessity of both.

To echo Barton, whatever the merits of Kendall's poetry, it cannot be denied that Kendall by 1860 had advanced the search for an Australian idiom in poetry further than Sangster had assisted the Canadian. In many ways the six Australian colonies in 1867 were more of a nation than was Canada. Within ten years, however, there was to be a very strong literary nationalist movement in Canada. It will be easier to understand the comparison between the poet and his environment in each country after considering the fate which befell Charles Mair and his friends.

The history of Canadian Confederation is complicated by many social, political, religious, and regional issues. Symptomatic of the manner in which national feeling lagged behind political development was the phenomenon known as the Canada First movement, which

---

[24]W. H. O. Smeaton, "A Quartette of Australian Singers," *Centennial Magazine*, Sydney, 1 (1889), 854.

[25]*Ibid*. The passage from Marcus Clarke appears on page 153 of this book.

had its origins in the idealistic and enthusiastic discussions between five young men in Ottawa in 1868. Their aim was to advance the growth of a national sentiment—to make Canada a reality in the hearts of her people as well as on the statute books. It is difficult to develop a programme designed to create a force as intangible as national sentiment, and it is not surprising that there were wide differences among the five concerning the means by which their common objective was to be reached. Kendall, Furphy, Paterson, and Lawson could, by the nineties, take the existence of an Australian national sentiment for granted, but in Canada it had to be self-consciously developed. Each one of the five approached the subject from his own point of view, stressing the aspect that interested him most.

Charles Mair, the son of Scottish pioneer settlers, believed that poetry was more important than politics—though he was later to see the close connection between them which existed in Canada—and saw himself as the Canadian Keats. For him the development of a national literature would solve the problem of creating a national sentiment, and in this he drew a measure of support from the other four.

George T. Denison was the proud descendant of a United Empire Loyalist family, a young cavalry officer *par excellence*, given to frequent sabre-rattling and occasional pomposity. Denison was a prey, more than the others, to that dual loyalty that could be seen in Howe, and which continued to reveal itself in Canadian writers throughout the century. He was torn by the claims of a local patriotism to Canada and by those of loyalty to the wider British connection. It is not surprising that the confusion in his mind was later to be resolved by his espousal of the cause of Imperial Federation. Typically, he saw the creation of national sentiment as a duty—to Britain as well as to Canada—and, as a good soldier should, he tried to inspire his countrymen to do their duty, even if it took a "rattling good war" with the United States to bring them to their senses.

Robert G. Haliburton, inheriting many of his famous father's aristocratic loyalties and sympathies, knew more clearly than the others what it was he wanted. Sharing his father's fondness for outspoken criticism, he introduced an element of patriotic pride which was not entirely divorced from a *Herrenvolk* theory. The Canadians were a northern race, which, he asserted, had been proved by history to be superior to the others. As the North had dominated European life for centuries, so the Canadians were the Northmen of the American continent. Theirs was the "manifest destiny," and to them would come the prize, not to the heterogeneous racial confusion inhabiting the United States. Five years older than any of the others, Haliburton, with his confident assertions, left his mark upon his more impressionable colleagues.

William A. Foster was a Toronto barrister, shy with strangers, enthusiastic among his friends, yet diffident about undertaking decisive action. He preferred, where possible, to stand aside and comment rather than to take the initiative. Yet, ironically, he found himself at the head of the group, principally because his was the most catholic idealism. In him the others could find neutral ground.

Henry J. Morgan, the youngest, was a journalist. He was the host of the gatherings, and frequently stirred himself into flights of impassioned oratory until he had almost convinced himself that he knew what he meant. Twenty years later, writing to Mair, he said: "Do you remember those evenings? Lord how I talked! I can almost hear it all now, and you, dear old Charlie, who always assured me that you understood what I was talking about. I don't think that I did myself— all I know was that I wanted something very much indeed. I only wish that I could remember what it was now."[26] There is a real pathos in this memorial to a lost vision, for in many ways it is typical of the fate that was to befall all five. Each of them, filled with a crusading zeal, went out to find a world to conquer, the exact nature of which was not quite clear. Denison, writing forty years later, described the spirit which had moved them:

Nothing could show more clearly the hold that confederation had taken of the imagination of young Canadians than the fact, night after night, that five young men should give up their time and their thoughts to discussing the higher interests of their country, and it ended in our making a solemn pledge to each other that we would put our country first, before all personal, or political, or party considerations; that we would change our party affiliations as often as the true interests of Canada required it.[27]

[26]Morgan to Mair, June 17, 1889; Parcel 17 of the unsorted papers of Charles Mair, held at the Douglas Library, Queen's University, Kingston, Ontario. The references given are to the parcel numbers assigned to the papers by the Librarian, as they were in January, 1954.

[27]G. T. Denison, The Struggle for Imperial Unity, 10–11.

These were the five who had pledged themselves to work unsparingly for the creation of a national sentiment; they were strongly united only in their personal regard for one another, and by the one pledge which had so many different meanings. An account given by Denison to Mair of a private dinner shows that there was no unanimity between them: "Foster and I argued points of public policy and for some reason our views were decidedly opposite to each other; the old gentleman (Morgan's friend) interposing the remark at intervals that he understood us both and that he entirely disagreed with the views expressed on either side."[28]

At first, their efforts to implement their pledge were haphazard and carried out individually rather than as a group. Then Mair left for the North West with a party of surveyors, and in the vast uninhabited stretches of Canada's unclaimed empire he found the direction in which he could aim his crusading energies. The influence of Haliburton's racialism, mixed perhaps with some native Scottish prejudice, had caused Mair to look with a suspicious eye on the half-breed population of the area, and he was only too ready to cry treason against those who had dealings with the United States. Mair found the North West fertile beyond his hopes, an empty country whose only access for much of the year was through the territory of a foreign land which was itself looking with interest towards the north. He made it his task to inform his comrades in far-away Canada that the Red River settlements were not located in a barren wilderness, and that the public should stir itself from apathy before a great realm was lost to it. In articles published in the Toronto *Globe*, Mair hammered away at this one theme: "Open the North West!"

Denison leapt on to the cause from Toronto, and, characteristically, in one letter to Mair introduced Haliburton's racialism, his own racial purity, his pride in ancient English institutions, and the need for Canadian ones. A book he had recently published had received rather patronizing reviews in the London press. He did not appreciate being told that he had done well—for a colonial.

I am very glad to hear such good accounts of the resources and fertility of the great North West. When filled up with a loyal population and a prosperous one, I have every confidence that in time it would prove a great source of strength to the Dominion, and that we, the Men of the North, as

28Denison to Mair, January 8, 1869; Parcel 40, the Mair Papers.

Haliburton says, will be able to teach the Yankees that we will be, as our ancestors have always been, the dominant race.

We Canadians must pull together, a national Canadian spirit must be encouraged. I am a life-member of the St. George Society, and as I am pure English by descent, entitled to be one, but it is all wrong. We want Canadian societies, and Canadian associations, the races must fuse here into one nationality if we ever hope to be a great people.[29]

This is a fair example of the confusion of Denison's mind; but he was not alone in such confusion. A character in Richardson's *The Fortunes of Richard Mahoney* provides an Australian counterpart to Denison. John Turnham has just been elected to the legislature, and he addresses his followers:

Our first cry, then, is for men to people the country; our next, for independence, to work out our own salvation. Yes, my friends, the glorious future of this young and prosperous colony . . . rests with ourselves alone. We who inhabit here can best judge of her requirements, and we refuse to see her hampered in her progress by the shackles of an ancient tradition. What suits our hoary mother-country—God bless and keep her and keep us loyal to her!—is but dry husks for us. England knows nothing of our most pressing needs.[30]

Yet Turnham too is a member of the St. George Society, and proud of it. But what was parodied in Australia was taken with deadly seriousness in Canada. When Haliburton, during a lecture tour of Nova Scotia, Quebec, and Ontario, developed his theory of racial superiority to its inevitable logical conclusion—complete independence for Canada—Denison rebelled. Enthusiasm for things Canadian could not submerge, in the life-member of the St. George Society, a strong sentiment for the mother-country. There was a difference between grumbling within the liberal tolerance of a constitutional monarchy and the frightening nakedness of a republican experiment. Denison drew back a step, and wrote anxiously to Mair as early as June 1869:

Haliburton is writing for independence but he is making a mistake, it is too soon. I don't want to see independence until just after a rattling war with the United States when we will have a common feeling against them, a common history with all our sister provinces, and when we have taught the States that we are determined to keep clear of them. If England stands by us we can always hold our own . . . and independence would be the worst thing for us now.[31]

[29]Denison to Mair, March 10, 1869; Parcel 3.
[30]Henry Handel Richardson, *The Fortunes of Richard Mahoney*, 269.
[31]Denison to Mair, June 8, 1869; Parcel 3.

The division in the ranks had already begun to appear, but Haliburton continued regardless. He too was fired with enthusiasm by the cause of the North West, and assumed that Mair also shared his eagerness for independence. He wrote: "Why don't you suggest that the North West Territory should be called 'Norland'? It would be an excellent wedge, and we might some of these days have the whole new free nation called Norland instead of Canada. Think this over."[32] Mair replied by sending further articles to the *Globe* in which he attacked more and more strongly the American influences on Canadian life. He warned, almost hysterically, against the annexationist tendencies of those who would throw away Canada's promising future for material ends. Denison echoed these sentiments. His reservations about Haliburton's advocacy of independence had become stronger, and though he said nothing publicly, his letters to Mair show that he was beginning to take a darker view of all those who supported either independence or annexation. Only two months after his letter expressing uneasiness at Haliburton's approach, he wrote:

I do not see the *Gazette* but I have read all your articles which have appeared in *The Globe* and with great pleasure. The true Canadian spirit which is breathed in them is specially gratifying at a time when some of our fools are saying "We can never hold out against the States, if they like they can annex us in spite of ourselves," and others, bigger fools still, if not worse, are agitating independence for fear England might throw us off.[33]

The next two years saw Denison on an extended lecture tour, taking as his text, "The Duty of Canadians to Canada." As was typical of the man, his appeal was based on the clearly defined responsibility which the citizen owed to his community. If jingoism and sounding patriotic generalities could bring a more vivid apprehension of this duty, then Denison did not hesitate to use them in his speeches. Coming out openly in opposition to independence, Denison made clear his stand as an Imperial Federationist in a speech on April 29, 1871. In it, he provides a significant and comprehensive statement of the position of the right wing of the Canada First movement. More than that, he points out a concept of nationalism, very different from the Australian variety, which had developed in the heart of the Canadian nationalist movement.

[32]Haliburton to Mair, July 14, 1869; Parcel 48.
[33]Denison to Mair, August 11, 1869; Parcel 40.

It must not be supposed that the growth of a national sentiment will have any tendency to weaken the connection between this country and Great Britain. On the other hand it will strengthen and confirm the bond of union. Unfortunately England has reached that phase when the manufacturing and commercial community have attained such wealth and affluence, have become so wrapped up in the success of their business and have acquired such a pounds, shillings and pence basis in considering everything, that national sentiment is much weakened. In fact sentiment of any kind is sneered at and scoffed at as being behind the age. This school of politicians, fearing the expense of maintaining a war to defend Canada, calculating that in a monetary point of view we are not a source of revenue to them, speak slightingly of us, and treat the sentiment of affection that we bear to the Motherland with contempt.

Nothing could be more irritating to a high spirited people. We have the gratifying reflection, however, that the more we rise in the scale of nations, the more will this class desire to keep us, until at length every effort will be made to retain our affection and secure our fealty. *It is our duty therefore to push our way onwards and outwards, to show England that soon the benefits of the connection in a material as well as a moral point of view will be all in her favour* [my italics].

I hope that the day will come when the British Empire will be united into one great power or confederation of great nations, a confederation for the purpose of consolidating power as to foreign countries, and on all international questions; and rest assured, if we Canadians are only true to ourselves, the day will come when Canada will be not only the largest, but the most populous, the most warlike, and the most powerful of all the members of that confederation, if not the most powerful nation in the world.[34]

Here is nationalism with a vengeance. It is the duty of Canadians to build up their country into the most powerful nation in the world in order to preserve and strengthen the British connection! It is possible that Denison was carried away by his own oratory, though his letters give every indication that the position outlined in his speech was a firm personal faith. The emphasis which he continued to place on the warlike virtues displays a curiously unrealistic appreciation of the military situation; as an army officer, an expert in cavalry, he is curiously naïve when he assumes that Canada must grow strong to retain the Imperial connection, and that during the time until this strength is built, must rely on the continued protection of the United Kingdom.

[34]Denison, *The Struggle for Imperial Unity*, 52–3.

The promise that Canada would be "biggest and best," as well as "most warlike," provides further illumination of Denison's views about the development of a national sentiment. He had already expressed privately his hope for a "rattling war" with the United States as a compulsory unifying force; now, publicly, he insists on aggressiveness as an ingredient of the new Canadian national spirit. Yet Denison's aim is Imperial Federation. It is interesting to see how an Australian nationalist interpreted a similar set of facts applied to his own country.

In the eighties the "Yellow Peril" was the Australian equivalent of the Canadian fear of American invasion. Thousands of Chinese had been admitted to Australia from Hong Kong and Malaya on the grounds that as they were British subjects they could not be excluded. This issue was one of the rallying points for the Australian nationalists, and for the whole of the labour movement, which regarded the Chinese as "scabs." Thomson, in his book *Australian Nationalism*, dismissed Imperial Federation in 1888 as a system "whose cardinal principle is that the centre should be nourished at the expense of the extremities."[35] This is typical of the manner in which Australians regarded Imperial Federation. Many of them thought it part of a plot to postpone Australian Federation and to perpetuate a state of colonial dependence. Discussing the Chinese situation, Thomson works an interesting variation of Denison's argument (pp. 104–5):

The question of whether the Chinese who come here are moral or immoral is a matter of comparative indifference to an Australian. Their crime is that they are a cheap race—cheap to a degree that is destructive to the white race. And, as we proudly hope that Australia shall one day be the seat of a mighty independent nation of the Anglo-Saxon race, to which Britain shall look in the far-off future with eyes full of trusting love and pride, it is our bounden duty as loyal and patriotic natives of the soil, to use every effort in our power to prevent the calamity which would bring about the one result, and so destroy our hopes and prospects of the other. In fact, it would be little short of treason to our land to stand by and see a cancer in her breast, which, though small at present, grows daily stronger in vitality, taking deeper and deeper root, and slowly but surely sending its noxious parasitical fibres hither and thither throughout our land.

Here, it is the bounden duty of Australians to oppose official British policy for the sake of future relations between Britain and an independent Australia. The parallel is more striking when Thomson goes on

[35]*Australian Nationalism*, 3.

to paint a glowing picture of the benefits of a war with the Chinese (pp. 112–13):

So far from thinking a Chinese war would be a calamity to Australia I fervently believe it would be the greatest blessing we could possibly receive. For it would give us an excuse to clear out every yellow alien from our midst; and there would be such an uprising of patriotism in Australia as has seldom been seen in Anglo-Saxon annals. . . . A Chinese threat of invasion . . . would immediately federate our states into one nation; it would give us a permanent national government, and, baptised with the certain halo of a glorious victory in a truly righteous and holy cause, the flag of our new-born nation, the blue banner of the Southern Cross, would be an emblem that henceforth to all time would inspire the sons of our country with patriotic pride and a firm resolution to live true to her, and, when necessary, to die for her.

Whether they be Americans or Chinese, the idea is the same—the threat of external conflict is offered as a means of forcing the issue. In Canada the issue is not the creation of a political unit, for that already exists; it is to make the nation one in spirit. In Australia the position is reversed; external aggression would make use of the national spirit which already is there in abundance to force the creation of the national political unit. With Denison the ultimate aim is Imperial Federation; with Thomson, it is independence. But both federation and independence had support even among the original five members of Canada First, and the variations which they reflected were to be repeated as the movement gained adherents.

The second stage in the development of Canada First took place during the evangelizing activities of the five founders. Schultz was admitted, then Edgar, then five others, and the "Twelve Apostles," as they were called, agreed to form an organization, non-political in character, called the North-West Emigration Aid Society. Mair continued to be the advance scout of the group. He wrote of the conditions in the North West, and the others, in Toronto, acted collectively as an information bureau and individually as recruiting officers. The North West provided the new focus of unity, perhaps the only point of policy on which they were all agreed. "National Sentiment and the Development of the North West"—these were the two aims, which, expressed in general terms, were subscribed to by all twelve. Wisely, no details were added; independence was not raised in public, and the mutterings of Denison against Haliburton remained only as a set of variations to be rehearsed in his private letters. It is evident from the Mair Letters that, during this second stage of the organization's life, there continued an undercurrent of uneasiness. Denison was later to remark that the failure of the movement was brought about by outside influences. These did assist in the disintegration of the party, but Denison's subsequent public assertions that only the original founding five remained true to the old spirit of unity are misleading. The seeds of dissension had been sown long before the Canada First movement entered its final stage of development.

The name "Canada First" seems to have sprung from a suggestion by Edgar. He proposed as a motto for the group, "Canada Before All" or "Canada First of All." Denison began to use the phrase "Canada First," but the name did not achieve widespread recognition until the publication in 1871 of Foster's famous lecture, "Canada First or Our New Nationality." Foster had been of a more retiring nature than the other members of the group, and had contented himself with writing articles for the Toronto *Telegram*. Denison tried to make Foster agree to read the paper at a meeting. Through a misunderstanding, however, the lecture was published before it could be delivered. It received wide circulation throughout Canada, and to Foster's surprise and gratification stimulated considerable interest and discussion.

"Canada First" appears a curious document to the modern reader. There is a core of romanticism in the style which erupts frequently into emotionalism, and into those purple patches that marked so much of the movement's propaganda. The influence of Haliburton's racialism is again evident: "The old Norse mythology, with its Thor hammers and Thor hammerings, appeals to us—for we are a Northern people— as the true outcrop of human nature, more manly, more real, than the weak marrow-bones superstition of an effeminate South."[36] It is extraordinary to find such doctrines advocated by a movement whose aim was the unification of all Canadians, French and English, by the propagation of a Canadian sentiment; for no matter how initially attractive such ideas might be to an Anglo-Saxon audience, they would inevitably act in direct opposition to the alleged aims of the movement. Foster launched an impassioned plea for consideration of Canada's achievements in the world. He recites—in epic catalogue

[36]W. A. Foster: *Canada First: a Memorial*, 25.

—the deeds of Canada's most noble sons, ending on a note dangerously near anti-climax. Canadian honour is safe. Admiral Watt has figured in a hundred engagements, and "not long ago, Plumb of Niagara was head-boy of Rugby."[37] The lecture is not well written. It is vague and loosely constructed, avoiding any definite statements, as Canada First literature nearly always did, and indeed had to, to preserve unity among its members. Foster had no illusions about his literary ability. He told Mair: "If any of my writing has achieved success it has not been on account of a fluent stream of words. That is a gift I cannot acquire, and must leave to you and Robert [Haliburton]."[38]

Nevertheless, Foster's words caught the attention of many Canadians. They seemed to make more urgent the need to defeat the sense of aimlessness and anxiety for the future which had beset the new Dominion in the first decade of its existence. The Canada First movement seemed to offer a rallying point around which theories could be argued, and it seemed to offer a definite plan. Interest was so great that the party's membership increased considerably, and the committee was filled with optimism for the future. It was as a result of this optimism that the suggestion was made that the movement should constitute itself a fully fledged political party. Daniel Spry urged this strongly, but there were many misgivings among the original members. Denison displayed considerable common sense in pointing out to the other members of the committee the objections to the scheme. He recounted these in a letter to Mair.

I can see no advantages at all in the proposal that we should attempt to enter politics on an official basis. I am completely against it. We can do more good by remaining a power to be reckoned with behind the scenes, where we can influence policy by offering the support of a substantial number of electors to the party which is pledged to carry out plans in the best interest of Canada, and by withdrawing it when we feel that those interests are not being served. If we go into it ourselves we shall draw the fire of both parties. Foster agrees with me, Haliburton is non-committal, but I have the feeling he would like to see himself in political office, perhaps the first President! Morgan is sitting on the fence. I hope to God that nothing comes of it.[39]

Over thirty years later, in his *Struggle for Imperial Unity*, Denison described the situation.

[37]*Ibid.*, 32.
[38]Foster to Mair, June 21, 1875; Parcel 6, the Mair Papers.
[39]Denison to Mair, April 19, 1872; Parcel 17.

Foster and I discussed the matter at great length, and my suggestion was that we should go on as we had been going, and that if we ever wished to hold public meetings Dr. Canniff, one of the "Twelve Apostles" and the oldest of them, the author of *The Early Settlement of Upper Canada*, would make an excellent chairman, and not being a party man would not arouse hostility. I said, "If we organise a party and appoint a particular man to lead, we shall be responsible for everything he says", and repeated that the Party press would attack him bitterly and injure the cause, which was all we cared for. Foster supported my views, and during 1872 and 1873 we kept quiet, watching for any good opportunities of doing service to the country.[40]

Denison contested the 1872 general election as a Reform candidate but was unsuccessful, and left for England in November 1873. Shortly afterwards a by-election was held, and the Canada First group decided to support Thomas Moss, a Liberal who was standing for West Toronto, and who had Canada First sympathies. Foster was brought around to the idea of giving Moss support from the movement, as a political party, and on January 6, 1874, the Canadian National Association was formed. The time was well chosen. The Pacific Scandal had broken, Macdonald had resigned, and there was a wave of popular feeling against the corruption of party politics. Canada First had always placed much emphasis on protests against this corruption, and its entry into the political field as a new force free from the unsavoury reputations of the older parties caused a flood of membership applications. It seemed as though the move had been a sound one. However, as a political party, Canada First was obliged to draw up a definite platform; the sounding generalities would no longer do. Foster became the leader of an Executive Committee and the platform was drafted. The eleven points which emerged concealed a core of irresolution behind a facade of determination. The first point was particularly ambiguous "British connection, Consolidation of the Empire, and in the meantime a voice in treaties affecting Canada." To the Federationists it meant Imperial Federation, though avoiding a definite statement to that effect. To the Annexationists and supporters of independence it meant either a front to placate the timid, or a guarantee that Britain's support would be preserved during the process of building an independent state. The key words were "in the meantime"—in the meantime until what? Each read his own preference into the answer. The platform managed to convey the impression of

[40]Denison, *The Struggle for Imperial Unity*, 56–7.

looking resolutely forward without assigning the route to be followed.

At first all seemed to be going well. Moss was elected, the party founded a weekly, the *Nation*, and set up the National Club in Toronto as a place where it was hoped that Canadian nationalists of all parties might meet. The year 1874 found the Canada First party rejoicing in the hope that at last it had found its true leader in Edward Blake. Blake's Aurora Speech, in which he seemed to support the platform of the party, was hailed as the beginning of a period when prominent men from all parties would break with their old affiliations and swing instead into the new national party. Blake's reference to national spirit was applauded by all sections of the group, and his remark that "We are four million Britons who are not free" was cheered by supporters of independence and Imperial Federation alike. To the enthusiastic members of Canada First, Blake appeared to endorse their entire programme. "The future of Canada, I believe, depends very largely upon the cultivation of a national spirit. We must find some common ground on which to unite, some common aspiration to be shared, and I thing that it can be alone found in the cultivation of that spirit."[41] Canada First was prepared to provide that ground. Foster wrote to Mair with a light heart: "You have read Blake's speech of course. Good boy, Blake! He will go on to perfection! As for the Grits, I do not object to your maledictions on 'em. The National club is in full blast—about 400 members, good furniture, excellent grub, fine company, best of liquor, unexampled cooking—great success! Canada First is well!"[42]

The future seemed bright, but Canada First was far from being well. At the same moment that Foster was confidently predicting the break-up of the existing political parties, Blake's enthusiasm was beginning to cool, and the many factions within the movement were beginning to make their presence felt. Foster reflects the first shades of anxiety over the independence question. He wrote to Mair:

I have just read your article in the C.M. and can't refrain from writing to say how pleased I am with it. It hits the nail on the head. *The Globe* you know is hammering away at Goldwin Smith and *The Nation* returns the fire; but the fight hurts us, as we do not trust our existence as a party to the Independence question. That question may be discussed ad nauseam but we do not want to be bored to death with it.[43]

[41]*Canadian Historical Review* II, 249 *et seq.*
[42]Foster to Mair, June 10, 1875; Parcel 48.
[43]Foster to Mair, August 10, 1875; Parcel 48.

There was no danger of the independence dispute producing boredom, though the rest of the phrase was closer to the truth than Foster knew. His letter was in response to a long article entitled "The New Canada," which Mair had written for the August issue of the *Canadian Monthly*. In it the more unfortunate influences of Canada First upon Mair's literary style are evident. After rehearsing the natural advantages of the North West, he began an intense and detailed tirade against American institutions, ending on a note of bathos which was no doubt intended to be inspirational:

Talk of annexation to such a state of affairs as this! There is not one fibre of our moral and intellectual nature which does not revolt at the coarse and unnatural suggestion. Is there any true Canadian who can think of these things without disgust and loathing? Is there any Canadian girl who can think of them without horror and shame? NO! Thank God, our young men are not afraid of the battle of life, our maids are innocent and pure. Their dreams are holy, touched with the hope of a true Canadian off-spring, and the consciousness that the world can bestow no higher honour than to be the virtuous and devoted mother of a Canadian child.[44]

In this article Mair comes out openly against both annexation and independence, and the split in the party began to reveal itself unmistakably. Mair was not the only one to express himself in such extravagant terms. The issues of the *Canadian Monthly* throughout 1875 display the tremendous interest which was felt in the controversy. It dominates all other subjects. Howland and Norris, both of the Canada First party, come out in favour of independence, with annexation as the probable ultimate aim. Foster, Mair, and Denison bitterly attack them. Others outside the party cheer from the sidelines. Jehu Matthews, in a series of articles, points to the spectacle which Canada First is presenting to the people of Canada. "What," he asks, "does Canada First mean? First to what?" but the party was unable to answer. The weakness inherent since its formation proved to be fatal. In the spring of 1875 Blake made up his quarrel with Mackenzie and Brown, and accepted office in the Liberal government. Cracked by internal dissension and deserted by the man they had come to regard as their leader, the members of Canada First dissolved the party.

This was the inevitable outcome for a movement so divided on the meaning of its alleged aims. The Canadian experience reveals the compensations which Australia received for her long-delayed federa-

[44]*Canadian Monthly*, August, 1875; 163.

tion. The *Bulletin* school of Australian nationalists adopted the cry of "Federation and Independence," but their greatest attention was drawn to the cause of federation as the first necessary step towards independence. Had federation come as early as it had to Canada, it is probable that Australian nationalism would have been as divided as the Canada First movement. As it was, federation remained the rallying point for nationalists of all opinions, the independence question being assigned more and more to the background, until, by 1901, when federation was finally achieved, the independence issue had ceased to play an important part on the political scene. The parliamentary Labour Party, which rose to a position of power early in the years following federation, found, as radical parties often find when they assume the responsibilities of office, that they had ample scope to implement their policies within the framework of the British connection. Added worries about the intentions of the Russians, and later of the Japanese, led to second thoughts about the desirability of throwing off the protection of the Royal Navy, even on the part of the most ardent republicans.

The essence of the Australian nationalist movement in the last forty years of the nineteenth century lay in the struggle for political federation; national sentiment already existed as a potent force throughout the colonies. The Canadian nationalist, on the other hand, had to whip up enthusiasm for a cause which had already been achieved. Only those who spoke for annexation or independence were advocating a change from the status quo, and though these speakers caused great excitement and violent opposition, the emotions they aroused were more *against* union with the United States, or *against* changing the tie with Britain, than they were *for* any definite concept of Canadianism. The search for a national identity, which is still going on, was then—as one is sometimes tempted to think it is now—the concern of a small minority of the population. With their genius for compromise, most Canadians are content to regard themselves as inheritors of the best of both British and American worlds and are happy to let it go at that. The long delay in adopting an official Canadian flag indicates more than an inability among the two major racial groups to come to an agreement. An ardently nationalist people would not have waited ninety-three years. It implies rather a distrust of any ideas which purport to define Canadian status or national identity with any degree of precision. Not only does Canada mean to the Nova Scotian something quite different from what it means to the Manitoban, it has different meanings for individuals within the same area. That there is a Canadian national spirit is undeniable, but the Canadian feels that an attempt to define it too rigidly would be a mistake—the intangible at least has the virtue of excluding no one.

This aspect of Canadian nationalism was the rock on which Canada First ran aground. Not only did they attempt to define the indefinable, but they were suspicious of the continuation of Canadian regionalism as an enemy to the growth of a national spirit. Such a recent critic as E. K. Brown has echoed them, claiming that in literature, too, a spirit of regionalism stresses the superficial and peculiar at the expense of the fundamental and universal. It is true that excessive fragmentation may be dangerous, but perhaps Professor Brown was caught up in a persuasive Canadian tradition. Insistence on the value of the universal may be found throughout the history of Canadian criticism. Didacticism must be stressed by means of "the fundamental and the universal," until one begins to think that the two terms are synonymous. For such critics, regionalism is the purgatory Canadian literature must endure before the coming of great books is a possibility, but it is a necessary purgatory. Canadian poets have cut across the borders of regionalism more than the prose writers, but we have seen that with the earlier poets this has been a source of weakness. With their eyes firmly fixed upon the parent tradition more than upon the object before them, they have been chasing, prematurely, a universal which cannot exist for them until it grows from local roots.

In Australia no regional literatures have developed, but not because the writers kept their eyes so firmly on the English tradition that family resemblances countered any regional differences. Canadian regionalism finds its equivalent in Australian nationalism. Apart from the universal division between city and country—with the balance of emphasis heavily in favour of the country—there is little to distinguish the Victorian or the Queenslander from the Western Australian. The bushmen were—and are—a shifting population. Shearers, drovers, timbermen, station workers, all moved freely from one part of the country to another, rarely staying long in one place. As the Bush Myth has developed from them, the picture they drew was composite rather than localized. They described what was "fundamental and universal" for bushmen all over the country, and this is the picture that has come to be accepted as a universal, even by the urban population. But it was a unity founded on the common factor of a continent-wide Australian sentiment, such as the members of Canada First were doing their best to create for their own country. They did not realize that what had happened in Australia could not be repeated in Canada. There nationalism was expressed through regionalism, and though for long unrecognized, as we shall see in a later chapter, the same type of strength was quietly working its way through the ballads and legends of Canadian regionalism.

This was beyond the understanding of the Canada First party. Denison records the apathy which greeted his attempts to stir up interest in a Canadian literature, an apathy which emphasizes the difficulty of the nationalist in Canada. He writes indignantly to Mair, describing a meeting at Brantford in 1871.

During my stay at Brantford, I arranged to speak to their local Literary Society. I saw from their programme for the year that they had addresses on Shakespeare, Milton, Keats (two), Scott, Southey and Wordsworth. Not one Canadian! I gave them a direct talk about the *duty* [my italics] of societies like theirs in building an awareness of Canadian literature. Would you believe it? They couldn't see it! They said that there *was* no Canadian literature, and that they saw no reason why they should waste their time on the third rate when there was so much to be done studying the works of the truly great. I do not know what to do with such people. They are so desperately afraid of being considered colonial that they concentrate on the very attitude that ensures they can never be anything else. These very societies which we had hoped would be of such great assistance emerge as the greatest enemies of our cause. How can they be so foolish![45]

The attitude of the literary societies is really a restatement of Smith's definition of literary colonialism, and Denison found himself unable to combat it. It was an attitude which was shared by the upper and middle classes in both Canada and Australia, but in Canada class barriers were not maintained, and in Australia they were strengthened. The class which was to play such an influential and unexpected part in Australian literary development represented itself as the oppressed majority straining beneath the colonial yoke, and therefore did not reflect any of the attributes of colonialism of which

[45]Denison to Mair, October 9, 1871; Parcel 33.

Smith speaks, and theirs was the attitude which was to influence the national one. The Canadian malcontent, on the other hand, was absorbed by a society where colonialism imposed no obvious economic burdens, and where there was little incentive for class barriers to be maintained. The study by Canadian literary societies of English authors exclusively was therefore a reflection of colonial literary dependence willingly embraced by the colonists themselves.

6. Advance and Retreat

AGAINST THIS BROAD background of the nature of nationalism in Canada in the years following Confederation, it becomes easier to trace the fate of the individual literary nationalist. Because Charles Mair took so prominent a part in the foundation of the Canada First movement, it is all the more curious to note in his work the dual influences of colonial romanticism and literary nationalism. The path of development he was to follow is representative of the direction forced upon the literary nationalist in Canada by virtue of the peculiar dualism of Canadian nationalism.

Mair had been writing poetry for some time before he became associated with the other four founders of Canada First. Several poems had been published in newspapers, and he received in 1858, at the age of twenty, a favourable review of one of them from Charles Sangster which highly delighted him and encouraged him to go on. By 1868 he had found a publisher, and his first volume of verse, *Dreamland and Other Poems*, appeared. The timing was fortunate and the book sold well, receiving good reviews from the critics. But it is important to note the differences between the public and private utterances of at least one of the critics. Mair's friend Haliburton had this to say in his published review of the 1868 volume: "The sunshine that pervades his poems is refreshing. Many poets, when they look on nature, are too prone to view it 'by the pale moonlight', and the voice that comes to us from their muse is far too solemn and sad to be an echo of that song of nature which, to the ear of the healthy and the happy, is as cheery and joyous as the carol of the song-bird."[1]

A year later Haliburton wrote to Mair strongly advising him to

[1]Quoted in Perceval (ed.), *Leading Canadian Poets*, 154.

examine the type of poetry he was writing. In the first stage of the growth of Canada First, all five members were insistent on demonstrating a conscious Canadianism, and it was felt that Mair, as the literary member of the movement, should provide the example. Haliburton wrote:

I shall be glad to hear from you. I have been reading the poems over, and like your "Fireflies", but these archaic words set me damning. For God's sake drop the old style—you're living in a new world, and you must write the language of the living to living men. I hope to see some new poems from you. There is more poetry in you than has yet come out of you, though what you have written is very "charming". Most Canadian poetry is still dominated by the sugary titles tacked on to them, such as "Midnight Musings", or, what is more to the point, "Nocturnal Missions."[2]

Chastened, Mair was in a mood to echo these views, and he set about the task of revising his earlier poems in the light of Haliburton's criticism. In addition to writing new poems on Canadian themes, he revised nearly every poem from the 1868 volume to give them what he hoped was a more Canadian flavour. The original version of one passage from a poem called "Summer" was as follows:

> Dreams of by-gone chivalry,
> Wassailing and revelry,
> And lordly seasons long since spent
> In bout and joust and tournament.
> And, mid visioned feats of arms
> Fierce attacks and rude alarms,
> Let my dreams run back to thee,
> Chastely fair Eurydice![3]

These were the types of images that had set Haliburton damning. The revision shows how hard Mair had tried to learn his lesson.

> Dreams of old-world chivalry,
> Bout and joust and revelry;
> Or, more suited to our land,
> Dreams of forest chief and band;
> Braves in paint and plume arrayed,
> Sunburnt youth and dusky maid
> Paddling down in days gone by,
> Spirit lake or haunted snie;

[2]Haliburton to Mair, August 24, 1870; Parcel 48, the Mair Papers.
[3]Charles Mair, *Dreamland and Other Poems*, 78.

> Huddling in their barks in fear
> When strange voices hit the ear;
> Or encamped where, mountain-throned,
> Star-lit, monarch pines intoned
> Earth's primeval homage, back'd
> By wild chute and cataract;
> Hearing Nature's Spirit then
> Talking to the souls of men![4]

In many of the poems which were to undergo this process of "Canadianization," Mair turned to Indian themes as though this in itself were sufficient to make his work distinctively Canadian. As may be seen in the above example, the change was more superficial than essential. For thirty years, while living in the North West Territories, Mair continued his private crusade for Canadian literature. A fellow prisoner, with Schultz, of Louis Riel in the first Riel Rebellion, Mair makes little of having escaped from the adventure with his life, and for the rest of his life bitterly thought of Riel as the man who had destroyed the only manuscripts of a new collection of poems he had prepared for publication. He went on writing what he called "The Canadian Poems," again revising the earlier ones, and, after the publication of the long verse-drama *Tecumseh,* he began to collect material for his memoirs.

In 1901, from Saskatchewan, Mair asked Denison to arrange for the publication of a new composite volume of poetry. The edition was published by Briggs of Toronto and contained *Tecumseh,* the poems from the 1868 volume, as revised over the years, and a new section of "Canadian Poems" written after 1868. The book was dedicated to "The Survivors of the Canada First Movement." Still sensitive perhaps to Haliburton's criticism of thirty years before, one poem, called "Midnight" in the 1868 volume, was left out altogether. But by 1901, what Mair was trying to do had already been done by men whose poetic ability far outstripped his own. Living in comparative isolation for most of his life, brooding on the fate of his early political and national ideals, Mair had relapsed politically into a staunch conservatism, and despite his dogged perseverance as a literary nationalist, these influences were evident in his poetry. There is no indication that he was aware of the work of Lampman, Roberts, Campbell,

[4]Charles Mair, *Tecumseh and the Canadian Poems,* 222–3.

Duncan Campbell Scott, and Bliss Carman, and in studying Mair it is hard to remember that the 1901 volume appeared after many of the most important works of those poets.

Mair was so earnestly Canadian that he came to believe that his was the only valid form of Canadianism, and he could not see that he had been passed by those with less self-conscious but more authentic voices. The comparative failure of the 1901 volume, and the indifference of the critics, did much to convince him that he had been on the wrong track. Despite Kendall's "plunder of perfumes," the Australian poet had captured some of the essence of the Australian scene. Mair, too, had his brief moments, but they came despite, rather than because of, his self-conscious searching. If Canada First failed because it tried too hard to define what was not yet ready to be defined, Mair's poetry attempted to do the same thing, and met the same fate.

But it is the attitude which Mair was to adopt towards his own revisions that provides the curious postscript to the story. The nationalist literary movement continued after the collapse of the Canada First party, but it was largely discredited by association. In politics, Mair and Denison reverted to extreme Toryism—based, as they asserted, on Canada First principles; and this reaction is also to be seen in their attitude to literature. The Mair Letters reveal the curious story of Mair's repudiation of his revisions. In 1925, John Garvin set out to edit a volume of Mair's work for a new series on Canadian poets. Garvin wished to include the texts of both the 1868 and 1901 volumes. Mair, then 87 years old, protested. In a letter to Garvin he said:

> As regards my poems, I do not see what use there is in publishing both the *full* and *abridged* poems. I cut them down and omitted "August" and the "Prologue to Tecumseh" and other verses in the 1901 volume in order to reduce its size, a matter of moment at that time. [The correspondence in the Mair Letters for 1901 contains full details of the publication of the 1901 volume, and these poems were omitted not for reasons of expense or size, but because Mair was not satisfied with them.] I am glad that they will be restored. Silly as some amatory verses are, I am not ashamed of them, they were *felt*, enacted [sic]; the truth that is poetry the world over.[5]

The difference between the two texts was far from being merely a matter of complete or abridged versions of the poems. In most cases

[5]Mair to Garvin, December 22, 1925; Parcel 4.

they were quite different in structure, emphasis, and content. Garvin tactfully tried to point this out to Mair.

You say: "As regards my poems, I do not see what use there is in publishing both the full and the abridged poem." I am sorry that you differ from me in this respect, but I feel very strongly that the 1868 edition of *Dreamland and Other Poems* should be republished exactly as in the original and the 1901 edition should also be reproduced exactly.

You are aware that there has been considerable discussion among the critics as to who was the real founder of Canada's distinguished nature school of verse. My contention for years has been that Charles Mair was the real founder. That is why I want the 1868 edition republished exactly.

It is also of tremendous interest to students of literature to know the changes made by the author himself thirty years or more later. Hence my exact reproduction of the 1901 edition. And I do want you to yield to my critical literary judgement in this respect.[6]

But Mair persisted and refused to allow the revisions to be included. He looked back fondly to the reception given to the 1868 volume when he had been called the "Canadian Keats." In 1901 he had been ignored, and refusing to face the implications he had assumed that the earlier volume must have been the better of the two.

To save expense I made a mess by mangling *Dreamland* and omitted some to shorten the 1901 volume; these "revisions" I need scarcely say did not afterwards commend themselves to my judgement. To be sure, there is some immature ["and puerile" crossed out] work in *Dreamland* which my critics pointed out in a friendly spirit, but really all the more reason why it should be preserved, as illustrating a young poet's imperfections.[7]

Garvin countered strongly. He threatened to resign the task, appealed to Mair again to respect his judgment, and all but told him that it would be fatal to his reputation were he to be known only by the 1868 volume. Mair indignantly refused to allow the publication of any of his poems unless his wishes were followed. The rest of the Mair-Garvin correspondence is marked by cool politeness, most of Garvin's early enthusiasm for the project having disappeared. Mair makes constant sniping remarks about the degeneracy of literary taste in the modern age, the incompetence of editors, and the sacred nature of the poetic fire. In a letter to Mrs. Gillespie, he reveals the nostalgia

[6]Garvin to Mair, December 28, 1925; Parcel 4.
[7]Mair to Garvin, May 3, 1924; Parcel 32.

for the past which coloured his judgment during the last years of his life. "I wish we could go back to quill pens, so delicate, so flexible, so responsive to a writer's emotions. They almost seemed to *think* with one. But like the world's good old things they have passed."[8]

Mair's was a dream that had failed, and at the end he was driven to repudiate his own methods. His position in 1925 was much more that of the "colonial poet" of Smith's definition than it had been either in 1868 or 1901. In 1868 he had followed, timidly, the parent tradition. He had gratefully accepted a place of subordination, humbly following in the footsteps of Keats; but his purpose was to rise above this subordination, and he was fired by an intense love for Canada and by a desire to see her produce her own accredited interpreters. Haliburton and Canada First provided the impetus to make this change an acknowledged part of his writing; but Haliburton had turned out to be a supporter of independence, and, looking back from the edge of senility, nationalism in poetry must have come to be associated in Mair's mind with political disloyalty. As a result, he repudiated much of his own achievement.

There is a lesson to be learned from this. Canadian literary nationalism, as much as its Australian equivalent, was intimately involved with many complex political, social, and moral issues. In Australia these issues encouraged literary nationalism. In Canada they did not. As a result, Mair's Canadianism itself often took the form of romantic yearning, looking backwards towards an idealized Canadian past.

The characteristics of Mair's poetry reveal almost a reflex response to traditional modes of thinking. As part of his backward glances a note of primitivism is introduced, an invocation of the Noble Savage in which relative values are always being raised. Lefroy, in *Tecumseh*, flies from a decadent civilization and from the false values of commercialism into the wilderness where untamed nature maintains an integrity that European culture has destroyed. The Indian leader, Tecumseh, himself affirms as his aim a programme for turning back the Indians to their old ways, away from the compromise and contamination that has come from contact with the white man. The plain romantic strain which thought of primitivism as not incompatible with progress was one that had been in vogue, and was on the wane by 1850. In the second half of the nineteenth century, the

[8]Mair to Mrs. Gillespie, March 27, 1925; Parcel 32.

simple idea of progress—reflected in man's increasing command over his environment—had replaced it. Mair was already out of date when he propounded his ideas, which were more typical of the late eighteenth century than of the late ninteenth century. One justification lay in the nature of the country. Here was an empty and presumably unspoilt country which was in danger of becoming corrupted. It was less a return to, than a preservation of, nature.

The theme of "pain and fret" was another inheritance from early romanticism that Mair adopted. The convention that the world was a place of suffering and tribulation which found reflection in the poet's gloomy melancholy was responsible for the most unfortunate aspects of colonial romanticism. Although, it will be remembered, Haliburton, in his review of the 1868 volume, praised Mair for his cheerfulness, such poems as "Werter" do not escape the influence of the convention.

> Wave high, ye overhanging woods,
> And whisper sadly of the tomb.
> Lonely I trace your solitudes,
> And haunt your melancholy gloom.[9]

"Midnight" (p. 145) follows the same trend.

> I could not tell what life-long ease or pain
> Found hoarse expression by the river's brink,
> Where moving things mysterious vigils kept.
> These had their joys perchance, whilst I did link
> Sad thoughts of bygone pleasure till I wept.

One remembers Haliburton's private letter to Mair on this type of poetry—"Midnight Musings" or "Nocturnal Missions." In the 1901 volume "Werter" was left out entirely, and "Midnight" had virtually become a new poem with its name changed, somewhat enigmatically, to "Germs." But these were part of the revisions that Mair repudiated, and both poems were back in their original form in the 1926 Garvin edition of his work.

In this discussion of Mair as a representative of literary nationalism, one must not overlook his principal claim to inclusion in Canadian literary history. Despite his descents into bathos and his later tendency to scatter Canadian place-names and themes as an earnest of his

[9]*Dreamland*, 110.

Canadianism, he did write with his eye firmly on the object, when that object happened to be Canadian nature. "Autumn" is a poem that is painstaking, almost painful, in the *minutiae* which are collected and recorded. The drone of the insects, which begins as a conventional background to a summer woodland scene, does not, as one might expect, lull him off into sweet dreams of romantic fantasy. Instead it becomes the most vivid factor in the poet's consciousness, and the poem proceeds from general description to a particular examination of what can be seen by one who sits in the grass and uses his eyes to look at the things that lie close at hand. There are "gangs of blue-flies," "dusty crackers snapping wings," the uneasiness of potential victims alert for sign of their enemies; there is the still spider trimming his web, waiting patiently, surrounded by discarded husks of his past visitors. The gnats, horse-flies, water-beetles, all belie the apparently torpid scene that first met his eye. The poem concludes (p. 124):

> Hail August! Maiden of the sultry days,
> To thee I bring the measured meed of praise.
> For, though thou hast besmirched the day and night,
> And hid a wealth of glory from our sight,
> Thou still dost build in musing, pensive mood,
> Thy blissful idyl in the underwood.
> Thou still dost yield new beauties, fair and young,
> With many a form of grace as yet unsung,
> Which ripens o'er thy pathway, and repays
> The toil and languor of the sultry days.

In spite of its lack of poetic distinction, this poem marks a most important development in the way in which Canadian poets looked at nature. Prevented by the heat-haze from surveying the broader landscape in general and diffuse terms, Mair surveyed the Lilliputian scene under his nose, and by minute description of this at once captured a portion of Canadian nature, rather than Nature with a capital letter. Someone had to number the streaks of the tulip. There was indeed "many a form of grace as yet unsung" on the Canadian scene, and Mair began the practice—which Lampman continued—of looking at particulars. Frogs, beetles, horse-flies, all were part of the tapestry-design of Canadian nature, and must be included in poetry seeking to interpret it.

Evident throughout Mair's poetry, too, is an admiration for stoicism and endurance that is later to be found in some of D. C. Scott's poetry, and later still in the work of E. J. Pratt. "The Iroquois at the Stake" combines nearly all of Mair's beliefs. The poem is a dramatic monologue spoken by an Iroquois warrior, captured and condemned to death by the Hurons. He taunts his captors for their betrayal of the brotherhood of the red man, and for their adherence to the French, warning them that the time will come when the whites, French and English alike, will drive all Indians, irrespective of their tribe, away from their ancestral homes. He does not fear death, and asks that it be made hard rather than easy, in order to test him the more, and to show his captors the way in which an Indian should die—in the hope that his example may shame them into resolution in their dealings with the white men. Mair in particular, and North American writers in general, found the Indian an admirable subject with which to point a moral and adorn a tale.

By contrast, the Australian aborigine—in whom no one could detect the image of a Noble Savage—for long scorned as a figure unworthy of the attention of literature, has recently been rediscovered. Xavier Herbert's *Capricornia,* Katherine Susannah Prichard's *Coonardoo,* and Rex Ingamell's poetry have aroused the national conscience to a sense of shame at the manner in which the natives have been treated. In all the arts, attention to the aborigines—their designs, legends, art, music, and dancing—to make up for past neglect has now gone to the opposite extreme. But they are not, as were the Indians, represented as the proud but conquered foe. They are rather the unremembered ones, squashed by white men—not necessarily by malice—as ants are squashed.

If the nineteenth-century Australian poet could not write of the aborigines as the Canadian could write about Indians, he had to turn to a subject that he knew about—the Australian bushmen.[10] For this reason, even a nominally academic poet such as Kendall, when he wished to turn from nature poetry to deal with human themes, found himself with no option but to describe incidents from the life of the bushmen whom he had so often met. Any attempt to introduce the

[10]One must remember that "bushman" as used in Australia does not mean an aborigine or half-caste, but refers to the white inhabitant of the outback regions, usually a member of the nomadic bushworkers described in previous chapters.

heroic element had to be done by means of the back door; for in his contempt for authority, and with his inherently iconoclastic attitude, the bushman was a merciless debunker of posing and of those who tried to strike attitudes—even when he was presented as the hero of the picture. Kendall was enough of a bushman himself to realize that though there were examples of real heroism in the bushman's constant struggle for survival, these could not be stated in terms considered suitable for such themes in the Old World. Instead, in his bush anecdotes, if Kendall wished to develop the idea that these men had skills and instincts and generosities that bordered on the heroic, he must be careful not to say so; he must mock such pretentiousness.

> No party is Jim of the Pericles type —
> He is modern right up from the toe to the pipe;
> And being no reader or roamer,
> He hasn't Euripides much in the head;
> And let it be carefully, tenderly said,
> He never has analyzed Homer.[11]

He has instead the knowledge of the bush and the love for it to be able to survive its most pitiless trials. He has an intense loyalty to his mates, and, swearing and grumbling, he will do all in his power to help them in trouble. Given the nature of the country and the hardships which were endured by those who worked in it in the early days of its development, it is almost inconceivable that they did survive. The fact of their survival is no mean accomplishment, and a modern Australian poet, A. D. Hope, has this comment to make on it:

> Without songs, architecture, history:
> The emotions and superstitions of younger lands.
> Her rivers of water drawn among inland sands,
> The river of her immense stupidity
>
> Floods her monotonous tribes from Cairns to Perth,
> In them at last the ultimate men arrive
> Whose boast is not: "we live" but "we survive"
> A type who will inhabit the dying earth.[12]

Professor Hope reaches his subject from a direction different from Kendall's (the starting point is very close to Barron Field's), but their

[11]Kendall, Poems, 192.
[12]Mackaness (ed.), Anthology, 148–9

conclusions are the same, and it is interesting to note the unity of theme as an example of the rationalizations of which Australians are capable. Here is a people still at grips with its environment; a great gap exists between the manner of life which is forced upon such a people, and the culture of a civilized society that has had time to develop leisure and knows how to employ that leisure profitably. Yet there are specific virtues that may arise even from a preoccupation with survival. They may be virtues different from the traditional ones, but they are virtues none the less. Professor Hope ends his poem on this note:

> Yet there are some like me turn gladly home
> From the lush jungle of modern thought, to find
> The Arabian desert of the human mind,
> Hoping, if still from the deserts the prophets come
>
> Such savage and scarlet as no green hills dare
> Springs in that waste, some spirit which escapes
> The learned doubt, the chatter of cultured apes
> Which is called civilization over there.

It is from the acceptance of these facts that any real contribution to Australian writing has come. Once the environment, with all its limitations, is accepted, then the values which have established themselves as a result of struggle with that environment may be recognized. It is not surprising that nineteenth-century Australia was so poor in academic poets. Romanticism was swamped by a realism more pressing than that known in Canada, and that is why the most original achievement in poetry was gained in the field of the bush-ballad, a form despised in Canada.

As we have seen, most traditional forms in writing were regarded either with indifference or with active hostility as unsuited to Australian conditions. The cult of the formless arose as part of the association of form with authority and with a way of life that was suspect among the most vigorous elements of the population—those who had inherited the manner of thought of the convicts. Adaptation of traditional literary forms did take place in Australia, but whereas in Canada the comparatively refined level of literary taste dictated the adaptation of more advanced and sophisticated literary forms, in Australia the nature of the environment and the absence of highly developed literary taste brought about the use of more primitive forms which had been bypassed by Canadian writers.

The ballads which were to achieve such great popularity, and the picaresque novels of Boldrewood and Furphy, were, of course, rooted in forms quite as traditional as those which influenced Canadian writers; but this apparent inconsistency was not considered important. The ballad and the picaresque tale were flexible forms for adaptation. The ballad appealed to the most basic of man's instincts for poetry; there was an easy rhythm and fast action in the narrative which dealt with subjects within common experience. To this extent only can an exception be made to the assertion that there was no cult of the primitive in Australia. There was no conscious reversion to the simplest of poetic forms because of any articulate philosophy teaching the superiority of simplicity. It was the thing itself rather than a copy of it, a primitive form of poetry adopted spontaneously to suit the requirements of what was essentially a primitive taste. The picaresque novel was also adopted as the most suitable form of fiction in a society which tended to celebrate the stories of rogues, vagabonds, and the more colourful lawbreakers.

As we shall see when discussing the growth of the ballad, there were ballad writers in Canada too—mainly Scots who had come from a homeland where the popular tradition had continued much more strongly than in England—but they made no real mark on the literary scene. Yet their influence was the same in kind, if not in degree, as that worked by their Australian counterparts on the development of Australian nationalism.[13] One is tempted to speculate that, in spite of the higher standard of poetry achieved in Canada in the nineteenth century, a Canadian national literature might now be in a more advanced stage of development had early Canadian writers drawn their own traditions from a less sophisticated level. Australian adaptations were made on the basis of traditions from which the later English forms had themselves evolved. A common ancestor of hardy stock was found in the ballad, one which was likely to survive the transplanting, even though the level of achievement was, at first, not comparable to the Canadian one.

The Canadian poet considered himself, rightly, the inheritor of an elaborate poetic tradition, but he did not always realize that the very

[13]See A. J. M. Smith's "Colonialism and Nationalism in Canadian Poetry," 83.

wealth and complexity of his riches could constitute a handicap in the new land. Catherine Traill's reaction was typical and natural.

It is the most unpoetic of all lands, there is no scope for imagination; here all is new—the very soil seems newly formed; there is no hoary ancient grandeur in these woods; no recollections of former deeds connected with the country. . . . The class of people to whom this country is so admirably adapted are formed of the unlettered and industrious labourers and artisans. They feel no regret that the land they labour on has not been celebrated by the pen of the historian or the lay of the poet. . . . They would not spare the ancient oak from feelings of veneration, nor look upon it with regard for anything but its use as timber. They have no time, even if they possessed the taste, to gaze abroad on the beauties of nature.[14]

In these echoes of Field's comments on Australia, Catherine Traill was, of course, quite right. These people did not have the time to indulge sensibilities developed in an ordered and civilized society. She could not see how she could adapt her values to those of the new country. She was right in saying that the unlettered were those to whom the new country was best suited—they had less to unlearn, and in this they shared the experience of the Australian bushmen. But their experience, though recorded, was seldom heard. New traditions, instinctively developed in response to the new soil, were overlooked in literary circles which were too busy attempting to preserve intact their elaborate English inheritance. What Catherine Traill did not see was the rise of new attitudes to replace the old—equally compelling and more suitable to a society busily engaged in creating itself and its values.

Isabella Valency Crawford was one of the few who could see the other side of the picture. There was no regret, but there was vigour and pride and hope which more than made up for the values that had been lost. And there was veneration too, not for antiquity, but for achievement; not for the past, but for the future—"anticipation."

> The lab'rer with trained muscles, grim and grave,
> Look'd at the ground and wonder'd in his soul,
> What joyous anguish stirr'd his darkened heart,
> At the mere look of the familiar soil,
> And found his answer in the words—*Mine own!*[15]

14C. P. Traill, *Backwoods of Canada*, 154.
15I. V. Crawford, *Old Spookses' Pass, Malcolm's Katie and Other Poems*, 51–2.

This was the type of achievement that emigrants from the United Kingdom had gone to Canada and to Australia to find. Many of them had found it in Canada; very few had been able to in Australia. The Australian bushman had to seek pride in other achievement: personal skills, independence, opposing what he considered injustice, outwitting the law, and even personal survival, and he sang his ballads commemorating these things.

The unself-conscious nationalist in Canada was writing his ballads too, but no one was listening to him outside his own community. The conscious nationalist, as represented by Mair, was ringing the changes on the more elaborate traditional forms. *Tecumseh* was a "closet-drama," and in this, his most ambitious and longest statement of a Canadian national theme, Mair was struck by no sense of incongruity at the use of this form. This is an example of the confidence with which Canadian poets felt they could draw upon traditional forms to tell Canadian stories and to describe Canadian scenes. Heavysege had used the closet-drama in Saul to tell a Biblical story; Mair used it to tell a Canadian one, complete with references to Indian mythology and with comic relief provided by boorish American soldiers. No Australian poet attempted to write a verse-drama in the period under review. The first notable work in the form did not appear in Australian literature until 1944, when Douglas Stewart's *Fire on the Snow* combined the narrative excitement of the ballad form with the introspection of Brennan's metaphysical poetry—in other words, though influenced by contemporary English poetic drama, the play was built upon Australian traditions.

Mair's *Tecumseh* was not, of course, built upon Canadian traditions of form, nor was it felt at all necessary that it should be. As a result there is little sense of integration between form and content. Some of the speeches in the play, when taken out of context, are not unsuccessful. For example, Tecumseh, abandoned by his allies, resolving to fight and die with his people, sees in the flamboyance of the autumn leaves a symbol of the approaching death of the glories of his race:

> This is our summer—when the painted wilds,
> Like pictures in a dream enchant the sight,
> The forest bursts in glory like a flame!
> Its leaves are sparks; its mystic breath the haze
> Which blends in purple incense with the air.

> The Spirit of the Woods has decked his home,
> And puts his wonders like a garment on,
> To flash, and glow, and dull, and fade, and die.[16]

But one has the sense that such passages are connected inadequately; the highlights resolve themselves into a series of tableaux.

In summary, the poetry of transition in Canada evolved into an idiom which, by Smith's definition, was marked by all the characteristics of colonial romanticism. In the case of one poet, Charles Mair, a partial adaptation of the romantic temperament to the needs of a political nationalist movement ended in failure and disillusionment, with an eventual repudiation of the compromise, and with a reaffirmation of faith in the virtues of colonial romanticism. Patriotic poetry, to avoid identifying its author with the Independence or Annexation groups, had to be imperial in nature. Progress had been made in the poetry of natural description which was beginning to incorporate specific details of the Canadian scene. Closer observation was training Canadians to see their country through their own eyes rather than through English ones.

Australian colonial romanticism made very little progress; the academic poets and critics were concerned with problems of distinctive Australianism, and nationalism in poetry was encouraged. Even Kendall, leader of the romantic poets, cast aside into other idioms and experimented with bush ballads, stanzaic forms, and Australian themes, and occasionally managed to reproduce what was considered to be an authentic echo of the Australian scene. In his failures Kendall fell farther than his Canadian contemporaries, but in his successes he reavealed a sensitivity and feeling for the essence of the local scene that rivalled Lampman at his best. The poetry of colonial romanticism was accepted and encouraged in Canada, and led to the greater successes of Lampman, D. C. Scott, Carman, and Roberts, while the indifference to its practitioners in Australia led to the virtual extinction of such romanticism beneath the boisterous folk-type literature of the eighties and nineties. When it reappeared again in the poetry of Bernard O'Dowd, it was in a very different form.

[16]*Tecumseh*, V, vi, 120–7.

7. Towards a National Tradition: Canada

THE LAST TWO decades of the nineteenth century saw the emergence of a national statement in poetry in both Canada and Australia. The preceding chapters have set the scene and have outlined the nature of the pattern which had evolved; it is now necessary to examine in detail the climactic moments of that evolution as it occurred in each country.

Within each country during the century, two parallel streams in literature developed which we shall call the Academic and the Popular. As these terms are used here, Academic poetry refers to that based directly upon sophisticated English models of the central tradition, whether the theory and practice of such poetry had university associations (as in Canada) or not (as in Australia). Popular poetry refers to that of folk-literature and to literary adaptations of it, based upon less sophisticated models of the central tradition. Academic poetry received the greatest attention in Canada, virtually driving Popular poetry beneath the literary surface. Popular poetry, on the other hand, came to dominate the Australian literary scene, obscuring the Academic.

The important point to remember here is the existence of the parallelism within each country; for, in each instance, the secondary stream continued, though largely unrecognized by the reading public, until the time came—early in Australia though only recently in Canada—when the two forces were in a position to draw strength from each other. This chapter proposes to discuss the triumph of the Academic tradition in Canada. First, the development of Canadian prose during the century will be examined very briefly; second, the

Academic tradition in poetry will be looked at through the central
figure of Archibald Lampman; third, the submerged stream of Popular poetry will be compared with its Australian equivalent; and, in
conclusion, an assessment will be made of the manner in which
the streams can be said to have followed the same pattern as their
Australian counterparts. If the two streams have merged in Canada,
what was the nature of the union, and how did the national statement
of the final twenty years of the last century influence the development
of Canadian poetry during the twentieth century?

We have seen that early Canadian poets, by adhering to English
traditions, achieved some measure of success within it. It was the
success of the provincial poet, but no less real for that. In Australia
the gap was too great to be bridged, and even Kendall, the best of
the Academic poets, floundered for most of the time trying to recon-
cile tradition and environment. We have seen too that in both
countries, expository prose was precise without pedantry and vivid
without affectation. Alexander Harris and Mrs. Moodie have left
invaluable pictures of the ordinary lives of the settlers in their respec-
tive countries. But while Harris did not try his hand at fiction,[1] Mrs.
Moodie did, and the contrast between *Roughing It in the Bush* and
her novels is a very strange one. When she was writing free of the
conventions which surrounded fiction, the shrewd and observant
comments of the writer reached the reader unimpaired. When writing
her novels, however, Mrs. Moodie is speaking in a different language,
and she felt bound to follow an elaborate ritual which smothered her
lively personality. We have already seen some of the reasons for this—
the conservative puritanism which emphasized the spartan virtues of
hard work coupled with moral righteousness, and which tended to
regard the reading of fiction as a waste of time, and hence morally
evil. But the ingrained human love of a story could not be suppressed.
In Canada it was channelled into a mould that fitted the prejudices
of society. If the novel had to exist, then at least it could meet certain
conditions; and as society was based on unyielding moral values, so
the novel was to be judged by the same inflexible criteria.

[1]If Colin Roderick is right in his contention that "Alexander Harris" was really
Samuel Sidney, an Englishman who had never been to Australia, the account of life
in N.S.W. attributed to him *is* fiction. That it should have been accepted as fact for
so long only emphasizes the point here being made. No one could possibly mistake
Mrs. Moodie's fiction for fact.

It has been suggested that the greatest single influence in the history of Canadian fiction has been that of Sir Walter Scott.[2] There is a great deal of evidence to support this claim, and it is certainly true that Canadian fiction shows comparatively little development during the century, certainly far less than occurred in Australia. Canadian poetry too was imitative, but at least successive Canadian poets were influenced by a steadily developing English tradition; they did not all attempt to follow the lead of only one man. In England and America the Scott influence was soon replaced by others; experiment and development in fiction was not inhibited. But in Canada the prejudice in favour of the moral excellence of Scott's novels hardened and consolidated itself until the Canadian novel was bound within its rigid pattern, and was so immune to later English patterns that no real attempt was made by Canadian authors to question the premises on which it was founded.[3]

John Richardson's *Wacousta*, which appeared in 1832, showed an almost slavish imitation of Scott's technique, blended with some of the North American adaptations to the romantic tale of adventure initiated by Fenimore Cooper. The book deals with the defence of the Detroit garrison against Pontiac's conspiracy. The characterization is all drawn in black and white—the pure are unbelievably pure, and the villains incredibly villainous. All this is quite suitable for a romance as long as one remembers the conventions of the genre and does not confuse the rival claims of romance and realism. But the book was popular in Canada as well as in England, and popular, it would seem, for what we might consider to be the wrong reasons. It is true that the reviews of the work in Canadian journals were mostly written by members of an urban community who had little more idea of the realities of frontier life than had readers in England; but the work was also popular in rural centres. Taking Scott as their yardstick,

---

[2]Professor R. L. McDougall of Carleton University, Ottawa, in an unpublished paper entitled "Scott and the Development of Canadian Fiction," traces the reception of Scott's influence by early Canadian critics and novelists, and shows by reference to periodical literature how the tradition became so entrenched that it proved too strong to be replaced by later English influences in the novel. Dr. McDougall cites Goldwin Smith's address "The Seven Lamps of Fiction," given in 1871, as the restatement of an attitude which rigidly defined the requirements of a good novel in terms of the practice of Sir Walter Scott.

[3]Professor McDougall quotes evidence of unfavourable Canadian critical reviews of new English novels, all made on the presupposition that Scott's works provided the standard of excellence.

critics praised *Wacousta* for its realism and faithfulness to the Canadian scene—and presumably the frontier settlers themselves agreed. One must turn again to Mrs. Moodie's example. Few people have shown themselves more acutely aware of the realities of everyday life in a frontier settlement, yet in her novels "reality" assumes a completely different meaning. This acceptance of the romantic novel into the body of Canadian literature by the Canadians themselves marks another point of contrast with the development of the novel in Australia.

It is a commonplace of Canadian criticism to admire William Kirby's *The Golden Dog*, which was published in 1877. Professor Pacey regards it as a work which blends admiration for the old regime with the new Canadian nationalism—a nationalism very close to that of Mair and Denison. It is unnecessary to rehearse the merits of the book, and foolish to deny its worth; but Kirby's debt to Scott must be heavily underlined. Professor Pacey acknowledges that a debt exists, but he does not feel that the example Kirby followed was a restricting one, or, if he does, he gives no hint of it in his commentary;[4] even in modern Canadian criticism it is not felt necessary to examine the question of whether, as late as 1877, the Scott influence was a healthy one for Canadians to follow. Professor Pacey judges the work within the framework of the Scott tradition and finds it, by comparison with *Wacousta*, a "minor masterpiece." This may be true, but it marks a limitation which is placed on the Canadian novel. It may only be judged in relation to the ceiling which the Scott tradition has placed upon its growth. With this handicap imposed before the novelist set pen to paper, it is not surprising that Canadian success in fiction during the century was fragmentary, and far below the level of achievement in poetry.

Sarah Jeannette Duncan is the only notable exception. She did not imitate Scott, but she left Canada too soon for the refreshing nature of her wit to have its full effect. She has been called the first Canadian woman journalist, but she was more than that. She attempted to do in Canada what Matthew Arnold was doing in England. From the columns of the *Week* she chided Canadian society in terms that were sharper, more sophisticated and worldly-wise than those used by any other contributor to that journal. Using terms that resemble Arnold's

[4]Pacey, *Creative Writing in Canada*, 71.

denunciation of the Philistines in *Culture and Anarchy,* Miss Duncan attacked the "Majores," the materialistic middle classes of Canada. In sharp contrast to the majority of literary critics who wrote for the *Week,* Sarah Jeannette Duncan put the case for the realistic novel, and, as a disciple of James and Howell, taught that the task of fiction is to give the appearance of life. But her only novel to deal exclusively with a Canadian background, *The Imperialist,* did not appear until 1904, when the century was over. The novel exploited material that had been waiting for interpretation for a long time. The social pressures at work in a small Ontario town in the eighteen-eighties was a fruitful subject, and in this work she displays an insight into the psychological analysis of provincial life that would not have disgraced George Eliot. Far from being provincial in spirit, she remained one of the most cosmopolitan of Canadian writers, equally adept in handling conversations in India, the Officers' Mess, Bloomsbury tea-parties, or Canadian small towns.

The power of tradition was just as strong in Canadian poetry as it was in Canadian fiction, but as there were more models held up for admiration there was more room for the poet to move around, and more opportunity for him to find a distinctive voice of his own. Some Canadians, with unconscious pessimism, look back on the last twenty years of the nineteenth century (much as some Australians do) as the Golden Age of poetry. As Paterson and Lawson represent the flowering of a native tradition in Australia, so four Canadian poets have become associated with Canada's national statement—Lampman, Roberts, Carman, and Duncan Campbell Scott. By centring attention on Archibald Lampman, it is possible to discover the nature and significance of the Academic poetry of the period. Though his work may differ in many ways from that of the other three, the picture is not changed in its essentials. Rather does Lampman's poetry represent and illuminate the dilemma which faced the Canadian poet at that time.

Archibald Lampman inherited from his family and from his environment many of the values which we have already assessed as typical of Canadian society as a whole. His family, on both sides, were of conservative loyalist stock. His father was an Anglican clergyman in an Ontario country town, and he was educated at a Church school and at the Anglican College in the University of Toronto. Most of his education was conducted by men who had not been born or educated in Canada and whose cultural orientation naturally inclined towards England rather than towards their land of residence. This might well have proved to be an insuperable barrier for a writer in Australia. That it was not a barrier in Canada shows the strikingly different mental climate, and the intrinsic difference in the nature of the Canadian achievement in poetry. E. K. Brown asserts that every element in Lampman's environment was against the development of Canadianism, and that hence when it came it was an instinctive Canadianism—the most precious type of all. But this seems only partly true. The peculiar structure of Canadian society and the orientation of Canadian values make it clear that there was, in fact, nothing really extraordinary and un-Canadian about Lampman's early environment. It is true that Anglicans were outnumbered by Presbyterians and Methodists, but while native traditions were developing around these two churches more rapidly than within the Anglican communion, these traditions had not grown very much by Confederation. The majority of teachers, in state as well as in private schools, had been educated in England or Scotland, and to a man their cultural orientation remained directed across the Atlantic. It is true that Lampman's instinctive Canadianism was of the most precious kind, but it seems a mistake to say with Brown that it had special obstacles to overcome; they were the obstacles faced by every Canadian poet, the obstacles of the Academic tradition in which they were all trained.

The Canadian Academic tradition has a long and honourable history. The time-honoured disciplines found able exponents and Canadian universities built early an enviable reputation for sound scholarship and thorough training. But as a testing ground for poets who had tried to build from nothing it had its drawbacks. The chief obstacle was, of course, the inability of most of its graduates to perceive that there was a need to build from nothing. They echoed O'Dowd's sentiments, and affirmed that they were the heirs of all the ages and the inheritors of the richness of the English tradition, without having—as O'Dowd did—Lares and Penates of their own. This training provided an admirable sense of form, a discipline unknown to the Australian poet. There was polished expression and an awareness of the meanings of words—a sensitivity that came occasionally to Kendall, but rarely to his colleagues. The sense of community, of enlightened cosmopolitanism, of belonging to a great fellowship of learning which refused to be bound by local geographical restrictions or to be put to work at the parish pump—all these things were admirable in their way, and lessened the feeling of isolation, the rawness of a new-born society. But those who would avoid the growing pains and the unsightly pimples of adolescence by trying to jump prematurely to precocious maturity must pay some price for their action.

There is little point in looking outside to the great world until one is able to see how the lessons that are learned there may be applied to the home acres. Australian writers spent a long time scrutinizing their own preserves, blind to the world outside. They paid the penalties for such close and exclusive preoccupation with themselves by the crudities and bumptiousness and offensive swagger that marks the worst results of the narrow outlook sometimes seen in their work. But when at last they raised their eyes to look beyond themselves and their own affairs, they knew themselves very well indeed; and they were able to select and discriminate among the wares that they now saw were available to them. They could look back, with their intimate self-knowledge, to see at once how certain things could improve their society and their ability to interpret it, and how others had nothing in common with it and were not worth importing.

The Canadians turned their eyes at once to the outside, paying little or no attention to their peculiar status as Canadians, and hence it was difficult to discriminate between all the good things they could see. Their knowledge of themselves was not deep enough for them to be able to judge instinctively whether this tradition or that, these ideas or those, would be suitable for them, and the only way to find out was by the principle of trial and error—bring them all in, then see which ones would work. There were many trials and many errors, but this was the Canadian way, and the successes that were achieved were a result of that way. The traditions that survived were essentially a compromise—not too rigidly English, but not exclusively local either. But at least these Canadians did see the necessity of applying their knowledge and of adapting it to their homeland. They saw that if they looked outwards, they must do so in order to look back in again with the added insight afforded by British and American experience. Those who looked out continually and did not see the need to look back in again, though calling themselves cosmopolitan and priding themselves upon the breadth of their vision, could have no roots, no soil in which to grow.

Lampman inherited the more enlightened aspects of the Academic tradition, but, like many of his English contemporaries, he was troubled by a social conscience. In the more restricted Canadian society there were fewer outlets than in England for the expression of humanitarian sentiment. Outside recognized charitable and religious foundations, fervent expression of concern over social injustice was evidence of a radicalism not accepted within the Canadian Academic tradition in literature. Lampman was thus prey to an inner conflict. His training would not allow him to defy the tradition in which he had been raised, and as a result he was left vaguely unhappy, bursting out occasionally towards the end of his career in poetry which seemed to reflect a pale socialism—pale because he knew only too well that there was a conflict between all the things he wanted to say, and the only way he knew in which to say them. As a result he was aware that he was losing touch with the group that he was most concerned to reach.

In the comparatively sparse field of Canadian criticism, one subject which has received much attention is Archibald Lampman's nature poetry. It is rightly claimed that his greatest artistic success was achieved in this area—a success of such proportions that he could be spared the fate of Alexander McLachlan, who was dropped from literary notice when evidence of his radical political ideas came to light. Many critics have pointed out that Lampman found in nature a refuge from the monotony of his Civil Service life, and from his doubts about the type of society which was evolving in the Ottawa of his day. The city, it was clear, both attracted and repelled him; for though it was the Ottawa of Sir John A. Macdonald, it was also the Ottawa of the Pacific Scandal, of corrupt politicians, and of great contrasts between the rich and poor. The opportunism of early Confederation politics caused his sense of idealism to turn in disgust back to a dream-world of the Ottawa valley which lay beyond the city—a world where the bitterness of man could be balanced by the dignity and grace of nature. If this were all he had done, one would expect little beyond Wordsworthian poems about nature providing man with the spiritual strength to go on. But there was more than this.

Lampman's meticulous powers of observation, first of all, enabled him to continue the tendency we have already noted in some of Mair's poems. No subject in nature was beneath the attention of the poet; but Lampman's sensitivity went far beyond Mair's limited range. In such a poem as "The Frogs" he perfected a technique that Mair was groping for but unable to find. From such gentle descriptions of nature as "April," with its strong memories of Keats, to the brilliant evocations of "Heat," the nature poems in *Among the Millet* proclaimed that here was a poet who could carry Canadian Academic poetry—based as it was on certain rigid principles, and pointed steadily in one direction—as far as it could go without changing course completely. Basing his poetry upon a composite picture of Canadian nature, made up of a multitude of sharply observed particulars, he gave the old images new meaning. "Morning on the Lievre" is a good example of this type of craftsmanship. Deceptively simple in its execution, the poem shows how Lampman was able to capture a moment and a scene with impressive authority.

> Far above us where a jay
> Screams his matins to the day,
> Capped with gold and amethyst,
> Like a vapour from the forge
> Of a giant somewhere hid,
> Out of hearing of the clang
> Of his hammer, skirts of mist
> Slowly up the woody gorge
> Lift and hang.
>
> Softly as a cloud we go,
> Sky above and sky below,
> Down the river; and the dip
> Of the paddle scarcely breaks,
> With the little silvery drip
> Of the water as it shakes
> From the blades, the crystal deep
> Of the silence of the morn,
> Of the forest yet asleep;
> And the river reaches borne
> In a mirror, purple grey
> Sheer away
> To the misty line of light,
> Where the forest and the stream
> In the shadow meet and plight,
> Like a dream.

From amid a stretch of reeds,
Where the lazy river sucks
All the water as it bleeds
From a little curling creek,
And the muskrats peer and sneak
In around the sunken wrecks
Of a tree that swept the skies
Long ago,
On a sudden seven ducks
With a splashy rustle rise,
Stretching out their seven necks,
One before and two behind,
And the others all arow,
And as steady as the wind
With a swivelling whistle go,
Through the purple shadows led,
Till we only hear their whir
In behind a rocky spur,
Just ahead.

This is the Canadian Academic tradition at its best. Employing no self-consciously Canadian terms, Lampman spins his web of imagery until the imagination is captured. His similes—"like a dream," "softly as a cloud"—are familiar enough, taken out of context, but when they are joined to "the misty line of light" of the Canadian river landscape with "sky above and sky below," the old images are enlivened with new meaning. The poem gives the reader the sense that something is about to happen; it sets the scene with a series of tranquil pictures that contain the threat of action, like the giant's hammer, just out of hearing. The seven ducks, with their seven outstretched necks— and note the sudden sharpening of the pictorial image which is evoked by the specific reference—burst upon the scene, and then, just as suddenly as they appeared, are gone. But they can be heard "just ahead," around the next bend, and the sense of impending action remains. The specific is blended with the general in a series of succeeding vignettes which merge into one impressionistic yet vivid picture.

One has only to compare Lampman's "Heat" with Harpur's "Midsummer Noon in an Australian Forest" or with Mair's "August" to see the extent to which Lampman advanced the tradition in Canada.

5Archibald Lampman, *Poems*, 19–21.

The first five stanzas again create an impressive objective picture of stifling summer heat. It is what Lampman does in the surprising last stanza that justifies the quotation of the poem in full, and points the way to what Lampman was to do with his nature poetry—not content to remain only with the descriptive techniques he had mastered.

> From plains that reel to southward, dim,
>   The road runs by me white and bare;
> Up the steep hill it seems to swim
>   Beyond, and melt into the glare.
> Upward half-way, or it may be
>   Nearer the summit, slowly steals
> A hay-cart, moving dustily
>   With idly clacking wheels.
>
> By his cart's side the wagoner
>   Is slouching slowly at his ease,
> Half-hidden in the windless blur
>   Of white dust puffing to his knees.
> This wagon on the height above,
>   From sky to sky on either hand,
> Is the sole thing that seems to move
>   In all the heat-held land.
>
> Beyond me in the fields the sun
>   Soaks in the grass and hath his will;
> I count the marguerites one by one;
>   Even the buttercups are still.
> On the brook yonder not a breath
>   Disturbs the spider or the midge.
> The water-bugs draw close beneath
>   The cool gloom of the bridge.
>
> Where the far elm-tree shadows flood
>   Dark patches in the burning grass,
> The cows, each with her peaceful cud,
>   Lie waiting for the heat to pass.
> From somewhere on the slope near by
>   Into the pale depth of the noon
> A wandering thrush slides leisurely
>   His thin revolving tune.
>
> In intervals of dreams I hear
>   The cricket from the droughty ground;
> The grasshoppers spin into mine ear
>   A small innumerable sound.

I lift mine eyes sometimes to gaze:
  The burning sky-line blinds my sight:
The woods far off are blue with haze:
  The hills are drenched in light.

And yet to me not this or that
  Is always sharp or always sweet;
In the sloped shadow of my hat
  I lean at rest and drain the heat;
Nay more, I think some blessèd power
  Hath brought me wandering idly here:
In the full furnace of this hour
  My thoughts grow keen and clear.[6]

This is not a wise passiveness, nor is it a realization of the terror of nature which instils moral values as a part of the education it gives. It is here an external condition, neither malignant nor benign, within which man is forced to react as his own nature dictates. Heat usually leads to lethargy, and the whole of nature, including the only other human figure involved, reacts as one would expect. But for the poet other considerations apply. Nature, in its extremes, allows man to recognize his own powers, and shows that "not this or that is always sharp or always sweet"—that he can make of it what he will. In this way, man is not passively receiving the influences of nature—the cows are doing that, "waiting for the heat to pass"—he is actively using them for his own purpose here: the unexpected opposite of the universal lethargy, the burning of the dross from his mind to leave him with sharper vision. Endurance against nature's extremes becomes, thus, not mere stoicism, but an active moral and humanistic principle.

There is nothing unusual in the romantic poet condemning materialism, sighing of his woe in a bitter world, and escaping to nature for the soothing and reviving forces needed to carry on in a vale of tears. This is stock equipment. But there are enough variations in the contrasts which Lampman poses to give the impression that more is involved than conventional poetic posturing.

Out of the heart of the city begotten
  Of the labour of men and their manifold hands,
Whose souls, that were sprung from the earth in her morning,
No longer regard or remember her warning,

[6]Ibid., 12–13.

> Whose hearts in the furnace of care have forgotten
> For ever the scent and the hue of her land;
>
> Out of the heat of the usurer's hold,
>   From the horrible crash of the strong man's feet;
> Out of the shadow where pity is dying;
> Out of the clamour where beauty is lying,
>   Dead in the depth of the struggle for gold;
>   Out of the din and the glare of the street;
>
>   Into the arms of our mother we come,
>   Our broad strong mother, the innocent earth.[7]

But this apparently Wordsworthian solution is not enough, for in nature there is also struggle. As we have seen in "Heat," nature's main virtue lies in its ability to provide a setting where man may strip away the artificial barriers that bar the way to self-knowledge. Though some of Lampman's early poems might seem to suggest that the only opposition being posed was that of corrupt city and idyllic countryside, he goes on, in others, to suggest that both are battlefields where man is struggling towards self-knowledge. In a poem written in 1887, but not published in his first volume, Lampman underlines his essential dilemma.

> Two noble trees together stand
> Silent in an autumn land,
> One is dead and bare;
> But the winds have stripped the other
> Brooding by its sapless brother
> In a grey despair.
>
> Two hearts that once were bound together
> Sit apart with broken tether,
> Thoughts that blindly grope,
> Between the two no word is said;
> Love in the one is dead
> And in the other hope.[8]

Man may appear rarely in the nature poetry, but elements of nature themselves symbolize, for Lampman, human and social relationships. The two trees lead the mind to the universal failure of communication of which Lampman was so conscious—failure between individuals,

[7]Ibid., 17.
[8]Lampman, At the Long Sault, 22.

sections of the community, and the opposed segments of the poet's own personality.

> Soul from soul we shrink and part,
> And no longer hail each other
> With the ancient name of brother.[9]

For the moment, the only thing to be done is to endure—the Canadian version of the Australian preoccupation with survival. It is not here a matter of physical so much as spiritual survival—the preservation of the sap. The emphasis on endurance, evident in "The King's Sabbath," "Vivia Perpetua," and "At the Long Sault," point to moral victories which result from enduring what cannot be changed. "The Weaver" (pp. 57–8) is a key poem in the presentation of this attitude.

> All day, all day, round the clacking net
>   The weaver's fingers fly;
> Grey dreams like frozen mists are set
>   In the hush of the weaver's eye;
> A voice from the dusk is calling yet,
>   "O, come away, or we die!"
>
> Without is a horror of hosts that fight,
>   That rest not, and cease not to kill,
> The thunder of feet and the cry of flight,
>   A slaughter weird and shrill;
> Grey dreams are set in the weaver's sight,
>   The weaver is weaving still.

The dreams are grey ones, but they are better than nothing. One has one's task, and one cannot fly from it, no matter what the cost. One cannot escape from oneself.

> "Nay, wife, what boots it to fly from pain,
> When pain is wherever we fly."

Man is here repeating the lesson of the earth itself. In one of his sonnets, "Earth—the Stoic" (p. 284), he compared the battering of the elements against the earth to the tribulations of man.

> Yet thou complainest not, O steadfast Earth,
>   Beautiful mother with thy stoic fields;
> In all the ages since thy fiery birth

9Lampman, *Poems*, 50.

> Deep in thine own wide heart thou findest still
> Whatever comforts and whatever shields,
> And plannest also for us the same sheer will.

"Sheer will" is the one thing that stands between us and the "grim Idiot at the gate" which presides over "The City of the End of Things" (pp. 181–2).

> But now of that prodigious race,
> Three only in an iron tower,
> Set like carved idols face to face,
> Remain the masters of its power;
> And at the city gate a fourth,
> Gigantic and with dreadful eyes,
> Sits looking toward the lightless north,
> Beyond the reach of memories;
>
> ....
>
> Alone of its accursèd state,
> One thing the hand of Time shall spare,
> For the grim Idiot at the gate
> Is deathless and eternal there.

Despite Lampman's protests, his is not completely the poetry of disillusionment. There are always traces of the recurring Victorian hope that progress will eventually bring changes for the better, but the spectre of mindless man walking mechanically through his iron towers haunts his later poems. Although much of his poetry is religious in tone, Lampman showed little belief in the doctrines of resurrection or salvation, and hence was unable to find comfort in the teachings of the Church.

Slow to make friends in Ottawa, Lampman for a time associated himself with a local group of free-thinkers—disciples of Kant, Spencer, and Huxley. He had previously complained of the lack of intellectual stimulation in his surroundings, where there had been no contact of minds to encourage and polish his thoughts. He held this to be the inevitable plight of the poet in Canada, where, he said, the poet was alone with nature and with himself. It is strange that this should be more true of Canada than of Australia. We have seen that the bushmen in Australia were a world to themselves, and that constant discussions about ideas and theories were always taking place. By a Canadian, these discussions would have been considered well below educated Canadian standards—they were so considered by educated Australians—but they provided a stimulation, coupled though it was with naïveté, that was rarely to be found in Canadian literary circles. The Ottawa Group represented a type of radical political and philosophical thought that was new to Canada. Lampman was stimulated by it, but he was also profoundly disturbed. "The Usurer" and "Epitaph on a Rich Man" were written in 1893, the year he apostrophized Fate in these terms:

> Thou art the wind and I the tree,
> The aspen trembling and distressed,
> The prairie bloom, the broken sea
> That cannot rest.[10]

The yeast of social conscience was working in his mind, and "The City of the End of Things" was a direct result. "The Land of Pallas," significantly omitted from the 1925 volume of his work, tries to find a solution in a visioned utopia conceived, like Morris's *News from Nowhere*, in largely pastoral terms.

The difficulties that beset Canada First members had also extended their hold over Lampman, though with different results. Canada First was handicapped by its lack of precision and the cloudiness of its ideals; Lampman's humanitarianism burnt as fiercely as Mair's patriotism had done, but as Mair found an indifferent audience for his message, so Lampman realized the impossibility of making any mark on the social order by the composition of such poems as he could write, phrased as they were in the cloudy idealism of the Canadian Academic tradition. A cloudy idealism certainly did not represent the specific sense of grievance that Lampman felt, but it was the best that he could do. The nearest approach he made to truly radical poetry was in the ode to "Liberty," which was not published until 1943, and it does little to enhance his reputation.

> Was it for this—for this? we cry
> That you made the peoples free,
> That your vessels plough the sea
> And your buildings climb the sky;
> ....
> For there comes at last the day
> When the meanest and most poor

10Lampman, *At the Long Sault*, 24.

> Having scanned the ages' flow
> Probed his hurt, and guessed the cure
> Shall rise up and answer—No![11]

The final choice was a bitter one, but Lampman felt it had to be made. He could do nothing with his grey dreams; they flashed with fire but it was a fire beyond his reach.

> The world goes by me an unfathomed stream
>   Too bright with flame, too dark with mystery,
> A shadowy glory and an ancient dream;
>   Its conflict and its pomp are not for me.
> By others let great epics be compiled,
>   Let others' songs in stormier measures flow:
>   I sit me in the windy grass and grow
> As wise as age, as joyous as a child.[12]

This passiveness, wise or not, represented Lampman's final position.

Unlike Mair, or O'Dowd or Paterson, Lampman did not write patriotic poetry, and he refused to do so when asked. In reply to such a suggestion from Roberts, he maintained that the poets would be better employed writing satires. His patriotism was not of the rhetorical nor of the political type, and because he was not an ardent nationalist, as Mair was, it is significant that his work should represent the national statement in nineteenth-century Canadian poetry. His was a nationalism more effective than Mair's because it gave more and demanded less, and because, above all, it reflected the Canadian's love for his country quite separately from controversial matters of politics and flag-waving. It is ironical that by his agonized retreat from the national capital into the world of nature, Lampman succeeded in interpreting Canada to Canadians with an authority that others had sought vainly to achieve.

The poetry of Duncan Campbell Scott differs in many respects from Lampman's, but the broader picture that he paints does not alter the validity of Lampman's claim to represent Canadian poetry in the period under discussion. In "The Height of Land" Scott branches out into a poem of ideas more provocative and more successful than any of Lampman's attempts in that field. There are obvious analogies to be drawn

[11]*Ibid.*, 29.
[12]*Ibid.*, 17.

between this poem and O'Dowd's "The Bush." Scott represents the poet as camped upon the height of land. On one side the watershed sweeps away to Hudson's Bay, and on the other is the crowded southern land "With all the welter of the lives of men." Poised on the border between the two, the poet senses an added perception and insight. Life is essentially simple as seen from this centre of a moving world, and he wonders—much as Keats wondered on the nature of beauty—whether it is possible to retain this intuitive power for all time, or will it change as the order of man changes? He comes to the conclusion that it is possible only here in the still centre.

> O Life is intuition the measure of knowledge
> And do I stand with heart entranced and burning
> At the zenith of our wisdom when I feel
> The long life flow, the long wind pause, the deep
> Influx of spirit, of which no man may tell
> The Secret, golden and inappellable?[13]

Scott's poetry is not as finely drawn as Lampman's but it presents more expansive vistas. The contrast between the two worlds presented in "The Height of Land" corresponds partially to the two worlds of Lampman's experience, but their relationship is made more dramatic by Scott's poised position between them. As O'Dowd went to the bush as the mystical mother, the purifier who opens men's eyes to themselves, so the insight is given to Scott to see the balance between the busy warm littleness of the civilized southern land, and the great brooding immensity of

> The lonely north enlaced with lakes and streams,
> And the enormous targe of Hudson's Bay.[14]

In this poem one obtains a greater sense of the force of Canada's sheer size applying a type of moral pressure against the insignificance of the small area man has yet managed to make his own. There is an equivalent sense of immensity in O'Dowd's "The Bush," and in both cases the poets are the interpreters of the mystical significance to their societies of the gigantic empty spaces which surround them. There is a great surface beauty in each. O'Dowd delights in the gum-tree blossoms and the waving grass, but there is also the burning crucible

13D. C. Scott, *Poems*, 51.
14*Ibid.*, 47.

waiting to anoint men's eyes. Scott delights in the glory of the sunrise from his height of land, but below is the charred earth and the burnt bone of the forest fire, and he suspects that even his new insight may only bear the same relation to the true vision—could he but see it—that exists between the primitive wall-drawings of a caveman and a masterpiece of modern painting.

Repeated even more strongly in Scott's poetry is the note of stoicism so evident in Lampman. Endurance is admirable, for man is at war with the blind forces of his environment, and may only win by inner moral strength. Scott's contribution to the national statement was the same in kind as Lampman's; he did not share his friend's inner conflict between the demands of the Academic tradition and social conscience, but by his own poetry and by his services as literary executor he consolidated Lampman's position as the representative of the national tradition in poetry.

Running parallel to the Academic stream of poetry in Canada was a vigorous Popular tradition. One looks in vain in histories of Canadian literature for mention of an indigenous ballad and lyric tradition equivalent to those found in surveys of Australian literature. A. J. M. Smith, in his *Book of Canadian Poetry*, includes several poems from the work of Alexander McLachlan—poems more Academic than the majority of his work—but makes no mention of folk-literature, or literary ballads based on folk-songs, beyond a sampling from French-Canadian sources. There are collections now appearing of Nova Scotian ballads, but no editions of Upper Canadian folk-songs appeared in any of the libraries until the 1960 publication of Fowke and Mills' comprehensive *Canada's Story in Song*. For all the impact that was made outwardly upon the Canadian literary scene, one might think that there was no parallel to the Australian movement, and that Canadians, when they wrote poetry, concentrated only on Academic forms.

This, of course, is not true. Though well-hidden—far more thoroughly concealed from the eye of posterity than the submerged Australian Academic tradition at the end of the nineteenth century—there begins to merge from obscurity not only a ballad tradition native to Canada, but a Popular literary movement based upon it. That all traces of this poetry have been so singularly effaced from the surface of the literary scene is eloquent testimony to the prejudices of Canadian criticism as moulding forces in Canadian culture. "Such songs are not poetry" was the general tenor of opinion—therefore let them not be mentioned. One is struck by the number of so-called "Popular" or "Family" song-books which were published in Canada between 1880 and 1900, yet a close examination of these reveals that they all contain English and American popular songs of the day, with perhaps "The Maple Leaf Forever" thrown in to show there was no prejudice. There are Temperance Readings but no drinking songs, nothing to reveal the existence of anything so low as a native folk-culture. Nor are such matters dealt with in the large and reputable periodicals of the day. The *Canadian Monthly*, the *Week*, and the *British American Magazine* make no mention of any undercurrent beneath the established literary scene. To find evidence, one must go to the files of long-forgotten and defunct country newspapers, and to slim volumes privately printed in local print-shops, seldom found in even the largest libraries. The sampling which has been obtained for the purposes of this discussion represents, it is certain, only a minute portion of the material which is available from local sources in small country towns, but it should be sufficient to support the observations made on the nature of the movement.[15]

For the first three decades of the last century the reception of British folk-ballads into the Canadian colonies followed much the same pattern that was evident in Australia. Mackenzie[16] lists the usual number of "come-all-ye" ballads, together with variations made upon them. The immigrant ballad was, by contrast to the Australian versions, extremely optimistic. Here is one which appeared as early as February 1750 in the *Gentleman's Magazine*:

> Let's away to new Scotland, where Plenty sits queen
> 　O'er as happy a country as ever was seen;
> And blesses her subjects, both little and great,
> 　With each a good house, and a pretty estate.
>
> There's wood, and there's water, there's wild fowl and tame;
> 　In the forest good ven'son, good fish in the stream,
> Good grass for our cattle, good land for our plough,
> 　Good wheat to be reaped and good barley to mow.

[15]Since this was written (in 1959), some of the popular Canadian material has been resurrected in anthologies, notably *The Blasted Pine* (A. J. M. Smith and F. R. Scott, eds.), Toronto, Macmillan, 1960.

[16]*Ballads and Sea Songs From Nova Scotia* (W. R. Mackenzie, ed.), 1928.

No landlords are there the poor tenants to teaze,
   No lawyers to bully, nor stewards to seize;
But each honest fellow's a landlord, and dares
   To spend on himself the whole fruit of his cares.

They've no duties on candles, no taxes on malt,
   Nor do they, as we do, pay sauce for their salt;
But all is as free as in those times of old,
   When poets assure us the age was of gold.

Once the immigrants had landed in the country they followed the Australian pattern of adapting folk-songs and ballads to suit their changed conditions. In many cases the changes are only superficial, matters of place-names. The original:

When I was young and in my prime, my age being twenty-one,
I hired as a servant unto a gentleman.
I served him true and honest, and very well, it's known,
And lately he banished me from Erin's lovely home.[17]

undergoes changes in places and occupations.

When I was young and in my prime, my age being twenty-one,
I hired as a plough-boy unto a farmer man.
I served him true and honest, for eighteen months and more
And now he would have me banished from Nova Scotia's shore.[18]

It is in the original songs that sprang from the country that one may begin to see the similarity between the Australian and Canadian traditions. The differences in the organization of society in the two countries ensured that the spirit of the original ballads changed less quickly in Canada than it did in Australia, but there is evidence that, from the very beginning, there was a division of the folk-songs into two categories, those that could be tolerated by polite society, and those that could not. It is most interesting to compare "The Indian Lass" as a product of the oral tradition with "The Lass of Mohee," the bowdlerized version that would be tolerated in print. First, here is part of the original version:

As I went a walking way down by the shore
I went into an ale-house to spend half-an-hour,
And as I was musing and taking my glass,
By chance there came in a fair Indian lass.

[17]Dan Bryant (ed.), "Shaun the Poet" Songster, 168.
[18]Journal of the Folk Song Society, II, 211.

She sat down beside me, she squeezed my hand:
"Kind sir, you're a stranger and not of this land.
It's I've got good lodgings, so with me you'll stay;
My portion you'll have then without more delay."

With a glass of good liquor she welcomed me in:
"Kind sir, you are welcome to everything."
And as I embraced her it was all of her moan:
"You are a poor sailor and far from your home."

We tossed and we tumbled in each other's arms;
All night I enjoyed her sweet lovely charms.
With love and enjoyment time soon passed away;
I did not go and leave her till nine the next day.[19]

The printed version of 1881 is very different and very proper. The relationship between the sailor and the maid is now sweetly sad, and notice the change in the first stanza—there will be no references to ale-houses in *The Canadian Companion*!

As I went a walking one evening in June
    A viewing the roses—they were in full bloom—
As I was a sitting down on the green grass,
    Who did I spy but a young Hindoo lass.

She stepped up towards me, she gave me her hand,
    Said she, "You're a stranger from some foreign land.
If you will follow, you're welcome to come;
    I live by myself in a snug little home."

The sun was a setting all o'er the salt sea
    As I rambled along with that pretty Mohee.
Together we rambled, together we roamed,
    Till we came to the cot where the cocoanut grew.

With fondest expression she said unto me,
    "If you will consent to live here with me
And go no more rambling across the salt sea,
    I will teach you the language of the lass of Mohee."

"O fairest of creatures, that could never be!
    I have a dear girl in my own counteree.
I'll never forsake her for her poverty,
    For her heart is as true as the lass of Mohee."[20]

[19]Mackenzie (ed.), *Ballads and Sea Songs of Nova Scotia*, 154. The editor gives the source as "the singing and recitation of John Adamson, Westville, Pictou County."
[20]Mackenzie quotes this ballad in his collection (p. 155) but it also appears in *The Canadian Companion*, a collection of sentimental songs and ballads, mostly English in origin, published by J. Bell of Montreal in 1881.

This is a good example of the type of moral censorship which was exercised over the early ballads. Most of these, even when far more innocent than "The Indian Lass," would be categorized as "low songs" and dismissed from notice.

Another interesting adaptation occurs in the appearance of a number of early Australian ballads in Nova Scotia. It is not clear whether these were imported directly by sailors who had been to Sydney, or if they came to Canada by way of Britain. Probably the latter is true, for Mackenzie in discussing "Jack Donahue" feels it necessary to say,"It is ordinarily supposed that 'Jack Donahue' is an Irish ballad, but the invocation and narrative details both suggest an Australian rather than an Irish origin."[21] He then goes on to write a page on why he thinks it is Australian. As Ingleton gives full details of the growth of this ballad as a convict song, and as it has been included in most major collections of Australian ballads from the eighteen-sixties, one might think Mr. Mackenzie's arguments superfluous. It underlines the lack of direct contact between writers in Australian and Canadian literature. There are some interesting minor changes in the Canadian version of the ballad. The word "Christians" has been substituted for "Convicts" in the line in the chorus, "Convicts all, both large and small, say prayers for Donahue!"[22] Mackenzie also records "The Wild Colonial Boy" and "Van Dieman's Land,"[23] but makes no mention of the manner in which they became current in Nova Scotia. It is interesting that the only ballads celebrating the exploits of outlaws—or, at least, the only ones readily available— should be Australian in origin. There is evidence that a strong tradition of occupational ballads, similar to the types that developed among the Australian drovers and shearers, was current among the lumbermen of the Maritimes and Upper Canada. Stated to be of New Brunswick origin, one of these songs, "The Lumberman's Life," consists of a series of reiterated complaints on the hardships encountered.

> O a lumberman's life is a wearisome life.
>   Some say it is free from care.
> O the winding of an axe, O from daylight till dark,
>   And the wild forests we must steer.

[21]Mackenzie (ed.), *Ballads and Songs of Nova Scotia*, 306.
[22]Ingleton (ed.), *True Patriots All*, 130.
[23]Mackenzie (ed.), *Ballads and Songs of Nova Scotia*, 304, 317.

When our camps they are dark and the piercing winds do blow,
And our limbs they are almost froze [couplet repeated twice];
O every rapid that we run they think it is great fun,
And they don't know the dangers we're in [repeated twice].[24]

The Scottish settlers who came to Upper Canada in the forties brought with them not only a large number of Scottish folk-ballads, but also the usual keen Scottish admiration for the work of Robert Burns. Vigorous and independent, the Scottish settlers worked hard and sang their songs; after a period of intitial hardship, they usually prospered, growing fond of their adopted country in the process. While many of their songs look back nostalgicly to Scottish mists and lochs, as the "Scottish Boat Song" does, a new oral tradition began, based on their experiences in their new country. These pioneers, who lacked the graces and the polish of sophisticated literary taste, left a record of their country which was more realistic and vivid than the products of the majority of the Academic poets, and, by their close attention to the local scene, laid the basis for a national idiom that could have added great strength to Canadian poetry had any attention been paid to it. In spirit the Canadian and Australian balladists are very close together. They avoided pretension and abstract philosophizing, and made shrewd comments on the significance of the events in their daily lives. Though they would have been condemned—and obviously were, by implication, from the way in which they were ignored by those with any pretensions to culture —as "non-poetic," they provided a virile native saltiness that was, as it proved in Australia, a valuable basis on which to build a distinctive literary idiom. The first important figure to write in the Popular tradition was the emigrant mechanic, Alexander McLachlan. The son of a Chartist and with Chartist sympathies himself, he would have been at home in the Australian outback. Instead, he came to Ontario in 1840, at the age of twenty-two. For ten years he tried farming, but in 1850 he settled down as a tailor in the town of Erin. By his death in 1896 he had published three volumes of poetry, and had gained a large audience in Canada, particularly among the working classes. Many of his poems were published in *Grip*, the Toronto radical magazine, and he gave numerous lectures to working-class organizations on the need for social justice. Chartists appear as sympa-

[24]*Ibid.*, 362.

thetic characters in those of his poems which are set in Scotland, but in his new country his doctrine was set out in the well-known passage from "Jack's as Good's His Master":

> Our aristocracy of toil
> Have made us what you see—
> The nobles of the forge and soil,
> With ne'er a pedigree!
> It makes one feel himself a man,
> His very blood leaps faster,
> Where wit or worth's preferred to birth,
> And Jack's as good's his master![25]

This is a common strain in Australia, but one hears it rarely in Canada. McLachlan continued to temper his Canadian patriotism with criticism of political corruption in local politics. In advice to "Young Canada" in the 1861 volume, he traces the path to success in the Ontario of that time, sniping at, among other things, the smugness of Toronto's material prosperity.

> 'Tis money rules the world now,
> It's rank and education,
> It's power and knowledge, sense and worth,
> And pious reputation.
> Get cash, and 'gainst all human ills,
> You're armed and you're defended,
> For in it even here on earth,
> All heaven is comprehended.
>
> And now my lads, if ye would reach
> The height of exaltation,
> Take my advice, let work alone,
> And stick to speculation;
> Work was not meant for gentlemen,
> It's low and it's degrading,
> And so, my lads live by your wits,
> And learn the tricks of trading.

Having made money, the time is ripe for the next move upwards.

> Now all the rowdies in the land,
> Around you, you must gather,
> By soft sawder and whiskey punch!
> You are a City Father.

25 Alexander McLachlan, *Poems and Songs*, 119.

And having grown by villainy,
To such exalted stature,
Set up your beaver, now you're fit
To be a legislator.[26]

The poem traces the newly elected politician through his career of "honoured corruption," until he retires lauded and respected by the nation he has plundered. On his death, the epitaph will continue the lie that he has lived. It would seem that the old-fashioned honesty of the pioneers is out of date in the city, but it is still kept intact on the frontier itself.

More important than McLachlan's satires of city life are his portraits of the pioneers. *The Emigrant* contains some effective passages describing the weariness of the pioneers working their way through the wilderness.

Through morasses, over bogs,
Wading rivers, crossing logs,
Scrambling over fallen trees,
Wading pond holes to the knees;
Sometimes wandering from the track,
And to find it turning back;
Scorning ills that would betide us,
Stout hearts and the sun to guide us.[27]

The humour of workmen in the bush is another attractive aspect of McLachlan's picture. Having selected a site for their clearing, the men set about felling the first tree—one of the forest giants that Catherine Traill had mourned. One of the workers says, deliberately, as the chopping goes on:

Sleep will heal the wretch's woes,
Longest days will draw to close;
Time and tide will hurry past,
Looked for long will come at last,
Whigs may wear a cheerful face,
Even when they're out of place,
Tories cease to rule the roost—
Britain learn to count the cost;
Radicals may yet have power—
Britain perish in an hour;

[26]Alexander McLachlan, *The Emigrant and Other Poems*, 207–9.
[27]*Ibid*. 36–7.

> Yankees cease their boasting, too,
> Who can tell what time may do?
> That would be a miracle,
> Yet the thing is possible;
> There is even room to hope
> For the Devil and the Pope—
> Changes strange we all may see,
> But we'll never fell that tree!

After the tree is felled, as though in answer to Catherine Traill, McLachlan has this comment to make:

> Trees, of which the poet sings,
> May be very pretty things;
> And these green-arched solitudes
> (Where no traveller intrudes—)
> May be fine, I do not doubt,
> Just to sit and sing about.
> Sentiments for those at ease,
> But, I fear it fells no trees;
> Not the sentimental tear,
> The strong arm is needed here.[28]

This is a note of realism that is heard all too seldom. The life of the pioneer, as we have seen, developed virtues different from the traditional ones, but virtues none the less. If there were celebration rather than regret at felling the venerable tree, it was not an unthinking one.

> 'Twas a kind of sacrament;
> Like to laying the foundation,
> Of a city or a nation.[29]

As the Australian bushmen felt a sense of solidarity grow among them, a sense which had its origins in experiences shared and hardships overcome, so McLachlan calls for a unity among the pioneers of Canada, based on the virtues they have learned together in the clearings.

> Each for all, and all for each,
> Is the doctrine that I preach;
> Mind the fable of the wands,
> 'Tis a fact that always stands:

[28]*Ibid.*, 43–6.
[29]*Ibid.*, 42.

> Singly we are poor and weak,
> But united, who can break?[30]

But the radical tailor's voice, though still lifted, found a steadily diminishing audience. The Academic critics ignored him for the most part, or, when they did notice his work, gave faint praise to the least admirable characteristics of his poetry: a vague mysticism and a tendency to over-moralize. They overlooked altogether the vigour of his pictures of life in the clearings. The prevailing note of radical idealism—present in Australian verse too, but sometimes distinguished by the more characteristic note of sardonic irony—was one with which Lampman could have sympathized, but he could not, any more than his literary colleagues, have countenanced the easy colloquial flavour of McLachlan's verse.

The second important figure to emerge in this examination of the Popular tradition in Canada is Alexander Glendinning. Glendinning arrived in Canada from Scotland in 1836 and settled on a small farm near Scarborough, Ontario, moving later to a larger one near Sarnia. In 1871 his local reputation as a folk-poet caused some six hundred of his admirers to raise a subscription to publish a volume of his verse, and a book of 240 pages, entitled *Rhymes*, was printed by the *Free Press* in London, Ontario. There seem to be no reviews of the work in any of the Toronto journals of the time, and Glendinning is never mentioned in any survey of Canadian literature. A. J. M. Smith drew his poetry to the attention of the Canadian Historical Association in 1944,[31] but contemporary references to the work remain elusive.[32]

It is extremely unpretentious poetry, but therein lies part of its charm. There is a directness rising from concrete personal experience that gives the book more than local interest. No radical as McLachlan

---

[30]*Ibid.*, 51.

[31]See p. 109, footnote 13.

[32]The only review of Glendinning's work which I have yet found is a newspaper clipping attached, presumably by a previous owner, to the inside cover of a copy of *Rhymes*. The clipping, which bears neither the date nor the name of the publication from which it was extracted, reads as follows: "The poems of Mr. Alexander Glendinning have been popular for many years among the Scottish community of this area [presumably Sarnia], and it is fitting that they should be preserved in the present volume. Mr. Glendinning describes many of his experiences as a settler in this country, and his views will, no doubt, bring back memories of their own early days to many of our readers, particularly those of Scottish origin."

was, Glendinning represents the shrewd, conservative Scottish crofter who grumbled and complained at his lot, but who formed the back-bone of the hard-working pioneer families of southwestern Ontario. His poems cover a period of over thirty years, and it is possible to see the changes gradually coming about in his attitudes as the environment and social climate worked upon him.

In an early poem called "Annandale Farming" he describes the rural scene in Scotland, telling of the circumstances that made him decide to leave his native country to try his fortune in the new world. His picture is a well-drawn piece of realism.

> Four or five horses, leaning 'gainst their stalls,
>   Eight calvers, high of bone and hard of skin;
> Some forty porkers, making hideous squals,
>   Through lack of murphies, pitifully thin,
> With savage snouts they undermine the walls;
>   Soon shall the half-rotten roof-tree tumble in
> And crack their rigbones, pound their hams and flitches,
>   And put a finisher upon the wretches.

The poem concludes with an ironic address to

> Ye happy few, ye owners of the soil,
>   Who feed upon the fat and drink the sweet,
> Just look and see how your poor tenants toil,
>   And, after a', have hardly bread to eat:
> Let down your rents, live and let live the while,
>   And we will be your servants, as 'tis meet;
> We'll gang and buy oursels new coats and breeks,
>   And never speak a word on politicks.[33]

In a subsequent "Epistle to the Laird of Davington" (pp. 45–52) written after his arrival at Scarborough, Glendinning describes his journey. He left Scotland with misgivings. He describes what was said about him by those who stayed at home.

> Poor fellow! his was a sad case;
> Hard fortune buff'd him back and face,
> And sent him frae his native place
>   As poor as Job.
> To scraffle on a wild goose chase
>   Half round the globe!

[33]Alexander Glendinning, Rhymes, 72–4.

His journey across the Atlantic is recorded with considerable feeling.

> Ye thinkna of poor luckless wretches
> In a ship's hold and under hatches
> 'Mang two three hunder lowsie bitches
>   Brood of blue ruin!
> These, as the vessel rolls and pitches,
>   Cursin' and spuein'.

Arrival at New York brought relief, and curiosity to see the Americans about whom he had heard so much. He was quite willing to be impressed, but his first reaction to their physique inspired this delightful comment.

> All hail! Columbia's forests green;
> All hail! New York, of cities queen;
> All hail! to Jonathan, our frien';
>   But, love me!
> What curious coons! how lank, how lean
>   Them Yankees be!

> Bare-faced, din, thin, cadaverous sights!
> They look as if they'd lien for nights
> Deep under Carlanrick's heights,
>   Or Borthwick wa's,
> Then bolted up for mortal frights
>   To scare the craws.

But while he is confident that such people could never beat the British, he has grudging respect for their energy and drive. On the trip up the Hudson River he was sure that a boiler would burst, but he imagines that if it did, they'd be able to fix it, and keep on going at their usual rapid rate.

> Them Yankees—guess the coons are clever,
>   For a' their talk,
> They make her go it now or never,
>   And that's a fact.

He arrived at Scarborough, and found that he had to start by clearing his land. After what seemed interminable chopping, he had a dozen acres cleared, and he planted a small crop before going ahead with the rest of the clearing. His clothes were worn out, but there was no one to see him.

> I whiles look down my cloutit breeks,
> The crutch just now wants two three steeks;
> But what care I for Fortune's freaks?
>   They need nae jacket
> Wha hae nought else to do for weeks
>   But trees to whack at.

Slowly he prospers; hard work is repaid, and there is time to describe the social activities of the new community, joined as most of them are to the work of the pioneer. There is a description of a logging bee:

> You muirland blades would laugh to see
> A band o' loggers at a bee—
> Smart chiels wi' handspikes working free
>   In shirt and breeches,
> And teamsters, loud wi' ha and gee,
>   Twirling blue beeches.

He goes on with an aside that marks the essential difference between settling on the land in Canada and small farming in Australia.

> Still Canada, say what they will on't,
> For my part, I can say nae ill on't;
> There's mony a gude-guan' busy mill in't,
>   And weel-fill'd ark,
> And every man gets bread and yill in't
>   That likes to wark.

This can be the basis for an unself-conscious nationalism that has its roots firmly in the soil. It is not rhetorical, but is more effective because it is not. In Glendinning's book are to be found comments on local politics and dry observations on social customs, at first from the viewpoint of an outside observer but later as an accredited member of the community. References to the "wee drap" are frequent in the early verses, and there is an ironical "Temperance Ode" (p. 106) obviously commenting with disapproval on the strength of the temperance forces in the country; he comes to the conclusion that it is because there is so little available worth drinking!

> That stuff they sell for whiskey now,
> 'Tis vile narcotic drugs;
> Just look at it, sae thin and blue,
> The thing would pizen dogs.

But twenty-five years later he is writing quite seriously against drink, and is repeating most of the sentiments found in the many "Temperance Readings" which were distributed in the province through the Presbyterian Church. One such tract distributed in 1860 describes the outward attractions of drink—sparkle, expansiveness, subtlety, colour— and then follows an exposure of the terrible dangers lurking beneath.[34] Using the same organization exactly, Glendinning wrote a poem entitled "That Drink!"[35] in which he is obviously sincere in his strictures. In other poems he thunders against those who would pervert "true Presbyterianism" by installing an organ in the kirk—those who would "praise their Maker by machinery."[36] Although increasingly conservative in social matters, Glendinning had been politically conservative since his arrival. He had seen the Americans, and though he thought the Canadians could beat them if they tried to invade Canada, he was not sympathetic to radical or Jacksonian democracy. In the year following arrival at Scarborough, William Lyon Mackenzie had raised his banner of revolt, and Glendinning was one of those in the loyalist ranks which put down the rebellion. After the affair had fizzled out, he wrote a parody of "Hohenlinden" called "The Battle of Yonge Street, 1837" (pp. 81–93).

> On Yonge Street, ere the sun arose,
> Stood the Queen's forces and her foes,
> With many a pale and bloodless nose
> And cheeks as chill as charity.

The mighty army of Scarborough, with Torrance swearing at its head, rolled up to join Montgomery. With drums rolling the line advanced, and the rebels promptly disappeared, leaving the army with nothing to do but wait until the pubs opened. Yet "'Twas a famous victory." The poem closes with mock-pathos befitting the occasion.

> 'Tis past: the wintry tempests sweep
> O'er the cold couch where warriors sleep,
> And mothers mourn and widows weep
> The flower of Markham's chivalry.

---

[34]The tract is in the possession of Mrs. James Gilchrist of Toronto. Originally the property of her father, it was distributed by the Presbyterian Church in Tottenham, Ontario.

[35]Glendinning, Rhymes, 222–4.

[36]Ibid., 167.

But in a later poem called "A Word to the Finnigans" (pp. 94–100), he is in deadly earnest about the reception he and the people of the Sarnia area intend to give any Fenians who show their noses across the lake. In a dispute about religious settlement in the province, Glendinning is strongly on the side of law and order. Though he disapproved strongly of the proposed Anglican Land Grants, he condemned those of his fellow dissenters who would take the law into their own hands. In a poem entitled "The Moderate's Garland" (pp. 117–18), he says:

> The Law of the Land! The Law of the Land!
>   Submit to the powers that be;
> Let talk who please of the Kirk and the Keys,
>   The Law of the Land for me.
>
> Give Caesar his due. Can we cancel our vow
>   To be loyal ?—to honour the king?
> Can we lift up our hand 'gainst the law of the land,
>   While we snugly sit under its wing?

One can imagine the reaction of the bushmen in Australia to such sentiments as these.

Glendinning has a poem on Confederation which provides an interesting contrast to the rhetorical productions of the Canada First party. He is doubtless one of those whom Denison found so infuriating; for his attitude is one of quiet interest at all the fuss which is being made. For him the main thing is to wait and see what it will all mean in terms of dollars and cents.

> So now Confederation is a fact,
>   And we are settled in our new Dominion,
> I hear a deal of folks begin to talk
>   (But this may be mere matter of opinion)
> About expensive government. John A.
>   Spends money rather foolishly, they say.

He regrets that George Brown is out of the picture, for Brown knows how to count the pennies. As for the rest of them, making their speeches—McDougall, Howland, Blair, McGee—only time will tell, but he is angry at the thought of extravagance. He concludes:

> But there's nae use in talking, I can see
>   The scamps will do exactly as they please:

> They care nae mair for folks like you and me,
>   As we were pyets chattering on a tree,
> There's one thing makes me aye as mad's a viper—
> Dance when they will, we have to pay the piper.[37]

It is clear that the main virtues of this type of poetry are its simplicity and directness. The men who wrote it were not burdened—for in these circumstances it may be a burden—by a literary awareness which had no application to their lives. The influence of Burns is obvious, but this is a healthy influence, for it too encouraged the strain of homely realism. There are many other figures in this movement. Robert Boyd was another Scot who lived in Canada between 1830 and 1880. A pioneer of the Guelph district of Ontario, he did for his district what Glendinning did for his.

"The Bachelor in His Shanty," a long and vividly descriptive poem by Boyd, describes his hardships when he first decided

> To come to this strange land o' trees,
> The vile abode o' frogs and fleas,
> Wi' no ane near to sympatheese,
>   Or yet to hate us;
> Devoured alive by slow degrees
>   By curs'd mosquitoes.

His troubles are almost as severe as the ill-fated Billy Barlow's. He is tormented by the insects, comes down with fever, is roasted in summer, frozen in winter, wolves carry off his lambs, hens and ducks disappear without trace; yet

> A farmer too I'm called by name,
> Nay—even a Laird—so much for fame,
> Which makes me blush wi' burning shame
>   The truth to tell
> For a' my craps scarce fill my wame
>   And nane to sell.

His "stock" consists of a dog and a cat, but, he hastens to assure us, they are both pedigreed. His troubles continue when he goes courting.

> Last week my humble suit I paid
> To bonnie, smirking Maggie Shade;
> She seem'd to list to what I said,

[37]Ibid., 122–4.

> But mark, ye fates,
> Straightway wi' guessing Sam she fled
> Aff to the States.

Other girls tell him to get a new house before they'll look at him, and he falls into a state of despondency, regretting his decision to come to Canada, but he regains his courage, and concludes:

> But oh! I fear sic hopes are vain;
> Auld Kyle I'll never see again;
> Weel, since its sae, I'll here remain
> Anither year yet,
> I may be blessed, for a' that's gane,
> Wi' routh o' gear yet.[38]

With Boyd as with Glendinning, the sense of independence, once the worst years and trials are over, turns to a feeling of pride in himself and affection for the land. This love is at first regional and local, but it expands eventually to take in the whole country. It is the most valuable type of patriotism, and while Mair and his friends were trying to impose national feeling as a doctrine to be lectured about, a more reliable national sentiment was growing before their eyes, and sought expression in country songs, and in the works of dozens of local poets. This pride in achievement was the one thing that could inspire and sustain the immigrant in his labour, and move him to a quiet patriotism that became national and lasting. There were few supporters for Imperial Federation from this class in Canada. Not as vocal nor as radical as their Australian counterparts, they wanted to "let things be," and in the meantime devoted their efforts to interpreting for themselves and their immediate neighbours on the land their ideas of the significance of the Canadian environment.

Isabella Valency Crawford attempted to combine aspects of both the Academic and Popular traditions, but divided her efforts too rigidly into separate compartments. Despite the very real power of "Malcolm's Katie"—where she does succeed in conveying the feelings of the pioneers—most of her poetry is reaching too consciously for effect. "Old Spookses' Pass," the story of a night stampede in a pass in the Rockies, uses its dialect too self-consciously and introduces notes of sentimentality which are out of character. In her Academic poetry,

[38]Daniel Clarke (ed.), *Scottish Canadian Poets*, 61–6.

she retains traditional forms, but is often in danger of losing the discipline of the form. Neither one thing nor the other, the compromise falls between the two.

Canadian folk-poetry shows strong similarities to the Australian in the spirit, if not in the form. It is closely identified with the Canadian frontier and the principal influence is Burns—a healthy influence for a community of small independent farmers usually working their own land. In Australia, the Irish influence is stronger than the Scottish, for the Irishman was more often a tenant than an owner of the land he tilled, and his feeling of resentment against the large landowners of his native country found a parallel in the attitude of the bushmen towards the squatters. In both countries folk-literature reveals a developing patriotism. In Australia this was based on pride in survival and the outwitting of those in authority. In Canada it was based not only on survival, but on positive achievement. Where the Australians were proud of their egalitarianism and of their accomplishments as a group, the Canadians were proud of the results of their achievements as individuals. There was a common earthy debunking of affectation, together with the substitution of basic values for superficial ones. The dignity of man's labour if it is on his own behalf or that of his friends, its servility and slavery if on behalf of an employer, loyalty to one's friends, pride in oneself either as an individual or as a member of a group—these are all common elements in the folk-literature of the two countries.

In Canada there was no clear merging of the two traditions as there was in Australia. The Popular tradition had been submerged too thoroughly for it to be able to break through the consolidated Academic tradition enough to influence it materially. Leftist poetry in Canada was not to emerge through the McLachlans or through any other vocal members of the lower classes, nor was it to be national in character as it was in Australia. Based on international doctrinaire socialism, twentieth-century leftist poetry, though not truly a part of the Academic tradition, is closer to it than to the Popular. Souster, Dudek, and Layton have denounced Academic poetry in Canada, but they have not become, in any sense, Popular poets. Theirs is a cerebral poetry, intellectual in conception and not concerned with reaching a mass audience.

Robert Service, though once very popular with his songs and ballads of the Yukon, has made little lasting impression on the Canadian literary scene. It is significant that of all the types of Australian ballads, the one that proved most ephemeral has been the prospecting ballad. Like the gold-rushes they celebrated, they soon died away because they were not identified with a sufficiently permanent state of society. The Australian outback, for all its shifting nomadic population, retained common factors that were stable and recognizable. The gold-rush ballads seldom survived for more than ten years after the strike was over. The attitudes that Service described were not familiar enough to Canadians all over the country to become the basis for any type of Canadian bush myth, and the folk-ballad, anyway, was not an important influence in Canadian literature. Service did fill a need or focus a dominant point of view, as Lawson and Paterson did in Australia. With the end of the Yukon gold-rush, therefore, the ballads of Service—never taken seriously by Canadian literary critics—faded back into the obscurity of the Canadian folk-stream. It seems probable that the Yukon and Klondike traditions will be kept alive as an extension of the American Western, and, as happened over a century ago with Sam Slick, yet another Canadian default will be assimilated by the United States to form part of the folk-lore on which their literature can build.

It is perhaps in the poetry of E. J. Pratt that one may see the best example of any fusion that has taken place. Pratt has combined the narrative excitement of one important type of ballad with the discipline and organization of the Academic tradition. He is fascinated by the concept of natural forces, of power, and of man's place in relation to them. He has the sweep of Canada's huge horizons presaged by Duncan Campbell Scott, but he has also an earthiness and a realism that was seldom found before in Canadian poetry. Perhaps his Newfoundland upbringing helped to develop this combination of the two forces. With rare exceptions, however, the Academic tradition continues to thrive in Canada, though struggling at times to re-establish contact with the public which threatens to slip away.

Many contemporary Canadian poets are concerned with recording universal experience, with little reference to the local scene. Intellectual and esoteric in its imagery, their poetry sets up barriers against all but a comparatively few readers. But this apparent lack of contact causes them no concern. The Australian professor, A. D. Hope, on the other hand, writes poetry which is more intellectual in its conception than that of many of his fellow-Australian poets; yet he is by no means indifferent to reaching what could be fairly called a mass audience. This is one important difference between contemporary Canadian and Australian poetry which can perhaps be seen more clearly against the social and historical background we have been investigating. One has only to turn to current "little magazines" in Canada to find further examples of the entrenched cosmopolitanism of the Academic stream. To find in 1960 literary magazines of a type that flourished in Canada in the middle nineteenth century underlines the tenacity of the Academic tradition.

8. Towards a National Tradition: Australia

WE HAVE SEEN that between 1880 and 1900 Canadian poetry developed a distinctly Canadian idiom. A national tradition in poetry also came into being in Australia during the same period, and Australian poetry, like Canadian, developed two parallel streams; but the relative importance of them was reversed. In Australia the Popular dominated the Academic. The significance of this difference will be clear if we repeat for the Australian scene the pattern of examination just conducted for the Canadian, looking first at the development of the prose, and then at the two streams of poetry. We shall note, as a final difference, the way in which, at the end of the century, the two streams of Australian poetry merge, their fusion projecting the future course of poetry in Australia.

In discussing the Popular tradition it is neither possible nor desirable to ignore the development of prose in Australia, for the attitudes which are revealed and the methods which are adopted continually cross the lines between poetry and prose in a manner not encountered in Canada. Henry Lawson, one of the leading figures in the bushballad movement, is equally famous for his short stories; Joseph Furphy, though no poet, revealed attitudes shared by the balladists. Hence, as an introduction to the *ethos* of the bush ballad it is useful to look briefly at the development of prose, particularly fiction.

Australian fiction followed the pattern that might be expected from discussion of the early poetry. For long it was assumed that the first important Australian novel was Henry Kingsley's *Geoffrey Hamlyn*, published in 1859. Kingsley's book was a conventional saga of colonial life, written for the English market. It was not until 1952 that Colin Roderick ran to earth *Ralph Rashleigh*, written by a convict, James Tucker, in 1845. Not only has the book been received as a valuable historical document, but the comparison it affords between the attitudes of Ralph Rashleigh and Furphy's Tom Collins has provided an opportunity for those who wish to examine the continuing nature of the convict influence in later indigenous writing. It is certain that Furphy knew nothing of the earlier work, written fifty years before *Such Is Life*.

Ralph Rashleigh was not directed towards a specific audience. It was an outlet for the self-expression of a bitter man, yet it employed an idiom in which bitterness is strangely mixed with hope and philosophical acceptance. As Cecil Hadgraft puts it, "It is the Convict's Lament followed by the Convict's Dream."[1] The same paradox is to be seen in *Such Is Life* in the eighteen-nineties, and among the outback bushmen well into the present century. It is a part of the compound that forms contemporary Australian political attitudes, a combination of seemingly bloodthirsty intolerance and of violent partisanship which never seems to come to a head. The class-war has been a part of Australian egalitarianism for over a century, quite divorced from any doctrinaire "ism." The Australian political climate is to the left of the Canadian, and the labels of communism and socialism have been used in attempts to define the position of the man who so aggressively calls himself the "Australian Worker." A glance at nineteenth-century literature, however, will reveal the same attitude under different names. "The Old Lag"—the emancipated convict— was talking about the "Revolution" as soon as the irons dropped from his legs at Port Jackson. Social protest was inevitable in an environment where both the political and social organization, and the parsimonious nature of the country's resources, seemed to conspire to make the emancipist feel himself to be the victim of a continuing oppression, and of discrimination exercised in favour of a privileged minority.

There were compensations. The camaraderie of the convict was replaced by the doctrine of mateship and the comfortable feeling that one had friends—a class solidarity against the common enemy. Then, too, there was the alternation of periods of hard work and long days

[1]Cecil Hadgraft, *Australian Literature*, 43.

of enforced or voluntary leisure. The convicts had no property worth speaking of, but they did not starve. While there was a squatter's flock there was always meat, and if the watchdogs knew their work too well, a spell of contract labour would provide ample meals and some spare cash to spend at the next pub. The nomadic workers demanded—and usually received—the best of meals, for the grazier knew that if his property were to be blacklisted there would be no labour available at shearing-time. The hard-working poor—whether "wage-slaves" or small selectors (farmers)—were despised as syco-phants or dupes. Work was an unpleasant necessity which had to be engaged in at intervals, but the real time for living came when work was over, and the bushman could echo the famous first line of Furphy's book: "Unemployed at last . . .!" From this came a fatalistic confidence that the future would take care of itself, and that in the meantime one was free to theorize about utopian schemes which had as their goal a state of affairs in which man was free from the need to work for a living! In one of the rare instances where the wild discussions of the bushmen found expression in action, the results were not en-couraging. William Lane, in 1894 during the great rural depression, gathered around him a group of enthusiastic workers and set off with them to Paraguay to found "New Australia" free from squatters and vested interests. The dismal failure of the expedition did not deter those who remained. Henry George perhaps found greater support for his financial theories among the Australian rural workers than among any other group in the world. For nearly twenty years *Progress and Poverty* was argued about in the outback pubs, and it was a standard work for any self-respecting bushman's library.

The remnants of this attitude survive among Australians today. The Canadian (and the American) who visit Australia notice a difference in the material values that prevail there. The Australian is reluctant to forfeit any of his leisure by working overtime to earn more; he values his leisure more than he does the additional goods which the extra money would buy. Part of this may be attributed to laziness, for it is unquestionably true that his aim is to receive the highest possible wage and the best working conditions for the least possible work. But once he has gained enough to satisfy what he considers the basic needs (and he would regard as luxuries many of the things that Canadians would consider as essentials), he has little ambition to earn more to buy the latest gadget. It would be foolish to conclude from this that the Australian is, therefore, less materialistic, or that he is more culturally inclined. He has less to be materialistic about, and with his notorious passion for horses and beer one might well question the uses to which he puts his valued leisure time. Yet it also remains true that since 1890 Australians have maintained more book-shops and have bought more books per capita than have the inhabitants of any other country in the world. While the anti-Academic prejudice in creative writing has been stressed throughout this argument, one must not confuse this with a prejudice against books and ideas.

George Carrington, an Oxford graduate who had spent some years among the Queensland rural workers, published a book in London in 1871, entitled *Colonial Adventures and Experiences* by "A University Man." His comments on the nature of the bushman reflect the surprise that visitors invariably felt whenever they took the trouble to meet him on his own terms. Carrington's experiences were dictated by necessity rather than preference, as his condescending but surprised observations indicate (p. 33 ff.):

While I was in Brisbane I had seen little, if anything of the working men, and had no expectation that I should ever be driven to associate with them. Now I was brought suddenly to their level, and I was astonished to find what an intelligent and companionable set of men they were for the most part. As far as I have been able to judge, they are far above the ordinary level. There is a total absence of that crawling deference to those who happen to have money in their pockets and good clothes on their backs, which may often be found in those of England and Ireland. Here I found realised much that I had been accustomed to consider high-flown and nonsensical; I could now understand the true meaning of the nobility of labour. When I say that the working men of Queensland are, as a body, far superior, both in mental and physical capacity, to the same class in England, I am saying little. A sense of independence conduces to the one superiority, and better food to the other. But besides this there is a leaven of education and information pervading the whole class, which is very remarkable. . . . This is more remarkable when you get further into the bush than it is in the towns. . . . These men, by constant mixing and rub-bing together, communicate their ideas to one another, and a taste for information is thus created. . . . But the worst of it is, from the first to the last, they all drink. . . . In Queensland men make a business of being drunk while they are at it, and allow no interval of sobriety to intervene until they have finished their money.

It was not true to say of Australia, as E. K. Brown said of Canada, that books were a luxury and writers an anomaly. As early as the eighteen-thirties a surprising amount of serious reading was done by drovers and shearers. When it appeared, the *Bulletin*—"The Bushman's Bible"—did not concern itself merely with entertainment. It published serious and essentially didactic material with a burning evangelism that was ignored by its opponents and argued by its supporters. That this did not happen in Canada is due to the lack of any continuing burning issues about class division, to the lack of leisure, and to the distrust of a collectivism that was forced upon Australian bushworkers.

Following *Ralph Rashleigh* and, as far as nineteenth-century Australians were aware, the first notable Australian novel was Henry Kingsley's *Geoffrey Hamlyn*. Popular in England, where it was published in 1859, Kingsley's book was harshly received by many Australian critics. The characters are never at home in Australia. Their ambition is to return to England after they have made enough money to spend their last years in the ranks of the English gentry. This was common enough among the early squatters, and was the justification for the bushworkers' taunts against them. The large graziers in the first half of the century regarded themselves as exiled Englishmen rather than Australians, and were frequently looking forward to the day when they could return "home." This was true even of some squatters who had been born in Australia. Kingsley's novel tells the story of a family who shared this attitude, and who were finally successful in achieving their aim—a happy ending from the English viewpoint, but hardly endearing to an Australian audience. One of the characters, Sam Buckley, sums up their point of view (p. 177): "Don't let me hear all that balderdash about the founding of new Empires. Empires take too long in growing for me. What honours, what society, has this little colony to give compared to those open to a fourth-rate gentleman in England? I don't want to be young Sam Buckley of Baroona. I want to be *the* Buckley of Clere." This was the chief convention of colonialism, and Kingsley felt he was speaking for the squatters when he echoed it. But the book did not reveal the realities of the situation— even the realities of the grazier class. It was the myth that the squatters accepted about themselves. Joseph Furphy was much closer to the mark in his comments; for while opposed to everything that the squatters stood for, he at least recognized the diversity that existed among them.

Those whose knowledge of the pastoral regions is drawn from a course of novels of the *Geoffrey Hamlyn* class, cannot fail to hold a most erroneous notion of the squatter. Of course, we use the term "squatter" indifferently to denote a station-owner, a managing partner, or a salaried manager. Lacking generations of development, there is no typical squatter. Or, if you like, there are a thousand types. Hungry M'Intyre is one type; Smythe —petty, genteel, and parsimonious—is another; patriarchal Royce is another; Montgomery—kind, yet haughty and imperious—is another; Stewart is another. My diary might, just as likely as not, have compelled me to introduce, instead of these, a few of the remaining nine-hundred and ninety-five types—any type conceivable, in fact, except the slender-witted, virgin-souled, overgrown schoolboys who fill Henry Kingsley's exceedingly trashy and misleading novel with their insufferable twaddle. There was a squatter of the Sam Buckley type, but he, in the strictest sense of the word, went to beggary; and, being too plump of body and exalted of soul for barrow-work and too comprehensively witless for anything else, he was shifted by the angels to a better world—a world where the Christian gentleman is duly recognized, and where Socialistic carpenters, vulgar fishermen, and all manner of undesirable people, do the washing-up.[2]

While Canadian idealization of backwoods life was accepted within the convention of the Canadian novel by the settlers themselves, the Australian bushman insisted on the presentation of reality. To him it is inconceivable that "the hero of the croquet lawn" should, in a moment of crisis, succeed in saving the situation, while resourceful bushmen looked on helplessly with admiration. However he might be opposed to them, Furphy at least gave his enemies the credit of knowing their jobs.

The convention of calling England "home" persisted among the upper classes into the second half of the century, but it gradually died away. More and more of the wealthy settlers returned from their pilgrimages to England disillusioned and surprised to find that home, after all, was not in Kent or Fifeshire, but was on the plains of the Riverina or the Darling Downs of Queensland. The classic description of this disillusionment occurs in Henry Handel Richardson's *The Fortunes of Richard Mahoney*. The hero, gazing on England, is overwhelmed by the small scale of everything, and by a claustrophobic

[2]Joseph Furphy, *Such Is Life*, 204–5.

feeling of restriction after the expansiveness of the Australian land-scape; and he feels suddenly ". . . the sense of an older, tireder wisdom" which makes of him the ancient, of them the young and untried. "How, knowing what he knows, can he placidly live through the home day, with its small, safe monotony? How give up for ever the excite-ment of great risks taken and met, on grander shores, under loftier skies?"[3] His discovery was the same as Howe's had been many years before, and he returned to Australia. Despite the continued conven-tion among the bushmen that the squatters were not true Australians, by the eighties there was a definite sense of nationality among squat-ters and bushmen alike. Perhaps for this reason, the nationalist litera-ture of the bushmen began to spill over beyond their own ranks, to gain general acceptance among all classes as the representative voice of the community.

Geoffrey Hamlyn provided the straw man for the realists to knock down, and though Marcus Clarke, in *For the Term of His Natural Life*, was not as scornful of Kingsley's colonial romanticism as Furphy was to be, his novel marked a definite swing away from romanticism. It too dealt with Englishmen who came to Australia, but they were not the Sam Buckleys. Clarke has presented a picture of the convict system in Van Diemen's Land (Tasmania). Searching the records for details of convict life, Clarke saw in them an opportunity to reverse the tendency which even then (1869) discounted the import-ance of the convict period in Australian history. If Field had spoken of the need for antiquity, this was the only one Australia had to offer.

Here again is the pervasive Australian pride in survival. Ralph Rashleigh had reflected the convict's sense of triumph at the very fact of his survival, as though his continued existence were a form of defeat he had inflicted on his oppressors. Furphy's Tom Collins took delight in his continued survival despite economic pressures. A. D. Hope has quipped about the "ultimate men" whose boast is they survive; and in Patrick White's *The Tree of Man*, the ability to endure pain, spiritual and physical, is the hallmark—indeed the privilege—of humanity.

In Clarke's *For the Term of His Natural Life*, there appears for the first time an accurate insight into the significance of the Australian setting as a dominant influence for a work of art. We have only to

[3]Henry Handel Richardson, *The Fortunes of Richard Mahoney*, 416.

compare two descriptions of the Australian scene, one from *Geoffrey Hamlyn*, published in 1859, and the other from Clarke's book, published eleven years later. First is this passage from *Geoffrey Hamlyn* (pp. 146–7):

A new heaven and a new earth! Tier beyond tier, height above height, the great wooded ranges go rolling away westward, till on the lofty skyline they are crowned with a gleam of everlasting snow. To the eastward they sink down, breaking into isolated forest-fringed peaks, and rock-crowned eminences, till with rapidly straightening lines they fade into the broad grey plains beyond which the Southern Ocean is visible by the white sea-haze upon the sky.

All creation is new and strange. The trees, surpassing in size the largest English oaks, are of a species we have never seen before. The graceful shrubs, the bright-coloured flowers, ay, the very grass itself, are of a species unknown in Europe; while flaming lories and brilliant parroqueets fly whistling, not unmusically, through the gloomy forest, and overhead in the higher fields of air, still lit up by the last rays of the sun, countless cockatoos wheel and scream in noisy joy, as we may see the gulls do about an English headland.

To the northward a great glen, sinking suddenly from the saddle on which we stand, stretches away in long vista, until it joins a broader valley, through which we can dimly see a full-fed river winding along in gleaming reaches, through level meadows, interspersed with clumps of timber.

There is little here to conjure visions of Australia. It is an exotic landscape, but with a few changes it would do to describe parts of Canada. Clarke, on the other hand, seizes this same note of strangeness as his point of departure, and weaves an impressionistic pattern from it, that probes beyond surface details to a more fundamental distinctiveness. This came in 1870:

In Australia alone is to be found the Grotesque, the Weird, the strange scribblings of Nature learning how to write. Some see no beauty in our trees without shade, our flowers without perfume, our birds who cannot fly, and our beasts who have not yet learnt to walk on all fours. But the dweller of the wilderness acknowledges the charm of this fantastic land of monstrosities. He becomes familiar with the beauty of loneliness. Whispered to by the myriad tongues of the wilderness, he learns the language of the barren and uncouth, and can read the hieroglyphs of haggard gum-trees, blown into odd shapes, distorted with fierce hot winds, or cramped with cold nights when the Southern Cross freezes in a cloudless sky of icy blue. The phantasmagoria of that wild dreamland called the Bush begins to interpret itself, and the Poet of our desolation begins to understand why free Esau loved his heritage of desert sand better than all the bountiful richness of Egypt.[4]

Clarke had not yet reached the stage when all this could be taken for granted, and when Australian nature was no longer fantastic but normal. He was half-way along the path stretching between Kingsley and the bush-balladists, who, by the eighties, had completely accepted the environment. But even so, Clarke was not an outsider trying to explain the scene in English terms; he was conscious of the strangeness of creation but felt himself to be a part of it.

The convict world, as presented by Clarke, is a microcosm where all sham has been removed; the world beyond remains a shadowy, unreal place—desirable, yet somehow artificial. This is a testing place for the insight which is obtained through suffering—a suffering so great that those who have survived are removed from the company of ordinary men. If still from the desert the prophets come, then this is the best place to look for them.

The closest prose equivalent to the bush ballads appeared in 1881 when Ralph Boldrewood published *Robbery Under Arms*, a story of bushrangers and gold-fields (and, incidentally, one of the few Australian books well known in Canada). The narrative is presented in the first person in Australian vernacular by Dick Marston, ostensibly one of the famous Captain Starlight's gang. He has been described as the first thoroughly Australian character in fiction. He is a likable rogue who rationalizes his way through moral judgments with a facility that Lord Birdwood, who admired the book greatly, described as "incorrigibly and typically Australian." His type is with us yet. He was a great favourite among the bushmen, and Mr. Ewers recalls that when the novel was being printed as a serial in the *Sydney Mail*, a group of shearers, impatient to know what happened in the next episode, sent a messenger forty-three miles on horseback to the nearest telegraph station to bring back the news. The book is still popular because of the unforced interest of the story, and the very easy conversational style which has not become dated. These are also attributes of the bush ballad. The book opens:

My name's Dick Marston, Sydney-side native. I'm twenty-nine years old, six feet in my stockings, and thirteen stone weight. Pretty strong and

[4]Marcus Clarke, *For the Term of His Natural Life*, x.

active with it so they say. I don't want to blow—not here, any road—but it takes a pretty good man to put me on my back, or stand up to me with the gloves, or the naked mauleys. I can ride anything—that was ever lapped in horsehide—swim like a musk duck, and track like a Myall blackfellow. Most things that a man can do I'm up to, and that's all about it. As I lift myself now I can feel the muscle swell on my arm like a cricket ball, in spite of the—well, in spite of everything.

Then comes the admission his muscle is presently restricted by the law—he is in prison. He then proceeds to tell the story of his life, his entry into the Starlight gang, and his subsequent adventures. The fresh, casual, and sardonic manner of telling the story was new in Australian fiction, but it was a technique that had been used for some time in the bush ballads. Both the prose fiction and the poetry of the period sprang from the same roots. As we shall see in the case of Henry Lawson, his short stories were based on the bushman's "yarns" told around the campfires, and his literary ballads were based on the bush songs that represented the same values, and, in many cases, the same subject-matter.

Joseph Furphy's *Such Is Life*, written in 1894 (though not published until ten years later), was the crowning achievement of nineteenth-century Australian fiction. The American, Professor C. Hartley Grattan, who has written much on Australia, has called Furphy's book "a primary document for any study of Australian attitudes,"[5] and the frequent appeals made to its pages throughout this discussion are based on a recognition of this fact. The narrator, Tom Collins, is the connecting link between varying facets of life in the Riverina of New South Wales.[6] Furphy's intention is to show that all these facets comprise one organic unit.

Without entering into the controversy over the origin of the bush-ballad tradition, it is necessary to insist on the link between the later ballads and the songs of the convicts in the early days of the settlement. We have seen that only recently has the importance of the convict

[5]J. K. Ewers, *Creative Writing in Australia*, 53.
[6]The Riverina is roughly a triangle bounded by the Australian Alps on the east, the Murray River on the south, and the Murrumbidgee on the northwest. Sometimes the term is extended to include the area around the Darling River system. It is one of the most important grazing districts in the country.

period been recognized in the history of the development of Australian attitudes, yet even some recent literary historians discount convict influences on the growth of the ballad. Geoffrey Ingleton's collection of broadsides from early Australia (*True Patriots All*) includes some convict ballads, and one representing convict morality has already been quoted; but no comprehensive collection of convict songs has yet been made. From the few examples now available, there seems to be a close connection between the adaptations made by the convicts, and the early immigrant songs which were versions of popular British ballads previously known to both groups. The note of rebellion is, naturally, stronger in the convict songs than in those of the settlers, where a nostalgic longing for home predominates. But there are also narrative ballads of the "come-all-ye" type which point a moral from the sufferings of the convict, and warn their audience that they should always obey the law or similar things will happen to them. These are too close in tone to popular English street ballads to be accepted as genuine convict songs, few of which echoed such pious sentiments. "Botany Bay," which exists in many versions, is an example of this type of ballad, attributed to the convict period, but not a product of the convicts themselves.

> Farewell to Old England for ever,
> Farewell to our rum-culls as well,
> Farewell to the well-known Old Bailey,
> Where I used for to cut such a swell.
>
> *Chorus*
> Singing tooral, li-ooral, li-addity,
> Singing tooral, li-ooral, li-ay,
> Singing tooral, li-ooral, li-addity,
> We're sailing for Botany Bay.
>
> 'Taint leaving Old England we care about,
> 'Taint cos we mis-spells wot we knows,
> But because all we light-fingered gentry
> Hops round with a log on our toes.[7]

"The Convict's Tour of Hell" is a genuine product of the convicts. It is a long narrative ballad which tells of the convict who, after death, in true humility knocks at the gates of Hell for admission, only to find

[7] Stewart and Keesing, *Old Bush Songs*, 15.

that Hell is full of his former gaolers, and that convicts automatically go to Heaven.

> "Fudge!" said the Devil, "you've gone astray,
> Convicts never come this way,
> They go to heaven in droves and legions—
> That's a place in the upper regions."[8]

The convict reaches heaven and is at once admitted on the grounds that he has suffered enough on earth. There he finds all his fellow-prisoners, executed outlaws, and victims of persecution of the past. Together they chat about their former ordeals, until the dreamer awakes and finds himself back in the reality of the convict settlement.

The Irish influence is prominent during this early period, as indeed it remained until the nineties. There were many Irish political prisoners with a traditional background of ballad-singing, and most early "come-all-ye" ballads were adaptations from Irish originals. Frank Macnamara, known as "Frank the Poet" (author of "The Convict's Tour of Hell"), and another called "Paddy the Poet" were responsible for many popular convict songs, although few of these have been collected. By the twenties and thirties, with the first influx of free immigrants in any numbers, many of these songs were adapted to the experiences they faced.

Perhaps the best-known early Australian ballad is "Billy Barlow in Australia." Billy's story is typical of the fate of many ambitious free settlers of small means who came to the country early in the century, when there were more convicts than free men. Having been left a thousand pounds, Billy Barlow came to Sydney. The ballad tells of the way in which he was sold a property, cattle, and sheep, by an obliging merchant who had no right to sell Crown land, and who accepted Billy's note for the supplies that he would need. His first misfortune came when he was robbed by bushrangers. He appealed to the troopers for help, but instead of attempting to recover his lost property, they quizzed him suspiciously about his identity. It will be remembered that the "ticket-of-leave" men were provided with a document which was virtually a passport within New South Wales. It was a guarantee of identity and good for travel within the colony. The free settler, of course, had no such official means of identification

[8]Ingleton (ed.), *True Patriots All*, 143–4.

unless, as seldom happened, it occurred to him to apply for such a document before leaving Sydney. As a result, free settlers, on reaching the outback regions, would often find that the police would suspect them of being escaped convicts, and would send them back to Sydney to be identified. This happened to Billy.

> Then he put on the handcuffs, and brought me away,
> Right back down to Maitland, before Mr. Day.
> When I said I was free, why the J. P. replied:
> "I must send you to Sydney to be identified."
>   Oh, dear, lack-a-day, oh!
>   So to Sydney once more went poor Billy Barlow.

No sooner was the question of his identity cleared up than Billy returned to the remnants of his property. The blacks had speared his cattle, and the country was experiencing drought.

> They at last let me go, and I then did repair
> For my station once more, and at length I got there;
> But a few days before, the blacks, you must know,
> Had speared all the cattle of Billy Barlow.
>   Oh, dear, lack-a-day, oh!
>   "It's a beautiful country," said Billy Barlow.
>
> And for nine months before, no rain there had been,
> So the devil a blade of grass could be seen;
> And one third of my wethers the scab they had got,
> And the other two-thirds had just died of the rot.
>   Oh, dear, lack-a-day, oh!
>   "I shall soon be a settler" said Billy Barlow.
>
> And the matter to mend, now my bill was near due,
> So I wrote to my friend, and asked him to renew;
> He replied he was sorry he couldn't, because
> The bill had passed into a usurer's claws.
>   Oh, dear, lack-a-day, oh!
>   "But perhaps he'll renew it," thought Billy Barlow.
>
> I applied; to renew he was oh! so content,
> If secured, and allowed just three hundred per cent;
> But as I couldn't do, Barr, Rodgers and Co.
> Quick sent up a summons for Billy Barlow.
>   Oh, dear, lack-a-day, oh!
>   They settled the hash of poor Billy Barlow.[9]

9Will Lawson (ed.), *Australian Bush Songs and Ballads*, 97–8.

Billy was brought back to Sydney, his property attached, and himself imprisoned for debt. Eventually he was freed, and penniless, with a prison record like so many of the other inhabitants, Billy Barlow threw in his lot with his fellow-nomads of the outback. The ballad is invaluable as a history of the manner in which the emancipists and smaller free settlers came to make common cause with one another. The circumstances of Billy Barlow's adventures are extreme, but they do much to explain the changes which took place in the attitudes of many British immigrants to Australia within months of their arrival.

There is no definite time which can be given to mark the merging of the convict and immigrant ballads into a native bush-ballad tradition. "Billy Barlow" already shows signs of that ironic realism that was to be one of the bush ballad's major strengths, and during the forties and fifties the new form began to emerge. There were fewer parodies and adaptations of British ballads, and more original ones reflecting the changing social attitudes of the singers. At the beginning of the thirties such parodies as "Sweet Alice" were quite common.

> Oh, don't you remember sweet Alice, Dan Holt,
>   The lubra so dusky and dark—
> The Warrego gin with a straw through her nose,
>   And teeth like a Morton Bay shark?
> The terrible sheep-wash tobacco she smoked,
>   In her gunyah down there by the lake,
> The grubs that she roasted, the snakes that she grilled,
>   And the damper you taught her to bake?[10]

From the sentimentality of the original "Ben Bolt" ballad has come a new bush realism based upon reminiscences of a startlingly different type, and using a set of terms native to the country, but which might well make a glossary necessary for non-Australian listeners. Such ballads still relied for their effectiveness, as all parodies do, upon a knowledge of the originals from which they were adapted.

The first extensive group of recognizably native ballads grew around the exploits of the early bushrangers. There is little difficulty in seeing the debt which many of them owe to the convict ballads, for not only is the brand of morality extolled identical with that celebrated by the convicts, but in many cases the terms used to distinguish varying shades of good and evil have their origin in convict

[10]*Ibid.*, 104.

slang. Even before the appearance of free settlers in any numbers, there had been convict songs and stories telling of the exploits of those of their number who had managed to escape to the mountains, to range the bush from hidden bases in a guerrilla warfare against the troopers and guards. As the propertied free settlers were identified with authority, their possessions also became fair game for the bushrangers. In spirit these songs had much in common with the Robin Hood ballads, and doubtless reflected much the same type of social outlook. The principal Australian bushrangers—as Robin Hood is reputed to have done—robbed the rich and helped the poor; or at least that was the way the ballads would have it. The most famous of them was "The Wild Colonial Boy" which was known throughout the country by 1840. The ballad celebrates the exploits of

> . . . a wild Colonial boy—Jack Dowling was his name:
> Of poor but honest parents, he was born in Castlemaine.

The Castlemaine district of Victoria was opened to small farmers and free selectors early in the thirties, but most of these had been driven from the land by 1840. A combination of bad seasons, bushfires, and the pressure of unscrupulous suppliers was responsible for the reversion of the area to large-scale grazing. Though this background is not mentioned in the ballad, it explains the reasoning of the second stanza:

> When scarcely sixteen years of age, Jack left his father's home,
> And through Australia's sunny clime, a bushranger did roam.
> He would rob the lordly squatters: their flocks he would destroy;
> A terror to Australia was the wild Colonial Boy!

The chorus, however, appears to be a survival from one of the older convict songs:

> Then come, all my hearties! We'll roam the mountains high;
> Together we will plunder—together we will die!
> We'll wander over valleys, and gallop over plains,
> For we scorn to live in slavery, bound down with iron chains![11]

The ballad provides an interesting example of the union of the attitudes of convicts and disgruntled free settlers. The hero of the ballad, among other things, holds up a mail coach and robs a judge, observing

[11]Ibid., 102–3.

primly as he does so, that he'd never rob "an honest judge who acted on the square." Eventually Jack Dowling is ambushed by three mounted troopers. Scorning the chance to surrender, he kills two of them before being killed by the third.

A very large group of ballads grew around the reputations of the more famous bushrangers. Ben Hall, Dan Morgan, "Starlight," Power, and the Ned Kelly gang all drew their tribute from innumerable unknown balladiers. In one of the ballads on the death of Dan Morgan one finds the note of sympathy repeated.

> O, Morgan was the travellers' friend; the squatters all rejoice
> That the outlaw's life is at an end, no more they'll hear his voice.
> Success attend all bushrangers who do the poor some good;
> But my curse attend a treacherous man who'd shed another's blood.[12]

It is with the coming of the Kelly gang, however, that the bushranger is elevated into the highest position in the bush-balladists' pantheon. As a result of the legends and songs, the expression "as game as Ned Kelly" entered the Australian vocabulary as the highest compliment that may be paid to a courageous person. Glenrowan, in Victoria, where the Kellys made their last stand against the police, has almost become a national shrine. The home-made armour Ned Kelly wore, the guns he used, and the most minute relics of his career have been preserved, and are displayed regularly at annual shows in Sydney and Melbourne as the relics of a patron saint, guarded, ironically, by the local constabulary. There are over three hundred Kelly ballads, but the first verse of one of them is representative of nearly all.

> On the head of bold Ned Kelly
> They have placed two thousand pound.
> And on Steve Hart, Joe Byrne and Dan
> Two thousand more they'd give,
> But if the price was doubled boys,
> The Kelly Gang would live.[13]

The Kellys were the last of the more spectacular bushrangers who plied the bush between 1810 and 1870. They are safely enshrined today as folk-heroes. Other nations have glamorized their outlaws— Jesse James has become the subject of American legends—but very

---

[12]Stewart and Keesing (eds.), *Australian Bush Ballads*, 35.
[13]*Ibid.*, 42.

few have concentrated almost exclusively on this category. The greatest figures of the American frontier were on the side of law and order, if they were not law-enforcement officers themselves. No trooper is to be found in an equivalent position in the Australian mythology. There were many epic hunts organized in the early days by parties of outnumbered mounted troopers whose job was made particularly difficult by the scarcely veiled hostility of the inhabitants of the outback. Yet no ballads celebrate the deeds of these men. The ballad-singers were all of the same camp: troopers were enemies, and when they defeated the bushrangers did so only because they had superior numbers or resorted to such treacheries as shooting their opponents when they were not looking.

> Throughout Australian history no tongue or pen can tell
> Of such preconcerted treachery—there is no parallel—
> As the tragic deed of Morgan's death; without warning he was shot
> On Peechelba Station, it will never be forgot.
>   ... McQuinlan was the man
> Who fired from his rifle and shot rebellious Dan.
> Concealed he stood behind a tree till his victim came in view,
> And as Morgan passed his doom was cast—the unhappy man he
> slew.[14]

Whatever is said about many of the others, there is very little that can be said for Dan Morgan. He had killed at least fifteen men without giving them any warning whatever, and was listed as one liable to be shot on sight. The note of moral indignation in the ballad describing his death was typical of the contemporary idealization of the bushranger by the bushman. No poetic distance was needed in which the less creditable aspects of the hero could be forgotten. These ballads were dealing with current incidents and personalities, and no subsequent attempt to debunk their heroes had much effect.

In the fifties came the gold-rushes, and with them came a flood of adventurers from all over the world to reinforce the bushmen who had gravitated to the gold-fields. Much has been made of the "digger" spirit, including the often repeated suggestion that it is here that one may find the true origins of Australian attitudes. As was the case with the smaller free settlers, however, though the newcomers undoubtedly added some leaven of their own, the composition of society and the

[14]Ibid., 35.

attitudes that existed before the gold-rushes were not materially altered. Eureka had been in the air for fifty years before it finally happened.

With the miners came a new crop of mining ballads, and the pattern which has been traced from the convict songs completed its cycle again, very quickly, on the gold-fields. There were adaptations from current English songs telling of how fortunes could be made overnight. These were rapidly followed by songs of increasing disillusionment, very like the "Billy Barlow" series. The young immigrant miner found himself beset by red-tape, swindled out of his claim by some unscrupulous official, or by the representative of a big mining concern. In effect, the battle for mining claims was very like the earlier struggle for small farms. As the large graziers had done all they could to discourage the dissection of their runs by small splinter properties, so the small prospector, when he had exhausted the ore which lay close to the surface, found himself squeezed out of his claim by companies which had the resources to extract the ore from deeper levels. Within several years of the initial strike, it was usual to find that the swarm of small individual claims had been consolidated into three or four large company ones. The large mine-owner began to occupy, for the miner, the same place the squatter occupied in the bushmen's minds.

One by one the diggers left the fields, and those who left with little more than they had when they came—and that was most of them—drifted from place to place, and, like the small free settlers before them, made common cause with the bushworkers. They occasionally worked as rouseabouts (sheep-pen hands) or jackaroos (cowboys), but more often they turned to droving, shearing, and bullock-driving, with the usual proportion of swagmen who did not want to do anything but wait to see what turned up.

There had been occupational ballads of droving and shearing since the thirties, and by the sixties these had multiplied greatly. There was, naturally, a great similarity in tone between these ballads, irrespective of the trade they celebrated, for the main facts of life in the bush remained the same for all of them. While there were no Australian equivalents of the American Pecos Bill and Paul Bunyan, who performed individual feats of heroic proportions, there were legendary places described in the ballads. Significantly, such places as "The

Speewah Shearing Shed" were utopias where every man assumed the power to perform heroic feats. The lawbreakers might be deified individually, but for other superhuman achievement everyone had an equal chance were he only able to reach this legendary place. Each of the main occupations had an equivalent utopia. The shearers had their Speewah Shearing Shed where the stalls were made of polished mahogany, the sheep combed and scented, and every shearer had at least three damsels bringing him beer whenever he wanted it. In these circumstances it appeared that prodigious numbers of sheep were shorn by men who had previously been indifferent tradesmen, and all this was done without effort, leaving plenty of time for story-telling and beer-drinking; and the pay was the wool itself which would turn to gold in the shearer's hands.

Though not as elaborate as the shearer's version, the drovers had their Mariella Plains where there was no such thing as drought, no stampedes, no squatters or dues to pay, and, above all, no troopers. The ideal of Clancy of the Overflow, who could ride all day, carefree and singing behind the cattle, was one held by all drovers. These songs are the only exceptions to the usual tone of sardonic realism to be found in the Australian bush ballad, and even here there are overtones which bring the songs back to earth again after their day-dreaming flights.

The independent attitude of the bushworkers aggravated a natural labour shortage in the rural areas. Though this scarcity was made acute at the time of gold-rushes, it had existed before then. If shearers as a group decided that they would not accept less than a certain sum for their work, then they were not seriously handicapped if the employers refused to agree. They could always avoid starvation in the bush, but the squatters could not manage without their help. There was sporadic attempts to import "non-union" shearers (the term was used even before there was an official union) but these were unsuccessful. In the brief shearing season, the shearers were thus able to make enough money to carry them, in many cases, right through until the next. For the rest of the time they lived cheaply with drovers in their camps, as swaggies, or as sundowners. The lines of bush-occupations were crossed so often during the year that individual differences between their songs began to disappear more and more. Though it was true that many of the songs had a utilitarian

purpose—as Brian Elliott proposes in *Singing to the Cattle* (p. 45)—
one cannot over-emphasize this aspect of ballad-singing and composition. Shearers, drovers, bullockies, and splitters all sang ballads in
the course of their occupations, but any folk-song is developed and
expanded by an increasingly large audience only if it reflects a
particular way of living and thinking, a distinctive set of social values
accepted by a large group. Australian bush ballads did this, and their
vigour and popularity sprang from needs more profound than that of
keeping the cattle tranquil—though this may have been a by-product
put to good use by the drovers.

"The Murrumbidgee Shearer" is an interesting example of the type
of folk ballad which had developed by the sixties. In common with
most of its kind, it attempts no direct description of the landscape;
the background was taken for granted. From this ballad may be
extracted most of the values we have been discussing.

> Come all you jolly natives, and I'll relate to you
> Some of my observations—adventures, too, a few.
> I've travelled about the country for miles full many a score,
> And oft-times would have hungered, but for the cheek I bore.
>
> *Chorus*
> So you can understand, my boys, just from this little rhyme,
> I'm a Murrumbidgee shearer, and one of the good old time.
>
> I've coasted on the Barwon—low down the Darling, too,
> I've been on the Murrumbidgee, and out on the Paroo;
> I've been on all the diggings, boys, from famous Ballarat;
> I've loafed upon the Lachlan, and fossicked Lambing Flat.
>
> I went up to a squatter, and asked him for a feed,
> But the knowledge of my hunger was swallowed by his greed.
> He said I was a loafer and for work had no desire,
> And so, to do him justice, I set his shed on fire.
>
> Oh yes, I've touched the squatter's house for sugar, tea and flour;
> And a tender bit of mutton I always could devour.
> I went up to a station, and there I got a job;
> Plunged in the store, and hooked it, with a very tidy lob.
>
> Oh yes, my jolly dandies, I've done it on the cross.
> Although I carry Bluey now, I sweated many a horse.
> I've helped to ease the escort of many's the ounce of gold;
> The traps have often chased me, more times than can be told.

Oh yes, the traps have chased me, been frightened of their stripes;
They never could have caught me, they feared my cure for gripes.
And well they knew I carried it, which they had often seen
A-glistening in my flipper, chaps, a patent pill machine.

I've been hunted like a panther into my mountain lair,
Anxiety and misery my grim companions there.
I've been planted in the scrub, my boys, and fed on kangaroo,
And wound up my avocations by ten years on Cockatoo.

So you can understand, my boys, just from this little rhyme,
I'm a Murrumbidgee shearer and one of the good old time.[15]

This ballad, ostensibly the story of a shearer, combines elements from the convict song, the parody—at least in the chorus—of an English ballad ("The English Gentleman"), and the bushranger ballad. The hero has done everything, from shearing to droving, from working on wages for a squatter to wandering as a swagman "humping his bluey."[16] His acts of dishonesty are all within the bushman's conception of the moral code. He has been in prison, been hunted by the police, but bobs up again as irrepressible as ever, the nameless symbol of a spirit the bushmen liked to consider typically Australian.

This was the position the ballad had reached when Adam Lindsay Gordon came upon the scene. Gordon was in many ways a "wild Colonial Boy" himself. He came to Australia when he was twenty, and was by turns a mounted trooper, a drover, a horse-breaker, a steeplechase-jockey, and finally a member of the South Australian House of Assembly. He committed suicide in 1870 at the age of thirty-seven, and in 1934 his bust was placed in Poet's Corner in Westminster Abbey. Statues of him are to be found in many Australian cities and towns, and for a while he was hailed as Australia's national poet. He is, of course, no such thing, but he did perform a very valuable service for the ballad. Gordon seemed to epitomize the national myth so well—a Byronic figure who flashed across the Australian bush and who gave the bush ballad its respectability.

Gordon was the first of the literary bush-balladists. He compiled traditional ballads which he heard during his wanderings, and began

[15]*Meanjin*, no. 3, 1954, 374.
[16]"Humping his bluey" means carrying his pack or "swag" for a long rambling journey. "Matilda" is another word for this pack—hence "waltzing matilda" means the same thing.

to write ballads of his own. With the beginning of Gordon's poetic activities, the Bush Myth began its slow march from the country on its way to capture the imagination of the city. Though he wrote some Academic verse, the difficulties Harpur and Kendall had faced were too much for him. He published four volumes of poems before his death, and his bush ballads quickly became incorporated in the repertoire of many a bushman. His are the first long narrative ballads which rely upon swift action and easy rhythm to carry them along. They are not as circumstantial as the traditional ballads, and lack something of their unforced vigour and refreshing absence of heroics. For example, there is this stanza from Gordon's poem, "The Wreck":

> The stockrider, Alec, at starting had got
> The lead, and had kept it throughout; 'twas his boast,
> That through thickest of scrub he could steer like a shot,
> And the black horse was counted the best on the coast.
> The mare had been awkward enough in the dark,
> She was eager and headstrong, and barely half-broke;
> She had had me too close to a big stringy bark,
> And had made a near thing of a crooked she-oak;
> But now in the open, lit up by the morn,
> She flung the white foam-flakes from nostril to neck,
> And chased him—I hatless, with shirtsleeves all torn
> (For he may ride ragged who rides from a wreck)—
> And faster and faster across the wide heath
> We rode till we raced. Then I gave her her head,
> And she—stretching out with the bit in her teeth—
> She caught him, outpaced him, and passed him, and led.[17]

Obviously, there is nothing particularly Australian about this. "The Murrumbidgee Shearer" was much more a product of the country than any of Gordon's ballads could ever be; yet Gordon prepared the audience and created a wider public demand and enthusiasm for ballad poetry. Henry Lawson gives an interesting sidelight on the type of reception which Gordon's poems received among the bushmen. In one of his short stories, "The Babies in the Bush," Lawson describes an exchange between a drover and his assistant. Both were fond of Gordon's work, and would quote it to each other at night around the fire.

The boss would straighten up with a sigh. . . . Then maybe he'd stand

---

[17]Adam Lindsay Gordon, *Poetical Works*, 47.

with his back to the fire roasting his dusty leggings, with his hands behind
his back and looking out over the dusky plain.

> "What mattered the sand or the whit'ning chalk,
> The blighted herbage or blackened log,
> The crooked beak of the eagle-hawk,
> Or the hot red tongue of the native dog?"

"They don't matter much, do they, Jack?"
"Damned if I think they do, boss!" I'd say.[18]

It remained for Henry Lawson and A. B. Paterson to complete the
process which Gordon had begun. But before discussing the work of
these two writers, it is necessary to say a little about a great Australian
periodical which, even more than Gordon, was responsible for pro-
moting not only the bush ballad, but a national Australian literature.

The Sydney *Bulletin*, under the editorship of J. F. Archibald, first
appeared in 1880 and is still flourishing today. From the first, the
Bulletin appealed to the bushmen. Here was a weekly journal which,
like Furphy's Tom Collins, announced its bias as aggressively Australian. In its first years, "Australia's National Newspaper" (as it called
itself) betrayed some of the same shrill note that could be heard at
times from the bushmen themselves, but with the acceptance of its
weekly message by an increasingly large number of subscribers, the
Bulletin assumed a greater degree of responsibility towards its readers,
and aimed at a high standard of journalism. The paper did not become
conservative; rather, like the labour movement with which it often
sympathized, early advent to power brought the *Bulletin* to a realization that it must weigh its words carefully. Within these limits, however, Archibald and his editors consistently followed their earliest
pledge to attack whatever they thought needed attacking, without any
consideration of the vested interests involved. Frankly based upon a
socialist platform, the *Bulletin* spoke so accurately for the outback
inhabitants that within five years the paper was known by the nick-
name it has borne ever since—"The Bushman's Bible." To Archibald a
paper was an organic unit rather than a collection of reports, and in
each issue he tried to make plain the basic issues of some controversial
subject. Spokesmen for Marxism, anarchy, George's Single Tax scheme,
pacifism, militarism, republicanism, monarchy—all found space provided for them in the *Bulletin*. In the famous Red Pages, aspiring

[18]Colin Roderick (ed.), *Henry Lawson*, 142.

poets were invited to submit their work for criticism, and stringent criticism it was. Archibald personally read thousands of manuscripts, and to the authors of those he thought showed real talent he wrote letters of encouragement and sent critical suggestions. To those whose work was accepted he sent cheques—and by current standards, substantial cheques too—with the demand for more as soon as possible. Above all, Archibald demanded conciseness of expression. He had no patience with pretentious or over-elaborate writing; a master of the précis, he would insist that his writers be as terse as possible. In reply to one correspondent he once wrote: "In writing to the *Bulletin* remember that it is only a little paper and not one to maunder in. We wouldn't allow three and a half columns to William Shakespeare."[19]

To join Archibald in his critical function came an obscure political writer named A. G. Stephens, who had caught Archibald's attention with a pamphlet on Queensland politics. Stephens was to be even more influential than Archibald in the cultivation and encouragement of Australian writers. He shared his employer's aversion to maundering, but he had a much more acute sense of discrimination in literature. Archibald had always disliked what he called "literary" verse, and was not interested in anything which did not at once appear to have a close connection with the lives and experiences of his readers. Stephens supported this view with some modifications; he was a widely read man who had considerable knowledge of English literary tradition and forms; but he rejected them, not through a prejudice against "bookishness," but because he could not see their value in the stage of development that Australian literature had then reached. He was quick to sense a genuine and distinctive Australianism in writing, even though it were hidden beneath a clumsy style, and he would work endlessly with authors helping them to revise and organize their material. The sketches of Steele Rudd owed their publications to Stephens, as did Furphy's *Such Is Life*, and nearly every other prominent literary work to emerge during the last decade of the century.

Paterson and Lawson were the two writers who brought the bush ballad to its highest level of popularity. Following Gordon's early promotion of the form, there had been a flood of literary balladists who followed, more closely than Gordon had done, the spirit and atmosphere of the anonymous bush ballads. Will Ogilvie, Barcroft

[19]The *Bulletin*, Sydney, March 2, 1895.

Boake, Edward Dyson, George Evans, and G. H. Gibson, to name only a few, had prepared the ground. Their work had been published frequently and the form was beginning to receive serious attention, even from some academic circles which had previously had little but scorn to heap upon the ballad movement. Despite tentative advances, however, the writers themselves would have nothing to do with the academic world of "Polite Letters." The time was not yet ripe, and the strong prejudice against university learning—as opposed to practical experience—had been one of the legacies inherited from an earlier period, and one which has not completely vanished even yet.

Paterson and Lawson came from very different backgrounds, and one of the circumstances attending their rise to popularity was the poetic "feud" which they carried on with each other through the pages of the *Bulletin*. Paterson, though brought up in the country, attended a private school and became a well-to-do solicitor in Sydney. As a result, he saw the bush through his early associations with it—his was an old and wealthy family of squatters. Paterson presents the bright side of life in the bush—the humorous incidents and the moments of lyric pleasure. For the first time, a representative of the squatters entered a field previously reserved for their opponents. Lawson was to make much of this, but he failed to obtain as much support as he expected, because by the nineties the sense of separation between squatter and bushworker, though still very real on an economic basis, had lessened in other respects. Both considered themselves to be Australians, and both of them loved the bush. Paterson, moreover, had not remained unaffected by the prevailing temper of society, and as many young men had done before him, he developed a strong social conscience—as strong as Lawson's, though he was less aggressive in displaying it. The pictures he presents are all from the point of view of the working man, and the bushmen themselves found no fault with his realism. Even as the son of a squatter, he shows the same attitude towards unionism and cheap foreign labour that bushmen shared all over the country. Paterson combined the ability to tell a story with the power to project a particularly Australian way of living and thinking —merging the best of the literary narrative ballad with the traditional ballad of social attitudes. Russell Ward[20] tells of an experience he had only ten years ago. When collecting material for research into bush

[20]"Australian Folk Ballads and Singers" (*Meanjin*, no. 3, 1954), 379.

ballads in the Albury district of New South Wales, he had repeated
to him as an authentic anonymous folk-ballad one of Paterson's, called
"A Bushman's Song." Ward cites this as a very late example of the
"folk" adopting a literary work that appeals to them, making it their
own. The ballad in question shows how far Paterson had come from
the traditional picture of squatter mentality, and how close he was to
the bushmen.

> I'm travelling down the Castlereagh, and I'm a station-hand,
> I'm handy with the roping pole, I'm handy with the brand,
> And I can ride a rowdy colt, or swing the axe all day,
> But there's no demand for a station-hand along the Castlereagh.
>
> So it's shift, boys, shift, for there isn't the slightest doubt
> That we've got to make a shift to the stations further out,
> With pack-horse running after, for he follows like a dog,
> We must strike across the country at the old jig-jog.
>
> This old black horse I'm riding—if you'll notice what's his brand,
> He wears the crooked R, you see—none better in the land.
> He takes a lot of beating, and the other day we tried,
> For a bit of a joke, with a racing bloke, for twenty pounds a side.
>
> It was shift, boys, shift, for there wasn't the slightest doubt
> That I had to make him shift, for the money was nearly out,
> But he cantered home a winner, with the other one at the flog—
> He's a red-hot sort to pick up with his old jig-jog.
>
> I asked a cove for shearing once along the Marthaguy:
> "We shear non-union here," say he. "I call it scab," says I,
> I looked along the shearing floor before I turned to go—
> There were eight or ten dashed Chinamen a-shearing in a row.
>
> It was shift, boys, shift, for there wasn't the slightest doubt
> It was time to make a shift with the leprosy about.
> So I saddled up by horses, and I whistled to my dog,
> And I left his scabby station at the old jig-jog.
>
> I went to Illawarra, where my brother's got a farm;
> He has to ask his landlord's leave before he lifts his arm:
> The landlord owns the countryside—man, woman, dog and cat,
> They haven't the cheek to dare to speak without they touch their
>   hat.
>
> It was shift, boys, shift, for there wasn't the slightest doubt
> Their little landlord god and I would soon have fallen out;
> Was I to touch my hat to him?—was I his blooming dog?
> So I makes for up the country at the old jig-jog.

But it's time that I was moving, I've a mighty way to go
Till I drink artesian water from a thousand feet below;
Till I meet the overlanders with the cattle coming down—
And I'll work a while till I make a pile, then have a spree in town.

So it's shift, boys, shift, for there isn't the slightest doubt
We've got to make a shift to the stations further out:
The pack-horse runs behind us, for he follows like a dog,
And we cross a lot of country at the old jig-jog.[21]

Paterson's poetry managed to combine, for the bushman, both the topical and the nostalgic, and that perhaps is the reason for his continuing popularity. In the nineties the old bush that had been sung about in the folk-ballads was beginning to pass away. There were many links with those days still, but one had to go to "the stations further out" to find them. The old bushman saw the new railways pushing into the areas once only accessible on horseback or by bullock-wagon; the great depression in rural Australia in the nineties saw financial institutions crashing, a succession of disastrous droughts, and, for almost the first time in the bush, the threat of starvation. The most bitter of Australian labour disputes took place during the decade, and it was refreshing for the bushman to turn aside to find in Paterson's poems a reminder of the past, and a reminder too that the present was not the normal state of affairs, that the bush had a brighter face than it was showing during the dismal lean years. Paterson's "Waltzing Matilda" is probably the only Australian bush ballad widely known outside the country, and it is the only song that one may be sure is known by everyone inside it. It has become a national folk-song because it performs the function of one, and this is true of many of Paterson's other poems. "Clancy of the Overflow," "Saltbush Bill," and "The Man from Snowy River" all have the air of genuine folk-creation behind them, yet they are all inventions by Paterson. Succeeding balladists and modern Australian writers who have no interest in the ballad have all been able to build upon an extension of the Australian mythology that Paterson built single-handed.

Apart from "Waltzing Matilda," the song that best represents Paterson is "Clancy of the Overflow." In these lines is the city man's longing for the bush, which is part of the great Bush Myth, and the lyrical celebration of the delights of the bushman's life. It is the

[21]A. B. Paterson, *Collected Verse*, 65-6.

Australian vernacular version, arrived at independently, of the Wordsworthian retreat to nature.

> I had written him a letter which I had, for want of better
> Knowledge, sent to where I met him down the Lachlan years ago;
> He was shearing when I knew him, so I sent the letter to him,
> Just on spec, addressed as follows, "Clancy of the Overflow".
>
> And an answer came directed in a writing unexpected
> (And I think the same was written with a thumb-nail dipped in tar);
> 'Twas his shearing mate who wrote it, and *verbatim* I will quote it:
> "Clancy's gone to Queensland droving, and we don't know where he
>   are."
>
> In my wild erratic fancy visions come to me of Clancy
> Gone a-droving "down the Cooper" where the Western drovers go;
> As the stock are slowly stringing, Clancy rides behind them singing,
> For the drover's life has pleasures that the townsfolk never know.
>
> And the bush has friends to meet him, and their kindly voices greet him
> In the murmur of the breezes and the river on its bars,
> And he sees the vision splendid of the sunlit plains extended,
> And at night the wondrous glory of the everlasting stars.[22]

There follow four stanzas describing the life of the city, sordid by comparison—the noisy dusty streets, the rushing people who have no time to grow, and the lack of real friendships such as are made in the bush. Paterson's values were those of his audience. His picture was half-way between the more Academic portrait of Kendall and the drought-filled horror-scene of the realists. There was both good and bad, and there was a sense of continuity between them. It was comforting for the bushmen to know that, after all the disaster of recent years, they were part of a society that had already grown roots and traditions of its own. That these traditions became those of the whole nation was part of Paterson's achievement.

In addition to his own poetry, Paterson, like Gordon, collected folk-ballads, but their influence was stronger on him than it had been on Gordon. He published a collection of them under the title of *Old Bush Songs*, for he was concerned that the old ways should not pass unsung and unhonoured. In one of his few poems in which he strayed from the ballad form, "Song of the Future," he expressed this concern.

[22]*Ibid.*, 10.

After tracing the history of the country in brief, he concluded:

> But times are changed, and changes rung
> From old to new—the olden days,
> The old bush life and all its ways,
> Are passing from us all unsung.
> The freedom and the hopeful sense
> Of toil that brought due recompense,
> Of room for all, has passed away,
> And lies forgotten with the dead.
> Within our streets men cry for bread
> In cities built but yesterday. . . .
>
> And it may be that we who live
> In this new land apart, beyond
> The hard old world grown fierce and fond
> And bound by precedent and bond,
> May read the riddle right, and give
> New hope to those who dimly see
> That all things yet shall be for good,
> And teach the world at length to be
> One vast united brotherhood.
>
> So may it be! and he who sings
> In accents hopeful, clear and strong,
> The glories which that future brings
> Shall sing indeed a wondrous song.[23]

It is obvious that this type of poetry is not Paterson's *metier*, but it is of importance as a pointer towards the attitude which Bernard O'Dowd was to adopt within ten years.

Henry Lawson was a very different personality. He too was brought up in the country, but as a member of the bushworkers. He had a strong sense of class-consciousness and, in his poetry at least, a sense of grievance that spoils much of his verse and turns it into shrill left-wing propaganda. It is for his short stories that Lawson is chiefly famous, and justly so, for in these there is none of the more blatant bitterness that may be found in the poetry. One extract from the short story, "The Union Buries Its Dead," will illustrate his quality of sardonic and detached observation. A man has been found drowned outside a small country town. There is no identification except a

[23]*Ibid.*, 135–6.

union card, but the local members of the union feel that they should arrange for his funeral. The description of the ceremony ends thus:

I have left out the wattle—because it wasn't there. I have also neglected to mention the heart-broken old mate, with his grizzled head bowed and great pearly drops streaming down his rugged cheeks. He was absent—he was probably "out back". For similar reasons I have omitted reference to the suspicious moisture in the eyes of a bearded bush ruffian named Bill. Bill failed to turn up, and the only moisture was that which was induced by the heat. I have left out the "sad Australian sunset", because the sun was not going down at the time. The burial took place exactly at midday.

The dead bushman's name was Jim, apparently; but they found no portraits, nor locks of hair, nor any love letters, nor anything of that kind in his swag—not even a reference to his mother; only some papers relating to Union matters. Most of us didn't even know the name till we saw it on the coffin; we knew him as "that poor chap that got drowned yesterday."[24]

When Australian writers of the Academic tradition used the local scene at all, they would often resort to the frequently repeated theme of Death in the Bush, with all its Bret Harte sentimentality. Not only is Lawson quietly poking fun at this old chestnut, but he is also parodying himself. In his verse he reveals all the worst features of sentimentality and melodrama that he attacks in his prose. In "Trooper Campbell" one stanza reads:

> The sad Australian sunset
> Had faded from the west;
> But nights brought darker shadows
> To hearts that could not rest;
> And Blackman's wife sat rocking
> And moaning in her chair.
> "Oh, the disgrace, disgrace," she moaned;
> "It's more than I can bear."[25]

Were all his verse of this quality, Lawson would be of little importance in a discussion of the bush-ballad movement; but he spread the range of his poetry over a large number of subjects and used many different forms. In his prose he is disciplined and convincing; yet a great deal of his poetry is very bad indeed. Perhaps verse provided him with an emotional outlet without restraining him within the discipline of the concrete subjects he was forced to deal with in his stories. His mind

[24]Roderick (ed.), *Henry Lawson*, 281–2.
[25]Henry Lawson, *Poetical Works*, 79.

was too cloudy when it attempted to deal with abstract ideas, and the result too often swings between the extremes of bathos and rhymed invective. "Star of Australasia" is little more than patriotic ranting, while the obsession of class distinction which underlies many poems is, for Lawson, a negative and destructive force, rather than the positive inspiration it was for Furphy and for many of the balladists. "Faces in the Street" (p. 5) carries with it echoes of Thomas Hood's "Song of the Shirt."

> They lie, the men who tell us, for reasons of their own,
> That want is here a stranger, and that misery's unknown;
> For where the nearest suburb and the city proper meet
> My window-sill is level with the faces in the street—
>   Drifting past, drifting past,
>   To the beat of weary feet—
> While I sorrow for the owners of those faces in the street.

But this, and the other poems that cry for revolution and the storming of the barricades, have not worn well. Popular once among the workers for whom they were written, these are not the poems for which Lawson is remembered. Of his lyric verses, the only one which remains well known is "The Water Lily," frequently put into anthologies and familiar to Australians as a song. It is the verse equivalent to Lawson's excellent short story, "The Babies in the Bush," and is one of his few good poems outside the bush-ballad form. There are traces of sentimentality, but they are not cloying as in so many of his other Academic poems.

> A lonely young wife
> In her dreaming discerns
> A lily-decked pool
> With a border of ferns,
> And a beautiful child,
> With butterfly wings,
> Trips down to the edge of the water and sings:
>   "Come, mama! come!
>   Quick! follow me!
> Step out on the leaves of the water-lily!"
>
> And the lonely young wife,
> Her heart beating wild,
> Cries, "Wait till I come,
> Till I reach you, my child!"

> But the beautiful child
> With the butterfly wings
> Steps out on the leaves of the lily and sings:
> "Come, mama! come!
> Quick! follow me!
> And step on the leaves of the water-lily!"
>
> And the wife in her dreaming
> Steps out on the stream,
> But the lily leaves sink
> And she wakes from her dream.
> Ah, the waking is sad,
> For the tears that it brings,
> And she knows 'tis her dead baby's spirit that sings:
> "Come, mama! come!
> Quick! follow me!
> Step out on the leaves of the water-lily!"[26]

Lawson is at his best when he is not taking himself too seriously. Ironic humour, which was the guiding spirit of his best short stories, appeared also in some of his bush ballads. "When Your Pants Begin to Go" is more effective social comment than are the embittered calls to revolution; and when he is dealing only with the bush and with bushmen, the two subjects he knew best, he managed to produce some first-rate ballads. Incensed by Paterson's sunny pictures of life in the bush, Lawson engaged in a poetic feud through the pages of the *Bulletin*. In reply to "Clancy of the Overflow," Lawson wrote "Up the Country." His picture is a very different one from Paterson's.

> "Sunny plains!" Great Scott! those burning wastes of barren soil and
>   sand
> With their everlasting fences stretching out across the land!
> Desolation where the crow is! Desert where the eagles flies,
> Paddocks where the luny bullock starts and stares with reddened eyes;
> Where, in clouds of dust enveloped, roasted bullock-drivers creep
> Slowly past the sun-dried shepherd dragged behind his crawling sheep.
> Stunted peak of granite gleaming, glaring like a molten mass
> Poured from some infernal furnace on a plain devoid of grass.[27]

Paterson replied with "In Defence of the Bush" and the debate was under way. The *Bulletin* published the poems, together with some of the peripheral material that had grown around the subject. The

[26]*Ibid.*, 110–11.
[27]*Ibid.*, 207.

publicity was extensive, and the bush ballad became even more widely known than before.

Bushmen continued to sing and compose their own ballads, for the advent of the literary bush ballad encouraged rather than inhibited the oral tradition. The last ten years of the century saw the final surge of nationalism sweeping on towards Federation, and it was not co-incidental that the ballad, as an expression of national sentiment and national unity, reached its highest point at the same time. The inhabi-tants of the crowded cities could share vicariously the breath of free-dom and sunlight that came to them from the expansive verses of the bush-balladists. Here was a form with which they could identify themselves, an inheritance held in common with the inhabitants of other cities, even if they had not ventured outside their own metro-politan areas. The outback was the great reality, the common factor uniting the whole continent. It was fortunate that this expression of national sentiment in literature came before the goal of the political nationalists was achieved. It provided a base of unity on which the new nation could build and a tangible expression of national sentiment on which all could agree. There was, after 1901, no need to repeat the Canadian experience of 1867, of searching for a unifying force, nor was there need to look for a distinctive national literature. The national literary statement and Federation had grown up together.

Accompanying the rise of the ballad, but comparatively unheard, was the steady parallel development of Academic poetry. There had been no major figures after Kendall, and only occasional entries in anthologies represent the work of the period. As we have seen, some of the balladists themselves attempted to write in more ambitious forms, but with scant success. More frequently, the would-be serious poets strayed over into the ballad form, and it is, ironically, for these poems that they are chiefly remembered. However, during the nineties the very success of the bush ballads provided the impetus for serious poets to work behind the scenes. Such poets as Christopher Brennan were disgusted by the lack of intellectual content in the ballad form; they were not content to allow it to become the unchallenged national statement in literature, and set out to remedy what they considered to be an admission of vacuity in the national mind. Hugh McCrae adopted some of the flavour of the ballads but distilled their essence until he had isolated the Pan strain lurking in the Australian character, and gave it expression in exquisitely formed lyrics. But the poet of the nineties who was to inherit the impulse of the bush-ballad movement, and who was destined to turn it into new directions in the decade following Federation, was Bernard O'Dowd.

O'Dowd represents the best and the worst of both Academic and Popular traditions. All his important poetry was published between 1903 and 1912, but his work has been chosen to close this survey of Australian nineteenth-century poetry, rather than that of the much more impressive Christopher Brennan, because in it the Academic and Popular traditions merge to point the way ahead to the path that twentieth-century Australian poetry was to follow. Like Lawson, O'Dowd was obssessed by class-consciousness and social conscience, but, unlike Lawson's his poetry rose above both invective and purely sectional appeal. Like Paterson, he drew upon those feelings which were common to all Australians, but, unlike Paterson, he injected an appeal to the intellect as well as to the emotions. O'Dowd greeted Federation in 1901 with all the enthusiasm and hope that Mair had displayed in the Canada of 1867. Unlike Mair, he did not have to concern himself with the creation of a national sentiment. His was an even more important task—to channel existing national sentiment towards worthy ends.

> An over-ozoned atmosphere,
>   An age of heavy days,
> Can bid a stolid race revere
>   The cult it held a craze.
>
> We smile when Austral troglodyte,
>   Adorned with ochre stain
> And blood-glued down, by wizard rite
>   Precipitates the rain.
>
> A fever of the soundest blood,
>   A too rebellious pain,
> Will with her flickering cities stud
>   Our common sense's plain.[28]

The idea of Australia obsessed him as much as the idea of America had obsessed Whitman, and the American poet remains the largest single influence in his work. We have seen that Paterson in one of his poems briefly expressed the hope that this new world would not

[28]Bernard O'Dowd, *Poems*, 153–4.

follow the bad ways of Europe, and this idea was the mainspring of O'Dowd's poetry. Here was a new nation, the world's youngest— though living in the world's oldest geological continent—full of hope, united in spirit, marching on to a future that could be the hope of the world or its despair. It was intolerable to O'Dowd that Australia should not profit by the mistakes of other nations, but should blindly proceed to imitate them. In one of his earliest sonnets he introduces the theme he is to repeat so often:

> Last sea thing dredged by sailor Time from Space,
> Are you a drift Sargasso, where the West
> In halcyon calm rebuilds her fatal nest?
> Or Delos of a coming Sun-God's race?
> Are you for Light, and trimmed with oil in place,
> Or but a Will o'Wisp on marshy quest?
> A demesne for Mammon to infest?
> Or lurks millennial Eden 'neath your face?
>
> The cenotaphs of species dead elsewhere
> That in your limits leap and swim and fly,
> Or trail uncanny harp-strings from your trees,
> Mix omens with the auguries that dare
> To plant the Cross upon your forehead sky,
> A virgin helpmate Ocean at your knees.[29]

After the terse style of the bush ballads with their concrete references to everyday life, O'Dowd's poetry was criticized for its constant use of abstractions and personifications. It was claimed that if the ballads had gone too far in one direction, O'Dowd had gone too far in the other. But with the production of more of his work, it became apparent that here was a genuine poet who had something of importance to say, and that though he was saying it in terms more profound than had been heard before in Australian poetry, his was not a break with, but an extension of, the national tradition. Democracy was O'Dowd's religion as it had been Whitman's, and in "Poetry Militant" —as he called his manifesto of 1909—he agreed that the poet is "The Answerer," and that poetry of purpose is the only true poetry at times of crisis when a nation stands at the crossroads of its future. Poetry, he repeated, has taken over the function once performed by the Church. It must be the conscience of man, and must expose the evil

29Ibid., 35.

and point out the good. More dynamic than Furphy, O'Dowd shared the novelist's belief that Australia was the crucible of democracy. America had had her chance and her prophet, but she had strayed and missed the road. Australia was not to do the same thing. Undeviatingly radical in his political thinking, O'Dowd was not bound to any doctrine except that of egalitarian democracy:

> That each shall share what all men sow:
> That colour, caste's a lie:
> That man is God, however low—
> Is man, however high.[30]

The land itself is identified with the moral choice which is involved. It is not merely a matter of communing with Nature and receiving the right answer, for O'Dowd found out, as Lampman did, that Nature has as many answers as there are men. Australian nature tests the human spirit first. The Silent Land can only speak to those who have died to the world of self, as represented by the values of European civilization, and who have been born again in the new spirit. Already many exist who have reached this state, for the spirit of Australian democracy, he affirms, has grown out of the soil and the sufferings the soil has imposed. Yet even in this state of grace, a conscious act of the will must be performed to keep us there. The Sirens of the Silent Land are always calling to make us forget the lesson that we have learned.

> Yet, lest our conscious urge to Right
> Indulgent guidance kill,
> They yield us clear or falser light
> According as we will.[31]

O'Dowd's doctrine finds its most elaborate expression in his longest poem, "The Bush." His habit of using personification, sometimes uncritically, is very evident here. But he has defended his habit strongly:

> Who fenced the nymphs in European dales?
> Or Pan tabooed from all but Oxford dreams?
> Warned Shakespeare off from foreign Plutarch's tales?
> Or tethered Virgil to Italian themes?

[30]*Ibid.*, 61.
[31]*Ibid.*, 80.

And when the body sailed from your control
Think ye we left behind in bond the soul?
What'er was yours is ours in equal measure,
The Temple was not built for you alone,
Altho' 'tis ours to grace the common treasure
With Lares and Penates of our own![32]

Harpur and Kendall had both found trouble when they attempted to
do this. They and their critics had found the adaptation so unsuitable
that they had been timid and apologetic about it. O'Dowd has no
regrets about "plunder of perfumes," but rushes in and aggressively
rides off with what he wants. This violence in associating Australian
and European poetic images sometimes has some curious results, but
the very swagger with which they are yoked together has its own
charm. The young and rather bumptious nationalist who proclaims

Our youngest hearts prolong the far pulsation
And churn the brine of the primordial sea:
The foetus writes the precis of Creation:
Australia is the whole world's legatee . . .[33]

is building upon a tradition which can no longer be called imitative.
Australia, he proclaims, has her own voice, and may now without
shame build upon it with adaptations not only from England but
from the best of the whole world's legacy. O'Dowd certainly tried to
follow his own principle. In his poetry can be found references to
Buddhism, Brahminism, Nordic myth, Dionysism, Isisism, and Nietz-
schean philosophy. "The Bush" (pp. 194–209) combines many of
these elements. The poem is not one of lyrical nature description;
the bush is the starting point—the symbol for the whole country
which it had become during the ballad era. There is a brief description of the variety with which nature manifests herself in Australia;
but there is one common factor which unites all regional differences:

But more we seek your undeflowered expanses
Of monotonous scrub.

The very words, "the bush," now carry connotations of a hundred
things. The bush ballads have given the words the power to create a
tapestry before our eyes.

[32]*Ibid.*, 205.
[33]*Ibid.*, 204.

When, now, they say "The Bush!", I see the top
Delicate amber leaflings of the gum
Flutter, or flocks of creaming greenleeks drop
Silent, where in the shining morning hum
The gleaning bees for honey-scented hours
'Mid labyrinthine leaves and white gum flowers.
Cantering midnight hoofs are nearing, nearing,
The straining bullocks flick the harpy flies,
The "hatter" weeds his melancholy clearing,
The distant cow-bell tinkles o'er the rise.

You are the brooding comrade of our way,
Whispering rumour of a new Unknown,
Moulding us white ideals to obey,
Steeping what'er we learn in lore your own,
And freshening with unpolluted light
The squalid city's day and pallid night,
Till we become ourselves distinct, Australian,
(Your native lightning charging blood and nerve),
Stripped to the soul of borrowed garments, alien
To that approaching Shape of God you serve.

Brooding, brooding, your whispers murmur plain
That searching for the clue to mystery
In grottos of decrepitude is vain,
That never shall the eye of prophet see
In crooked Trade's tumultuous streets the plan
Of templed cities adequate to man.
Brooding, brooding, you make us Brahmins waiting
(While uninspired pass on the hurtling years),
Faithful to dreams your spirit is creating,
Till Great Australia, born of you, appears.

O'Dowd uses the Brahmin idea that human progress and the rise
of civilizations are cyclical, each reaching fulfilment in its Great Year,
until at last shall come the "long, cold night of Brahm" when consciousness shall disappear with man, and all creation is reabsorbed
into nothingness. With this idea is merged the belief, so often repeated in Australian literature, that it is from the deserts the prophets
come.

But under all we know, we know that only
A virgin womb unsoiled by ancient fear
Can Saviours bear. So, we, your Brahmins, lonely,
Deaf to the barren tumult, wait your Year.

The reality with which O'Dowd is dealing is a spiritual one, and he insists that on the acceptance of that reality depends the future. It is by no means a foregone conclusion; one can only hope.

> Yea, you are all that we may be, and yet
> In us is all you are to be for aye!
> The Giver of the gifts that we shall get?
> An empty womb that waits the wedding day?
> Thus drifting sense by age-long habit buoyed
> Plays round the thought that knows all nature void!
> And so, my song alternate would believe her
> Idiot Bush and Daughter of the Sun,
> A worthless gift apart from the receiver,
> An empty womb, but in a Deathless One.

At the end of the poem, O'Dowd sums up his message. These stanzas have often been quoted in isolation, but taken in context they lead naturally out of the poet's argument. "The Bush" is, among other things, an intellectual rendering of the bushman's major themes.

> Where is Australia, singer, do you know?
> These sordid farms and joyless factories,
> Mephitic mines and lanes of pallid woe?
> These ugly towns and cities such as these
> With incense sick to all unworthy power,
> And all old sin in full malignant flower?
> No! to her bourn her children still are faring:
> She is a Temple that we are to build:
> For her the ages have been long preparing:
> She is a prophecy to be fulfilled!
>
> All that we love in olden lands and lore
> Was signal of her coming long ago!
> Bacon foresaw her, Campanella, More,
> And Plato's eyes were with her star aglow!
> Who toiled for truth whate'er their countries were,
> Who fought for liberty, they yearned for her!
> No corsair's gathering ground, or tryst for schemers,
> No chapman Carthage to a huckster Tyre,
> She is the Eldorado of old dreamers,
> The Sleeping Beauty of the world's desire.
>
> Yet she shall be as we, the Potter, mould:
> Altar or tomb, as we aspire, despair:
> What wine we bring shall she, the chalice, hold:
> What word we write shall she, the script, declare:

Bandage our eyes, she shall be Memphis, Spain:
Barter our souls, she shall be Tyre again:
And if we pour on her the red oblation
All o'er the world shall Aeshur's buzzards throng:
Love-lit her Chaos shall become Creation:
And dewed with dream, her silence flower in song.

With the poetry of Bernard O'Dowd the two streams of Australian poetry begin to merge into one. Academic forms are re-established, and after him it is possible to combine central and local poetic imagery without self-consciousness and without the need to justify its use. But the Academic forms themselves are used with a difference. The ballad has placed an indelible mark on succeeding poetry. The values they expressed are now general ones, and the anti-sentimental influences they reflected have prevailed. Australian poets writing in the present century have been less influenced by foreign trends than were their Canadian contemporaries. Australian poetry did not pass through a phase in imitation of T. S. Eliot, for there were native traditions established that were more influential. O'Dowd performed the marriage that made possible the birth of new offspring who could look back for support to their own native-born parents.

Bibliography

1. PRIMARY SOURCES

A. *Collections*

BARTON, G. B. *Poets and Prose Writers of New South Wales.* Sydney: Gibbs, Shallard, 1866.

BRYANT, DAN. *"Shaun the Poet" Songster.* New York: R. M. DeWitt, 1870.

CLARK, C. H. M. (ed.). *Select Documents in Australian History, 1788–1850.* Sydney: Angus and Robertson, 1950.

INGLETON, C. C. (ed.). *True Patriots All, or News from Early Australia.* Sydney: Angus and Robertson, 1952.

LAWSON, WILL (ed.). *Australian Bush Songs and Ballads.* Sydney: Angus and Robertson, 1955.

MACKANESS, GEORGE (ed.). *An Anthology of Australian Verse.* Sydney: Angus and Robertson, 1952.

MACKENZIE, W. R. (ed.). *Ballads and Sea Songs of Nova Scotia.* Cambridge: Harvard University Press, 1928.

PRESCOTT and SANDERS (eds.). *An Introduction to American Poetry.* New York: Crofts, 1932.

SMITH, A. J. M. (ed.). *The Book of Canadian Poetry* (revised edition). Toronto: Gage, 1953.

STEVENS, BERTRAM (ed.). *An Anthology of Australian Verse.* Sydney: Angus and Robertson, 1906.

STEWART, DOUGLAS and NANCY KEESING (eds.). *Australian Bush Ballads.* Sydney: Angus and Robertson, 1955.

——*Old Bush Songs and Rhymes of Colonial Times.* Sydney: Angus and Robertson, 1957.

B. *Individual Authors and Writings*

BOLDREWOOD, ROLF. *Robbery Under Arms.* Sydney: Angus and Robertson, 1947.

BRACKENRIDGE, HUGH. *Modern Chivalry: or the Adventure of Captain*

Farrago and Teague O'Regan, ed. C. M. Newlin, New York: American Book Company, 1937.

CAMPBELL, THOMAS. *Poetical Works*. Oxford: Clarendon Press, 1907.

CARRINGTON, GEORGE. *Colonial Adventures and Experiences of a University Man*. London [n.p.], 1871.

CLARKE, MARCUS. *For the Term of His Natural Life*. Oxford: Clarendon Press, 1949.

CRAWFORD, I. V. *Old Spookses' Pass, Malcolm's Katie and Other Poems*. Toronto [n.p.], 1884.

FIELD, BARRON. *The First Fruits of Australian Poetry*, eds. Richard Edwards and Roderick Shaw. Sydney: The Barn on the Hill, 1941.

FOSTER, W. A. *Canada First, a Memorial*. Toronto: Hunter Rose, 1890.

FURPHY, JOSEPH. *Such is Life*. Chicago: University of Chicago Press, 1948.

GLENDINNING, ALEXANDER. *Rhymes*. London, Ontario: Free Press Printing Company, 1871.

GOLDSMITH, OLIVER. *Poems and Plays*. London: Dent, 1936.

GORDON, ADAM LINDSAY. *Poetical Works*. Sydney: Brooks, 1898.

HALIBURTON, THOMAS CHANDLER. *Sam Slick*, ed. R. P. Baker. Toronto: McClelland and Stewart, 1941.

HARRIS, ALEXANDER. *Settlers and Convicts*. Melbourne: University Press, 1948.

HOWE, JOSEPH. *Poems and Essays*. Montreal: Lovell, 1874.

KENDALL, HENRY. *Poems*. Sydney: Robertson, 1886.

KINGSLEY, HENRY. *Geoffrey Hamlyn*. Sydney: Angus and Robertson, 1948.

LAMPMAN, ARCHIBALD. *Poems*. Toronto: Morang, 1900.

—— *At the Long Sault*. Toronto: Ryerson, 1943.

LAWSON, HENRY. *Poetical Works*. Sydney: Angus and Robertson, 1951.

MAIR, CHARLES. *Dreamland and Other Poems*. Montreal: Dawson, 1868.

—— *Tecumseh and the Canadian Poems*. Toronto: Briggs, 1901.

MALONEY, PATRICK. *Australian Union*. Sydney, 1869.

McLACHLAN, ALEXANDER. *The Emigrant and Other Poems*. Toronto: Rollo and Adams, 1861.

—— *Poems and Songs*. Toronto: Rose, 1888.

MOODIE, SUSANNA. *Roughing It in the Bush*. Toronto: McClelland and Stewart, 1923.

O'DOWD, BERNARD. *Poems*. Melbourne: Lothian, 1944.

PATERSON, A. B. *Collected Verse*. Sydney: Angus and Robertson, 1951.

QUICK, J., and R. R. GARRAN. *The Annotated Constitution of the Australian Commonwealth*. Sydney: Angus and Robertson, 1901.

RICHARDSON, HENRY HANDEL. *The Fortunes of Richard Mahoney*. London: Heinemann, 1938.

ROUSSEAU, J. J. *Oeuvres de J. J. Rousseau* (IV, *Discours*). Paris: Lefèvre, 1819.

SANGSTER, CHARLES. *The St. Lawrence and the Saguenay*. Kingston: Creighton and Duff, 1856.
—— *Hesperus*. Montreal: Lovell, 1860.
SCOTT, DUNCAN CAMPBELL. *Poems*. Toronto: McClelland and Stewart, 1926.
THOMSON, R. *Australian Nationalism: An Earnest Appeal to the Sons of Australia in Favour of the Federation and Independence of the States of Our Country*. Burwood near Sydney: Phipps, 1888.
TRAILL, C. P. *Backwoods of Canada*. London, 1836.
TROLLOPE, ANTHONY. *North America*. London: Chapman, 1866.
TUCKER, JAMES. *Ralph Rashleigh*. Sydney: Angus and Robertson, 1952.
WHITMAN, WALT. *Leaves of Grass*. London: Dent, 1948.

C. Manuscripts
Douglas Library, Kingston. The unsorted papers of Charles Mair.
McDOUGALL, R. L. "Scott and the Development of Canadian Fiction." Unpublished MS.

2. SECONDARY SOURCES

BISSELL, C. T. "Literary Taste in Central Canada during the late Nineteenth Century," *Canadian Historical Review*, XXXI (1950), 237–51.
—— "A Common Ancestry: Literature in Australia and Canada," *University of Toronto Quarterly*, XXV (1956), 131–42.
BROOKS, VAN WYCK. *The World of Washington Irving*. London: Readers' Union, 1945.
BROWN, E. K. *On Canadian Poetry*. Toronto: Ryerson, 1943.
CHITTICK, V. L. O. *Thomas Chandler Haliburton, "Sam Slick."* New York: Columbia University Press, 1924.
CREIGHTON, D. G. *Dominion of the North*. Boston: Houghton, Mifflin, 1944.
CUNLIFFE, MARCUS. *The Literature of the United States*. London: Penguin Books, 1954.
DAWSON, R. MACGREGOR. *The Government of Canada*. Toronto: University of Toronto Press, 1947.
ELLIOTT, BRIAN. *Singing to the Cattle*. Melbourne: Georgian House, 1947.
EWERS, J. K. *Creative Writing in Australia*. Melbourne: Georgian House, 1945.
FITZPATRICK, BRIAN. *The Australian People, 1788–1945*. Melbourne: University Press, 1946.
GREEN, H. M. *An Outline of Australian Literature*. Sydney: Whitcombe and Tombs, 1930.
HADGRAFT, CECIL. *Australian Literature*. London: Heinemann, 1960.
INGAMELLS, REX. *Handbook of Australian Literature*. Melbourne: Jindyworobak, 1949.

JEBB, RICHARD. *Studies in Colonial Nationalism*. London: E. Arnold, 1905.

LEGOUIS, E., and M. CAZAMIAN. *A History of English Literature*. London: Dent, 1940.

LOGAN, J. D., and D. G. FRENCH. *Highways of Canadian Literature*. Toronto: McClelland and Stewart, 1924.

MACMECHAN, ARCHIBALD. *Headwaters of Canadian Literature*. Toronto: McClelland and Stewart, 1924.

MCCOURT, E. A. *The Canadian West in Fiction*. Toronto: Ryerson, 1949.

MILLER, E. MORRIS. *Australian Literature* (2 volumes). Melbourne: University Press, 1940.

MOORE, J. SHERIDAN. *The Life and Genius of James Lionel Michael*. Sydney: Ferguson, 1868.

PACEY, DESMOND. *Creative Writing in Canada*. Toronto: Ryerson, 1952.

PALMER, VANCE. *National Portraits*. Melbourne: University Press, 1940.

—— *The Legend of the Nineties*. Melbourne: University Press, 1954.

PERCEVAL, W. P. *Leading Canadian Poets*. Toronto: Ryerson, 1948.

RHODENIZER, V. B. *Handbook of Canadian Literature*. Ottawa: Graphic, 1930.

RODERICK, COLIN, ed. *Henry Lawson*. Sydney: Angus and Robertson, 1950.

SCOTT, ERNEST. *A Short History of Australia*. Melbourne: Oxford University Press, 1953.

SMITH, A. J. M. "Colonialism and Nationalism in Canadian Poetry Before Confederation," Canadian Historical Association, *Report*, 1944, 74–85.

STEVENSON, LIONEL. *Appraisals of Canadian Literature*. Toronto: Macmillan, 1926.

TENNANT, KYLIE. *Australia, Her Story*. London: Macmillan, 1953.

Index